Aspects of Consciousness

The Authors in This Book

The authors in this book are the presenters at the Aspects of Consciousness conference held by the Academy for Spiritual and Consciousness Studies in Durham, North Carolina, June 10—14, 2015. For information about the conference, the book containing conference presentations, and DVD or audio recordings, go to the Academy website:

http://ascsi2.ning.com/conference

Editor
R. Craig Hogan, Ph.D.

The papers in this book have been included with the permission of the authors. The authors hold all rights and copyrights to the text, with no claim to copyright or ownership by ASCS or the editor. No part of this book may be reproduced in any written, electronic, photocopying or other copy media without written permission of the author. The exception is in the case of brief quotations embodied in the critical articles or reviews and pages where permission is specifically granted by the publisher or author.

ASCS Publications contact:
    Academy for Spiritual and Consciousness Studies
    P.O. Box 84
    Loxahatchee, Florida 33470

Greater Reality Publications
23 Payne Place
Normal, IL 61761

Contents

PREFACE VII

A WHITE CROW SPIRIT 1
    GARY E. SCHWARTZ, PH.D.

GETTING OUT OF THE BOX: REDEFINING WHAT IS REAL 15
    SUZANNE GIESEMANN, M.A.

EFT AND ADC FOR PHYSICAL MANIFESTATIONS OF GRIEF 39
    LARRY BURK, MD, CEHP

ENERGY PSYCHOLOGY: A BRIEF INTRODUCTION 45
    DAVID FEINSTEIN, PH.D.

AN EXPERIENTIAL APPROACH TO SURVIVAL OF DEATH 51
    NANDINI SINHA KAPUR, PH.D., JNU

ENERGY MEDICINE AND REGRESSION 63
    DONNA EDEN AND DAVID FEINSTEIN, PH.D.

DREAMING THE FUTURE: EVIDENCE FOR A HOLISTIC
CONNECTING PRINCIPLE 67
    DALE E. GRAFF, M.S.

NIGHTMARES: URGENT MESSAGES FROM THE GUIDING SELF 85
    HOWARD W. TYAS, JR.

YOUR SOUL IS YOUR REAL SELF & HOW EMDR & THE
VAGAL NERVE SYSTEM CLEANSE YOUR SOUL 111
    KAREN E. HERRICK, PH.D.

A CASE OF SPONTANEOUS MEDIUMSHIP? 123
    STANLEY KRIPPNER, PH.D.

MAGIC, SHAMANISM, AND TECHNOLOGY 137
    MICHAEL PETER LANGEVIN, M.S.

THE BRAIN IS SUPERFLUOUS: EVIDENCE FROM THIS LIFE AND THE NEXT 143
    R. CRAIG HOGAN, PH.D.

MUSCLE TESTING: COMMUNICATION TOOL FOR THE UNCONSCIOUS AND SUPERCONSCIOUS 179

    Larry Green

BELIEF SYSTEMS AND YOUR PERSONAL POWER 191

    Matthew Thie, M.Ed.

MARKERS: HOW TO RECOGNIZE VERY YOUNG CHILDREN WHO MAY HAVE HAD A NEAR-DEATH EXPERIENCE 217

    P. M. H. Atwater, L.H.D.

HOW TO SEE SPIRIT: A PERSONAL AND SCIENTIFIC INVESTIGATION 235

    Rhonda R. E. Schwartz, M.A.

CONTINUING PSI EXPERIENCES SUGGESTIVE OF AN AFTERLIFE 249

    Sally Rhine Feather, Ph.D.

SPIRIT AND THE SOUL PHONE: WHO WILL USE IT "HERE" AND "THERE"? 253

    Gary E. Schwartz, Ph.D.

EDGAR CAYCE ON DREAMS: YOUR PATHWAY TO PERSONAL GUIDANCE AND INTUITION 263

    Kevin J. Todeschi, M.A.

LUCID DREAMING AS A PATH TO PERSONAL GROWTH, HEALING AND SPIRITUAL WISDOM 281

    Robert Waggoner

BREAKTHROUGH OR BREAKDOWN 299

    Theresa A. Yuschok, MD

UNDERSTANDING THE HUMAN SOUL AND THE PURPOSE OF LIFE 307

    Lee Lawrence

LEADING EDGE SCIENCE OF THE AFTERLIFE AND MEDIUMSHIP 315

    Alan Ross Hugenot, Ph.D.

Preface

This book contains the proceedings of the June 2015 40th annual conference of The Academy for Spiritual and Consciousness Studies. The Academy's mission is to discern, develop and disseminate knowledge leading to an increase in the understanding of all aspects of human consciousness: its existence, survival, and environmental interaction. The mission is also to gain insights into the purpose of life in order to enhance the development of the human spirit.

This year's conference is titled "Aspects of Consciousness." It includes three sub-themes based on the special interests of Academy members:

- Spiritual Mysticism and the Spiritual Transformative Experience
- After-Death Experience and the Survival of Consciousness
- Mind/Body Medicine: An Integrative Approach

Recently, I received a call from a woman asking for information about a troubling experience. She is a married, stay-at-home mother of three young children who was raised Catholic but has since strayed from the church. As is the case with many people, she considers herself more spiritual than religious. She began hearing voices from spirits with no physical bodies. Troubled by this, she asked her husband to take her to the hospital emergency room where they prescribed medications to suppress the symptoms. Her question was, "Are the voices real?"

A family member of an elderly woman who often holds conversations with non-existent people asked me "Is she really speaking with someone or is it her mind playing tricks on her?"

Another individual, a male approximately fifty years old, who is a successful businessman on the church council of a large congregation and very active in his religious community, shared with me recently that he is hearing voices when he prays. Being both troubled and puzzled about this, he inquired as to what I thought of his experiences. These are just a few of the ever-increasing number of questions being posed to me by people seeking answers.

The underlying questions all three were seeking answers to are "Is it a mental illness or is there another explanation for these experiences? Is it a breakdown or a breakthrough? What are the symptoms of a spiritual awakening?" The answers are not simple.

This conference sought to address the issue of mental illness vs spiritual awakening objectively by looking at evidence from both the medical and spiritual perspectives given by psychiatrists, psychologists, university-based researchers, spiritual teachers, and religious scholars from the diverse backgrounds of Christianity, Sufism, Hinduism, Buddhism, and others.

Please visit us at our website ASCSI.org and join our forum of discussions on various articles of cutting-edge science of consciousness and book reviews relevant to the interests of our members.

To provide a venue for those who wish to publish, the Academy prints two scholarly quarterlies, *The Journal for Spiritual and Consciousness Studies* and *The Searchlight*, available to members of the Academy. Also available to members and free to the general public is our bi-monthly e-newsletter, *Spirituality Matters!* To learn more and to opt-in to have it delivered directly to your email inbox, visit our website home page and subscribe.

Thank you for your interest in the Academy for Spiritual and Consciousness Studies, our publications, and the conferences. Please join us in the future to help others in this great quest for human understanding.

namaste'

Lee Lawrence
Conference Committee Chair
June 2015 Durham/Chapel Hill NC Conference
Academy for Spiritual and Consciousness Studies

A White Crow Spirit

What Susy Smith Has Taught Me about the Other Side After She Died

Gary E. Schwartz, Ph.D.

This address is dedicated to Susy Smith and the many gifted mediums who have received evidential communication from her over the years.

> *In order to disprove the law that all crows are black, it is enough to find one white crow.*
>
> William James, PhD

Abstract

This paper begins by describing Susy Smith, who knew many of the most distinguished mediums and leading afterlife scientists of her day. Life after death research was the primary focus of her life for almost fifty years. After she passed into spirit, she became a collaborator in research from the other side. The paper describes twelve lessons Susy Smith has taught the author. It then focuses on describing how she taught him one specific lesson: that spirit can visit specific people on the earth plane to pose for a sculpture. The paper includes photos of example sculptures that mediums created based on her inspiration.

From "White Crow Mediums" to "White Crow Spirits"

The "one white crow" quote from Professor William James of Harvard University introduced my book *The Afterlife Experiments: Breakthrough Scientific Evidence of Life After Death* (Schwartz, 2002). James used this example to illustrate how it took only one "exception to the rule" to establish that a given rule was not absolute—and therefore not universally true. In his instance, and my instance too, we referred to the indisputable logic that indicates that it takes a solid demonstration of only one "genuine" medium to disprove the "law" that "*all* mediums are frauds."

In *The Afterlife Experiments* book, I provided extensive evidence documenting the existence of not only one "white crow medium"; the total was actually five. In my subsequent books, *The Truth About Medium* (2005) and *The Sacred Promise* (2011), the total number of white crow mediums increased to over twenty. And at the time I was writing this brief chapter (April 2015), I could report that I had at this point observed a total of over thirty white crow mediums.

Though most mediums do not like to "fly together,," we can imagine that if they did, this would be quite the "murder of crows."

Using the white crow metaphor, I have had the opportunity to observe striking and compelling evidence from the "other side" for what can be called "white crow spirits." For those of you who prefer terms other than spirits—for example, many scientists use the term "discarnates"—you can think of these "post-physical people" as "white crow discarnates."

I prefer to use the term spirits for three reasons: (1) spirit is a term used by mediums, (2) spirit is a word understood by the general public, and (3) spirit seems to be a more honorable and personable term, especially when speaking of specific white crows. For example, if we are going to refer to deceased persons as "discarnates," then we should label the mediums who hear them—and the scientists who investigate them—as "incarnates."

Whatever term we prefer—spirits or discarnates—is not of primary concern; what matters here is that some of these post-physical people are providing extensive—and often extraordinary—evidence not only that they are still "here," but that they care deeply about their loved ones, the human species, and the planet as a whole.

I have had the privilege to observe extensive and extraordinary evidence from a number of "white crow spirits," and I will be presenting some of this evidence in a future keynote address at the "Life in the Afterlife" Conference (September 25-27, 2015, in Scottsdale, Arizona). For the present address, I will feature the first white crow spirit I had the privilege to work with—and learn from—after she passed, Ms. Susy Smith.

Who is Susy Smith?

Very briefly, Susy Smith is a professional journalist and writer, lay scientist, and claimant psychic who published a total of 30 books in parapsychology and life after death over her distinguished career. I have written about Susy in five of my books, two while she was living (*The Living Energy Universe,* 1999, and *The Afterlife Experiments,* 2002), and three after she died (*The Truth about Medium,* 2005; *The Sacred Promise,* 2011; and *Super Mind,* 2015).

I met Susy when she was 85 years old, retired, and living in Tucson. In lay audience presentations I fondly explain that Susy became my "adopted grandmother"—she used to call me her "illegitimate grandson"—and that she often told me that she "could not wait to die" so that she "could prove that she was still here." Susy received this opportunity in the spring of 2001, a few months prior to her 90th birthday.

Susy knew many of the most distinguished mediums as well as leading afterlife scientists of her day. Life after death research was the primary focus of her life for almost fifty years. If anyone was going to provide compelling and replicated evidence of survival of consciousness after physical death, it would be Susy.

Twelve Lessons Susy Smith Taught Me After She Died

Over the past fourteen years, extraordinary evidence about survival of consciousness after physical death has been provided by Susy. Susy has come through more than a dozen mediums, many times under completely unexpected (i.e., to me and the mediums) circumstances. Table 1 (next page) summarizes twelve lessons Susy has taught me about the other side since she died. Table 1 reflects a partial and exemplary list of demonstrations that are especially memorable and meaningful.

A book could (and should) be devoted to this extraordinary evidence and I plan to write this book when time permits.

Table 1

Twelve Lessons Susy Smith (Spirit) Has Demonstrated "From the Other Side"

1. Spirit can come through a medium within 24 hours of physically dying. (LC)

2. Spirit can provide information that only the sitter knows about plans for her life in the next life. (LC)
  a. Dancing
  b. Raising an infant
  c. Participating in future research

3. Spirit can "drop in" unexpectedly to a person unknown to the person or the spirit's loved one, and specifically ask this person to contact the spirit's loved one.
  a. JM
  b. SG

4. Spirit can "watch over" loved ones in controlled experiments. (JM)
5. Spirit can "foresee future events."

a. Warning of "ambush" (spontaneous, Allison D)
   b. Tires (experiment, Janet M)
   c. Changing decision in a court case (experiment, Janet M)
   d. Dragonfly meeting (Janet M)
   e. Car not starting (spontaneous, Suzanne G)
   f. Highlighting a special day (Katherine Y friend)

6. Spirit can visit specific mediums for specific purposes.
   a. Pose for a sculpture (PS)
   b. Validate watching over by providing new evidence—"talk about the curtain" (SG)

7. Spirit can intentionally appear younger than she was when she physically died. (PS)

8. Spirit can interrupt and intervene in an experiment to protect the sitter and the experimenter. (SM)

9. Spirit can show up anywhere at any time.
   a. Restaurant (NM)
   b. Golf cart (SG)

10. Spirit can bring other spirits to mediums under blind conditions.
    a. Deceased sister (JM)
    b. Multiple family members (JM)
    c. Deceased significant other (NM)
    d. Deceased scientist (SG)

11. Spirit can confirm events associated with other spirits. (presence and meaning of bird, MO)

> 12. Spirit can play a behind-the-scenes role in bringing two people together. (KY)

I have chosen two examples to share in this report. They are Lessons 6(a) and 7.

Seeing Spirit and Sculpting Them?

Only a subset of psychics and mediums claim to be able to see the deceased. Of those who claim to see, the majority report seeing spirit in their "mind's eye" (that is, in their head). It turns out that only a small minority of mediums actually fit the well-known phrase "I see dead people" from the movie *The Sixth Sense*.

Of the more than thirty gifted mediums I have worked with over the years (Schwartz, 2002; 2005; 2011), less than a handful have reported actually seeing the deceased. One of them happens to be Rhonda Schwartz, a professional artist (and my wife), who unexpectedly began seeing spirit a few years after meeting me. Rhonda is giving a presentation on the process and evidence for seeing spirit at this meeting. Another happens to be a professional sculptor—usually of animals—and curiously, she began sculpting deceased people after she met me.

The psychic sculptor is Patricia Sahlin, author of the book *Mediums, Migraines, and Magnetite* (Sahlin, 2008). Pat's moving accounts of seeing ghosts, having conversations with deceased people, tracking down mysterious meteorites, exploring connections between headaches and magnetic crystalline structures and psychic abilities, comprise in her words "a very strange story."

However, it is prudent to remember the old saying "Truth can be stranger than fiction." Pat is adamant in reminding us that her book is not fiction. In her words:

> It's true. Bizarre? Weird? Completely out of the box? Oh definitely. Probably all that and more. But nonetheless true.

I will briefly review the "bizarre, weird, and completely out of the box" circumstances that led me to conclude that Pat had the capacity to create recognizable three-dimensional models of deceased people—even of people she did not know—who came to her unannounced, and she had no idea who they might be.

The Surprising Origin of Pat's Psychic Sculpting

Below is how Pat described her experience in *Mediums, Migraines, and Magnetite.* I have inserted some commentary as appropriate.

> That sort of leads to another interesting experiment we've conducted, nearly by accident. In working with Dr. Gary Schwartz, we've done some very interesting things and sent him some unique communications. There have been times when I felt I had a message from someone who has gone on, and that it is to be passed along to someone who is still here.
>
> There was one particular case when someone seemed to want to reach Gary. I tried to describe the person to him, but without much success. He didn't really know who it might be. Then I tried using an IdentiKit, one of the devices used by many police departments to do a composite sketch, since I simply can't draw. That was also a failure. But, in the meantime, we had been discussing the fact that apparently we can contact specific people who have gone on, and Gary had asked us to *"Find someone for Grace."*

At the request of the deceased widow "Grace" (a pseudonym I selected), I did not use the widow's or her husband's name. What is important in this context concerns the potential implications for psychic sculpting, not the particulars of this particular deceased person or his family.

> I had no idea who that might be, but Kate immediately said "tweedy, as in soccer and that sort of thing; probably

European; educated, connected with the publishing industry and with agriculture." Within minutes, an image began to come to me.

Kate, Pat's daughter, has mediumship gifts as well. Kate's mediumistic impressions, reported in italics above, turned out to precisely fit my request for Pat to "Find someone for Grace" (more details below).

As I said, I cannot draw. But, I'm a sculptor. I've only done the human figure twice before, years ago. My forte is in animal portraits [sculptures], but someone clearly wanted to reach Gary and all our attempts to identify the person, to *show* Gary who it was, had failed.

I finally said to myself "Okay, dummy. You're a sculptor; so sculpt!" So I gave it a try.

I did a little bust portrait of the man we could see, to the best of my ability, and then took some photos of it to send on to Gary. It wasn't wonderfully accurate, but apparently was close enough. This time he had no problem with recognition, particularly when I said I felt the person wore glasses.

In our conversation right after that, he let slip the name *Bruce*. That was all I had to go on. I still had no clue as to who the person actually was.

For the record, I accidently said the deceased man's first name to Pat. However, since this happened *after* the sculpture had been created it did not contaminate the intentional blinding of the sculpting process.

In a conversation with Dr. Dean Radin of the Institute of Noetic Sciences, I explained what had happened and told him that all I had was the first name. Dean asked "Bruce *Baxter*?" I told him that I had no idea, and he asked if I'd email him the photo.

> I did, and it was only a few minutes later when his reply came back. *"That's Bruce Baxter all right. The only thing missing is his glasses."*

Some commentary is useful here. During this particular time period, I was conducting a university-based double-blind mediumship experiment with my then postdoctoral fellow Dr. Julie Beischel, currently Research Director of the Windbridge Institute. We had been requested by "Grace," wife of the late "Bruce Baxter" (also a pseudonym)—a distinguished European parapsychologist—to include her in our ongoing experiment.

Given Bruce's deep interest in life after death, it occurred to me that maybe Bruce had decided to "drop in" on Pat and see if he could goad her to make some sort of picture of him. The reason was that Pat had spontaneously called me within days of our conducting the Baxter double-blind research reading.

For the record, I was subsequently invited to present our findings publicly at one-day conference in Europe in honor of Mr. Baxter.

> So the upshot was that it turned out to be Bruce Baxter, a friend of Gary's from Europe who was indeed involved in publishing and agricultural journals, as well as a very active voice in the study of the paranormal and life in the hereafter.
>
> Bruce had passed on at a testimonial dinner a few months before, while essentially in the midst of a debate on the subject of life after death. His wife's name? *Grace.* Of course. Both the man who was trying to make contact and the man Gary asked us to find were one and the same. Bruce apparently worked for years toward proving the theory of life after death. If the little sculpture means anything, he has not only proven his point, but he's *still* taking a very active interest and perhaps an active part in developments.

Following on the heels of that remarkable event, Gary asked me if I could contact Susy Smith, the author of many books on the afterlife, and if I could do a portrait of her, but this one was a bit different. Susy was someone Gary had known and worked with as an old lady in her lifetime.

He had an early photo of her and wanted to see if I could match it.

Correction—it was <u>not</u> actually a photo, but a self-portrait that Susy had painted of herself, probably when she was in her forties. Also, I did <u>not</u> tell Pat ahead of time about the self-portrait. <u>*It was only upon seeing Pat's sculpture of Susy that I saw the striking match to Susy's special self-portrait.*</u>

Susy was another one who was highly active in paranormal work and has several books published about it. I believe she still wants to continue to prove her point, long after her passing.

I did manage to contact her [psychically] and completed another sculpture, once again sending the photo to Gary. He was able to match up points from the photo, using a series of scientific measurements, and felt that it actually was a portrait of her. I had mixed feelings about it, and I'll tell you why.

If it had been my choice, I would not have tried to match an existing photo that Gary owns. Obviously I could be tapping into his vision of it and doing a sort of mental cheating to create the portrait. I strongly prefer to have the person come to me as an unknown and present an image for me to do, and then see if I can have it identified.

I agree with Pat here. The Bruce sculpture was truly "blind," though I had taken a photo of Bruce in Europe while he was alive; hence I had an image of Bruce in my head as well.

Of course, unlike with Susy, where I had asked Pat to attempt to contact her, I had not asked Pat to attempt to contact Bruce. As stated earlier, I had no idea that Bruce might, of all people, attempt to contact Pat, nor would I have guessed, in a billion years, that Pat (or anyone, for that matter) might make a spontaneous sculpture of a deceased European parapsychologist!

> In this case, the first thing I saw of Susy was *not* the image Gary wanted, but of a young lady, perhaps in her mid-teens. I felt a need to complete it, and I did so, long before I ever saw any photo of her. Some months later I found an image of her in her later years online. Could my interpretation be of a young Susy? You decide.

The image on the left is a digital photo I took of the self-portrait made by Susy. I did not email Pat this image until after she had completed her sculpture of Susy on the right. The images are displayed below.

A Third Surprising Sculpture

Apparently, sometime after the Susy sculpture, another unknown deceased male was seen by Pat, and she made a sculpture of him. She sent me a copy of the sculpture and asked me who it might be. Initially I had no idea, and told her so. Pat has wondered whether he might be a deceased astronaut.

Meanwhile, a few weeks later, I happened to glance at a wall that displayed an early photograph of my father and mother taken when they were first married in the early 1940s. To my surprise, there was a resemblance between Pat's third sculpture and my father.

Below is a set of images. The set contains a digital photo I took of the old photograph of my father (my mother is not included), with Pat's two male sculptures below it.

I will let you determine which of the two sculptures you believe best matches the image of Howard.

Notice that because neither of the sculptures is smiling, whereas the photo is smiling, the resemblance of the sculptures to the photo requires some inference. However, if you focus on components, such as (1) hair, and (2) noses, you will begin to make a reasonable discernment.

A   B

Future Research with Psychic Sculptors?

If Pat is correct, it should be possible to perform future controlled research with psychic sculptors.

Imagine if we combined psychic sculpting with the "double deceased" paradigm (where one deceased person brings a second deceased person to a medium under blinded conditions (Schwartz, 2011) in future experiments.

Imagine if we requested that sometimes the deceased wear disguises, and even intentionally impersonate other deceased individuals. Could they fool the sculptor?

Can the deceased, as it is sometimes claimed, show themselves at different ages, and be sculpted accurately at different stages of their life?

Future research can address challenging and meaningful questions such as these.

References

Sahlin, P. (2008). Mediums, Migraines, and Magnetite: Making the connection. Bloomington, IN: Xlibris Corporation.

Schwartz, G. E., and Russek, L.R. (1999). The Living Energy Universe: A fundamental discovery that transforms science and medicine. Charlottesville, VA: Hampton Roads.

Schwartz, G. E. (2002). The Afterlife Experiments: Breakthrough scientific evidence for life after death. New York, NY: Atria Books / Simon & Schuster.

Schwartz, G. E. (2005). The Truth about Medium: Extraordinary experiments with the real Alison Dubois of NBC's Medium and other remarkable psychics. Charlottesville, VA: Hampton Roads.

Schwartz, G. E. (2011). *The Sacred Promise: How science is discovering spirit's collaboration with us in our daily lives.* New York, NY: Atria Books.

Schwartz, G. E. (2015, in press). *Super Mind: Extraordinary evidence for super-synchronicity in contemporary life.* Vancouver, BC: Param Media.

Author Bio

Gary E. Schwartz, Ph.D.

Gary E. Schwartz is a Professor of Psychology, Medicine, Neurology, Psychiatry, and Surgery, and Director of the Laboratory for Advances in Consciousness and Health, at the University of Arizona. He is also the Chairman of Eternea (www.eternea.org). He received his Ph.D. from Harvard University in 1971 and served as an Assistant Professor of Psychology at Harvard before moving to Yale University in 1976. There he was a Professor of Psychology and Psychiatry, Director of the Yale Psychophysiology Center, and co-Director of the Yale Behavioral Medicine Clinic before moving to the University of Arizona in 1988. He has published more than 450 scientific papers and chapters, including six papers in the journal *Science*, and co-edited 11 academic books. He is a Fellow of the American Psychological Association, the American Psychological Society, the Academy of Behavioral Medicine Research, and the Society of Behavioral Medicine. His research integrating body, mind, and spirit has been featured in numerous documentaries and television shows, including the documentary *The Life After Death Project* (2013), produced and directed by Paul Davids. His books for the general public include *The Afterlife Experiments*, *The G.O.D. Experiments*, *The Energy Healing Experiments*, and *The Sacred Promise*.

For more about Gary, visit drgaryschwartz.com.

Getting Out of the Box
Redefining What Is Real

Suzanne Giesemann, M.A.

Abstract

How do we know what reality is? Former by-the-book Navy Commander Suzanne Giesemann used to think reality was only what we perceived with our physical senses. In this mind-expanding presentation, she shares verifiable evidence of a greater reality beyond the physical senses. She begins with irrefutable details received in communication with beings who once walked the earth in human form. The evidence she provides goes beyond a reasonable doubt to show that consciousness survives death. But can consciousness take other forms? If consciousness is limitless, then theoretically, the manifestations of that consciousness should be limitless as well. If so, can we receive evidence of higher and higher aspects of that consciousness? Prepare to expand your concept of what is "real" as Suzanne provides a glimpse of a boundless existence where reality takes on new meaning.

My presentation is entitled, "Getting Out of the Box: Redefining What Is Real." What is this box we're in? The concept of a box is something physical with four sides. It may also have a lid. These sides and the lid limit what can be contained within it. The main point I wish to convey to you this evening is that we put ourselves in a metaphorical box when we think that reality has boundaries—limits—of any kind.

I have a fairly by-the-book background. I served as a U.S. Navy officer for twenty years, following the rules and very much focused on this physical reality. Today I sit one-on-one with people who have lost loved ones and reunite them with those who have passed. I had no idea until 2009 that consciousness continued after death or that I could communicate with those on the other side of the veil. Now I connect daily with what I refer to as the "greater reality."

Here you see photos of a few of those souls who once walked in this reality, but who are now part of that greater reality. I could regale you all evening with stories from the readings I have given, but how about a quick one?

My husband Ty and I were packing our coach for six months on the road sharing the messages of hope. A woman called who was in such grief over losing her son that she was in tears. I had her come to my house right away. I wasn't sure how well I would be able to connect because I was a bit distracted with all I had to do for our trip. I need not have worried.

I immediately sensed the presence of her son, who gave me the name "Mikey." He showed me that he had taken his own life by jumping, and gave me the exact place where he jumped: the Verrazano Bridge. He showed me that his suicide was not premeditated, but he had been off kilter because he had not been taking his medication for bipolar disorder. He gave me his doctor's last name. He also gave me the name of his best friend and showed me that they had both played in a rock band. He told me to speak about a tattoo and the lyrics to a song. At that point his mother rolled up her sleeve and showed me the tattoo that she and Michael's best friend now had on their arms with the lyrics to Michael's favorite song.

I then asked Michael silently what kind of work he used to do. He pointed out the window of my study. His mother had no idea that I had asked the question and she could not see out the window as Michael said to me, "What your husband is doing right now." I saw Ty bent down at the rear of our coach stripping wires, so I turned to Michael's mother and said, "Your son was an electrician." And he was.

That, my friends, is what I mean by evidence. This is evidence that I was not reading my client's mind, for she had no idea I had asked the question and she could not see what my husband was doing. All of the evidence showed Michael's mother that there is another reality beyond this one and that consciousness survives the transition we call death. This is the main objective of evidential mediumship.

It is the evidence that those on the other side have given me in the sessions I do with their families that lets us know they are very real and very much with us. Without that evidence, some might think the information I bring through from the greater reality is a fabrication of my imagination.

After I spoke at last year's ASCS conference, a man came up to me and told me that his friend had asked him, "Do you think those things really happened to her?" I laughed and assured him that all of the stories I had shared were 100% true, without any embellishment. I was not at all offended by his question. That man didn't know me. He could only take my word for it, just as all of you can. So, take my word for this: I would not be where I am today if I were not one to play by the rules.

In my last tour of duty with the Navy, I served as aide to the Chairman of the Joint Chiefs of Staff. Rather than going through the standard interview process for a new aide, the Chairman specifically asked me to fill the position as his "right-hand man." One of the reasons he asked me is because he trusted me to tell him like it is, with no B.S., even when he didn't always like what I had to tell him.

I vowed long ago never to lie or B.S., for many reasons, but one of the main reasons being to honor the memory of my stepdaughter, Susan, a sergeant in the Marine Corps who was killed when struck by lightning in 2006. It is because of her that I do this work. Another reason that truth is so important to me is because my main mission is to bring hope to people who have suffered loss. I would not denigrate Susan's memory or give anyone false hope by telling anything that is not true. There is no need to make up stories. Why even *stretch* the truth, when those on the other side give me such good evidence?

I will be talking with you this evening about reality beyond the physical world. Some of the things I'm going to share with you may very well stretch your belief system. I know they've done so with mine. But as my friend and colleague Temple Hayes—senior spiritual leader at First Unity of St. Petersburg—told me, "If you're not making your audiences squirm every once in a while, you're not doing your job."

So, it's time for me to do my job.

I will be sharing with you stories that I have documented and saved in a file labelled "No Other Explanation." No other explanation for what? Than that there is a greater reality. You cannot experience this greater reality with the side of you that is human. The human mind assumes an "either/or" stance. There are three keys to understanding and accepting that there is a reality beyond the physical world. To do this, you must

- Get outside of the "either/or" mentality of the human mind.
- Acknowledge that the intellect can only take you so far.
- Move on to a more integrative way of knowing.

Instead of "either/or," see the greater reality as two worlds, distinct, yet interconnected. An integral mind sees the underlying whole that exists prior to the emergence of duality. This whole includes the formless and the formed, the transcendent and the immanent, the eternal and the temporal, the absolute and the relative, the impersonal and the personal, the one/whole/undivided and the multiple, partial/divided.

What is real? Is it only that which we see, feel, and so forth? The manifest? Or is all that is an expression of Consciousness in limitless forms?

The All is the state of pure Consciousness, with no differentiation: that formless, transcendent, eternal aspect of Consciousness that we call the One Mind, or the Absolute. How does Consciousness manifest? The All manifests in limitless forms, such as majestic mountains, beautiful flowers, you, and me. The All appeared to Christians early in this era as Jesus. The All manifested to Muslims in the 7th century as the voice of Muhammad, to Hindus in the content of the Vedas, to Buddhists as Gautama Siddhartha.

All of these physical manifestations of The All describe our reality ruled by opposites: the world of duality. I attended a conference last fall where a lot of really smart people used a lot of really big words to discuss the subject of NON-duality—that state of wholeness beyond this manifest world. To them it was all theory. I sat there and said, "It's not theory! I experience that state of wholeness on a regular basis!" I know that our essential nature is pure consciousness. One experiences this through meditation. It is in an expanded state that one dis-identifies with the contents of the mind and comes to rest in and as pure consciousness.

This repeated experience with consciousness has afforded me the ability to connect at times with extreme clarity with the greater non-physical reality, not just mentally, but physically. One of the most memorable examples of this was when I brought through a young man known as Michael "Wolf" Pasakarnis. I shared Wolf with many of you at last year's ASCSI conference. His story became the subject of my book, *Wolf's Message*.

What initially caught my attention when I learned about Wolf was how he died. He was killed the same way as my Susan. It was interesting that Susan came to me in a vivid dream before she was killed, as if her soul knew she was going to pass. Wolf certainly had an awareness at a soul level that this reality is not the only one. He walked in both worlds at once: the physical and the non-physical.

Wolf had difficulty turning off his awareness of what he considered his true home. If you haven't read *Wolf's Message*, I won't spoil the story by sharing the amazing proof he left before his death of what the soul knows. He sent me many signs of his presence after the reading I did for his parents. The most memorable for me shows how those on the other side can shift our reality to get our attention.

I had been drawn to go into my neighborhood Barnes and Noble store because I was told by my guides that there was a book there for me. I stood in front of the shelves of metaphysical books and something happened that had never happened to me before: one of the books moved. It moved twice, in fact.

I knew when this happened that it was an illusion—that anyone else standing with me would not have seen or heard the book move as I did. I also knew that it was done by my unseen helpers as a way of drawing my attention to that particular book to help me solve one of the puzzles Wolf left me. You see, in a reading, those on the other side can manipulate my senses to replicate a physical symptom from which they suffered. These symptoms are highly evidential, and the moment I report them, the pain or sensation goes away.

Reality for most of us is what our brain tells us. We humans rely upon our brain to interpret our reality. To the brain, everything is a frequency. So, to create a meaningful feeling in my body, Spirit simply creates the right frequency that the brain interprets as "real." This is probably fairly easy for those on the other side, who are dealing with higher frequencies. The lesson here is to not be fooled by what your brain tells you.

Perception is reality. If reality is relative, then what is real? Reality differs based on how we perceive things with our senses. A bee's brain processes signals much faster than the human brain. A bee flying past a fluorescent light would see the light as strobing. To us the light is solid. Our two realities are different, but both are equally real.

Is there anything beyond our brain's range of perception that we can't see or hear? Certainly. Take a dog's perception as a comparison. Dogs hear frequencies that our brains can't detect. Dogs see differently as well. Their sense of color is muted in comparison to ours. Try to tell a dog that there are colors more vivid than they can imagine in this world—something those on the other side have told me in sessions with them—and a dog could not comprehend such a concept (beyond the obvious communication challenges). But can we imagine how there could be things and experiences beyond our brain's ability to perceive? Of course.

When things happen to us that are beyond our current understanding, we call these "miracles." My definition of a miracle is simple: A miracle is an effect at this level of reality from a cause at a level of reality that we simply can't perceive. Let's use the example of a snail, whose brain perceives signals much more slowly than our human brains. Imagine a snail is looking at an apple on a table and a human hand reaches in and snatches the apple away before the snail's brain has time to process the visual image of the hand. What did the snail see? One moment the apple was there, and the next moment it appears to have vanished because the snail never perceived the hand.

To the snail ... it's a miracle! What is the snail's reality? The apple vanished. But with our greater perspective, we know the cause of the apple's disappearance. Could an unseen helping hand be reaching in to our reality when what we call "miracles" occur?

I have experienced many miracles in this work—those "no other explanation" experiences I mentioned. It was a big leap of faith at first for me to be doing this job. I thought I had gotten out of my box when I began communicating with loved ones who had passed, but I had a ways to go in taking the lid off my self-imposed box.

Through my meditations I have been introduced to a team of helpers with whom I commune every day after touching that non-dual state and coming down just a bit. This collective consciousness advised me to call them Sanaya. I found out when they first appeared that Sanaya is a Sanskrit name meaning "eminent, distinguished, and of the gods." It was only a few months ago that I found out it is also a Muslim girl's name meaning "flash of lightning"—quite an interesting choice of names considering how my stepdaughter was killed.

Today, I occasionally share Sanaya's words aloud in special group sessions. It is the evidence they bring through that has allowed me and others who were skeptical of this type of spirit communication to trust that the words are coming from consciousness beyond this limited self known as Suzanne. In a recent session, while I was in an expanded state of consciousness, a woman claimed her daughter was having trouble with bronchitis, and asked Sanaya about her daughter's health. Sanaya stated that a more serious issue her daughter was dealing with was diabetes. The next day, the daughter told the woman that blood work done because of her bronchitis revealed that she had diabetes.

This kind of experience with consciousness more refined than loved ones who have passed has allowed me to explore reality in ways I never could have imagined. I realized that this higher level of spirits we call "guides and angels" exists and that we can enjoy two-way communications with humor, cleverness, and intelligence. I feel their presence and they prove it to me every day. But what about communicating with even higher levels?

I was pondering that possibility one day while reading works allegedly channeled by Jesus. Two of these include the highly respected *A Course in Miracles* and *The Jeshua Letters*, written by a former skeptic like me named Marc Hammer. After reading about Marc's early encounters with Jesus, I set his book down and said, "Jesus, if you can come to normal people and skeptics like Helen Shucman and Marc Hammer, then I would like to experience your presence. I would like to feel you."

Sitting there on my couch, I felt an incredibly powerful presence step into my field of awareness. I mentally acknowledged this presence and said, "If this is really you, Jesus, please give me a Bible quote that is relevant." Immediately I heard words that stunned me, for I don't know the Bible well at all. I heard "Thessalonians First, 2:13." When I repeated this to my husband, Ty, he did a double take because he had never heard "Thessalonians" cross my lips. So I dusted off the only Bible we had in our house, just as Marc Hammer had done, and I read the verse given to me:

1 Thessalonians 2:13 And we also thank God continually because, when you received the word of God, which you heard from us, you accepted it not as a human word, but as it actually is, the word of God, which is indeed at work in you who believe.

The study notes to the side read, "God can use humans as instruments to deliver his truth." I found this to be a highly relevant verse in light of my request to be given some kind of evidence to show me that I was communicating with the consciousness of Jesus.

The next afternoon as I was reading more of *The Jeshua Letters* I again felt the presence of Jesus. I heard guidance about how my doubts were holding me back, and that if I would only surrender, I could hold the link with Jesus for as long as I wanted. Without asking, I was given another Bible verse as I heard, "Corinthians 2:14. Blessings be upon you. First Corinthians. The words you find will speak to you. Trust them when they speak to the heart."

I came out of the meditation and looked in my Bible for 1 Corinthians 2:14. The verse read, *"The person without the Spirit does not accept the things that come from the Spirit of God but considers them foolishness, and cannot understand them because they are discerned only through the Spirit."* The study notes explained: "Paul's point was that his wisdom originated from God's spirit, not from human intellect. Paul consistently maintained that the Holy Spirit was available to all believers." It was the same message as Thessalonians 2:13.

A few weeks later, Ty and I were preparing for a month's vacation in Key West. As we were packing, a voice inside me said, "Find the small book by Joel Goldsmith." I searched all of my shelves for *The Infinite Way*, the smallest of Goldsmith's books I own, which I had read years earlier. I could not find it, but the voice clearly said a second time, "Find *The Infinite Way*." I looked again with no luck.

On the morning of our departure, I was loading the car. The voice told me to look one more time. I looked again, and there it was on a shelf in the bedroom where I had already looked. On the eight-hour drive to Key West, I pulled out the book and begin to scan it. I could tell from the highlighted and dog-eared pages that I had read the book in its entirety. A date in the margin showed that I had read it two years earlier.

I was suddenly overcome with the presence of Jesus. I heard, "Read the book from the beginning." I turned to the front of the book and began at the beginning, as directed. There were a few Biblical quotes here and there. When I reached page 27 I found what sounded like a quote from the Bible, but there were no footnotes or references, just quotation marks. It sounded strangely familiar. I wondered if this could possibly be one of the two verses Jesus gave me when I felt and channeled him earlier. I read it again, but I could only wonder, because none of the quotes in Goldsmith's book gave references to chapter and verse.

I read on in the book. There were no additional Bible quotes until two pages later. I got to page 29 and read another quote that seemed strangely familiar. I grew very nervous, but excited. As soon as I could, I logged on to the Internet. I did a search for the quotes on page 27 and 29, and in that moment my whole view of the world and reality changed: On two separate pages in a book that I was so very clearly led to find were two Biblical quotes: Corinthians 2:14 and 1 Thessalonians 2:13.

There are 33,000 verses in the Bible. Goldsmith never gives references. If I had read these in the past, I glossed right over them and had no idea where they came from. These two references were given to me by a higher consciousness as an immediate that I felt as Jesus, in answer to my asking for a Biblical reference.

Goldsmith wrote, "Trust the words you hear when they speak to the heart." These words hit me like a blow to the chest, because Jesus had said to me that morning when he gave me the second Bible verse, "Trust them when they speak to the heart."

This was when I truly knew there is only One Mind. There is no other explanation for this. I realized then that this One Mind is not some limited being, but one Consciousness, and we are part of it.

Joel Goldsmith was a pretty sharp guy. In his book, *The Infinite Way*, on page 27 he wrote, "How frequently do we attempt to understand spiritual wisdom using our human intellect?" And on page 29 he wrote, "To receive the word of God or spiritual sense we need to feel rather than reason. This is referred to biblically as receiving the word 'in the heart.'"

What is your intellect telling you about communicating with deceased loved ones? About direct communication with Jesus? Is there even more to reality than this? If it is possible for humans to communicate with this refined energy, what about other beings who are allegedly at the same level? Are you ready for another "miracle"?

My main focus is always on improving the connection with the spirit world. The reason I've been able to tune in to these different frequencies is because everything is energy and we are made up of that same energy. I know that the energy around us is first detected through our intuition, a sense unto itself that is connected with our human energy field. One day I decided to play with this field and see if I could fine-tune it like an antenna. I chose a specific shape for my antenna, one of the more powerful shapes in sacred geometry known as the star tetrahedron.

If this sounds a bit "out there" for you, it did to me, too, but I have learned to play with new concepts. I sat in meditation and pictured this shape around me. Using my consciousness, I made it bigger. As I did so, I felt physically and mentally more expansive and open.

Suddenly, I became aware of several very familiar spirits on the other side. I had brought through these same spirits when conducting experimental investigations with Dr. Gary Schwartz in his laboratory of human consciousness at the University of Arizona. The accuracy of the evidence given to me that day was around 90%, and the energy I felt sitting in my newly tuned antenna allowed me to feel them just as clearly. I hadn't heard from them in quite some time, and they passed along some messages for Gary. I later shared these with him by email. He responded, "Amazing—and perfect timing."

At the same time that I heard from Gary's spirit team members, I heard my own guides, Sanaya, saying, "Get the latest book by Lynn McTaggart." I knew of Lynn's work from when I read her previous book, *The Field*. That book explained to me how the work I do is possible, from a scientific perspective, introducing me to concepts in the field of quantum physics.

After that meditation with the antenna, I went online and saw that Lynn McTaggart did have a new book. I immediately downloaded it to my Kindle. When I read the table of contents, my faith in the spirit world was confirmed yet again. Chapter 2 of the book I had been guided to buy the first time I played with the concept of visualizing an antenna in my energy field was "The Human Antenna."

The surprises continued when I opened Chapter 2 and read the first paragraph. It mentioned Dr. Gary Schwartz, the man whose spirit team had come to me during that same meditation when I was advised to buy that book.

The next day Ty and I flew to Arizona, where I was going to give a presentation in Sedona. We spent the night at a hotel in Phoenix. During my meditation the following morning in the hotel room, I decided to play again with the antenna visualization. As I did so, I felt a dramatic increase in energy. The presence was as strong as when the consciousness of Jesus had been present, but this felt slightly different. When I asked whom I was feeling, I experienced a bit of dismay. The answer I received was "Archangel Michael." My dismay stemmed from the remnants of doubt about the spirit world honed in my career as a naval officer. I had only recently learned to trust that guides and angels were real, but could I allow myself to believe that archangels also existed?

I decided to follow my own advice and play. I welcomed Michael for coming and asked what he had to share with me. The words that followed pertained to my work as a spiritual teacher and medium, with instructions as to how to increase my attunement. I always meditate with a pad of paper and pen to write the messages from Sanaya, so I wrote Michael's messages as well. The message ended with these words:

Hebrews. This is coherence. This is coherence. A gift.

I came out of the meditation and immediately googled "Hebrews." Jesus had given me the two Bible verses in the past that were undeniably relevant. I wondered if perhaps Michael—if this was indeed him—had been trying to lead me to the book of Hebrews in the Bible. This time there was no particular verse mentioned. I had written a few numbers on the page, but scratched them out, as I felt I was making them up. I scanned the book of Hebrews on my iPad, but saw nothing relevant to anything going on in my life. I did not tell Ty about the special presence I had experienced, because I did not want him to think I was being foolish. I truly thought the experience was the result of a fanciful imagination.

We left Phoenix and headed for Sedona. On the way, I called Gary Schwartz. As we chatted, we discussed my recent antenna synchronicities relating to finding him in Chapter 2 of McTaggart's book. Gary mentioned that he had lectured at Canyon Ranch the night before about antennas. He said something about one of the men present that I didn't catch, but I perked up when he said, "Michael was in Sedona." I immediately thought it was strange to hear that name just after my possible first-ever encounter with the presence of Archangel Michael. I made a mental note of this synchronicity and sent out the thought, "If that was really Archangel Michael, give me a very clear sign in Sedona." I did not mention my meditation experience to Gary for fear he would think I was suddenly leaning to the looney side, and he would want no more to do with my work.

We arrived in Sedona and began looking for the trailhead Ty had picked out for our day's hike. We missed the turn, so we decided to go to the Little Horse Trailhead, which was nearby. I changed into hiking gear in the small restroom in the parking lot and off we went. It was gray and snowing, so we were the only hikers on the trail.

Twenty minutes into the hike, we heard voices ahead. We caught up to another couple and began to overtake them. I detected a foreign language and slowed down to try and figure out what it was. I was a foreign language major and found it intriguing that I could not identify a single word of the language they were speaking.

As we passed the couple, I gave them a cheery "Good morning," then asked, "What language are you speaking?" The woman said, "Guess." I told her I didn't have a clue. She replied, "Hebrew."

I was stunned to hear this word after my experience in meditation hours earlier. Ty asked them where they lived, and they said near Tel Aviv. We hiked on and I remarked to Ty that I had just had a wonderful synchronicity, but I would explain it later.

Five minutes up the trail we stopped for Ty to take a photo. The couple caught up to us. They asked why we were in town and Ty uncharacteristically said, "For my wife to give a presentation." (We don't usually bring up anything that will lead to a conversation about my work until we can feel out who we're talking to). When the woman asked what it was about, I uncharacteristically gave her the full story. I said, "It's about my unusual transition from U.S. Navy commander to my current work as a medium."

The woman gaped and said, "Medium? U.S. Navy I can believe, but medium I cannot. I am a scientist."

I said, "Oh, but this is all about science! It's all about tuning in to a frequency that we simply can't tune in to with our current technology. It's all consciousness."

Her husband said, "I understand frequency. I am an electrical engineer."

I said, "Recently I've been learning about antennas because by visualizing an antenna, I'm able to fine-tune my reception." Ty confirmed that on the flight to Arizona the day before we had had a long talk about antennas and frequency. The man said, "My specialty is antennas."

I felt as if I were in an alternate reality. Here were these "Hebrews" on the trail and one of them was an antenna specialist. We were not even supposed to be on that trail, yet it seemed as if it was already known at a different level of reality that we would meet this couple.

I told the couple about hearing "Hebrews" in my meditation that morning and how it related to my antenna work. They appeared surprised, but the woman especially looked as if she did not know how to process this information.

We hiked on ahead of them and came to the end of the trail. I noticed the couple 100 yards away looking over an edge. I suddenly knew I was supposed to ask the man if his name was Michael. I thought, "That would be too much!" At the same time, I had a knowingness that his name was NOT Michael, yet I was supposed to ask him anyway. The reason why soon became clear.

I trotted over to them, feeling a bit foolish, and said to the man, "Your name isn't Michael is it?" He smiled tolerantly and said, "No." I explained, "I also heard the name 'Michael' in meditation this morning. He glanced at his wife, who said, "I am Michal." With her accent she pronounced it like Michael in Russian, with three syllables (*Me-hah-el*).

I asked the woman how to explain this further synchronicity and she said, "If you are so good, tell me what kind of scientist I am." I laughed and told her that my attunement doesn't work like that. I need to be in an altered state. She looked vindicated, until her husband said, "Use your antenna!" His suggestion made perfect sense, and I realized I had nothing to lose if I tried.

I turned to the side, closed my eyes, pictured the antenna array, and asked the question of my guides about her specialty. I turned back to her and said, "Cellular biology." She blinked, hesitated, and then said, "Not cellular." I smiled and said, "But it is biology." She looked defiant and said, "Biology is a big field." Her husband said something to her in Hebrew. I said, "And you do something with DNA." She said, "Not exactly," and again her husband spoke to her in Hebrew. His tone both times was exactly as if he were saying, "Come on. You know she's close. Give her a break."

I invited them to come to the movie that night and told them about my website. Ty and I hiked back to the trailhead. We quickly lost them from sight. I was lost in thought the whole way. We passed the trail register, which we had very uncharacteristically not signed. I opened the lid, and there was a foreign name, the word "Israel," and "party of 2"on the second line. I copied down the name to look them up online later.

When we got to the car, I heard clear guidance that if I changed my clothes, the couple would arrive back just as I finished so that I could show them the notebook with my meditation notes. The timing was perfect, exactly as predicted. When I showed them my notes (*Hebrews. This is coherence. This is coherence. A gift.*) They exchanged glances once again, and the man said, "We both specialize in coherence." I couldn't help but notice that the phrase "This is coherence" was given to me two times, just as there were two of them.

I said, "How do you explain this?"

The woman said, "So these abilities you have ... You use them to talk to people who have died, correct?"

I said yes, and she said, "Don't you do anything USEFUL with it?"

In spite of the off-handed insult, she must have been interested enough to look at my website, because she sent me an email later that day. There in the email was her name and title: a Ph.D. professor at a university in Israel in the subject of structural biology—a field I had never heard of. It would have been too hard for my guides to get that through to me, so they used a term I had heard before: cellular biology. I learned that structural biologists are interested in the function of cells and work with nucleic acids. It wasn't exactly DNA (Deoxyribo Nucleic Acid), but it was close enough for me.

I browsed through a book about Archangel Michael in a Sedona bookstore later that day. In it I read a phrase that sounded familiar to me, so I googled it. The phrase said, "You will know

Michael is present when you entertain certain strangers, for by so doing, some people have entertained angels without knowing it." Do you know where I had read that phrase, just hours earlier? *Hebrews* 13:2.

I know that those two Hebrew-speaking scientists on the trail were "real people," but what is the definition of an angel? A messenger. Those two were *the gift* Michael spoke about when he came to me that morning. This gift allowed me to expand my concept of reality and what is real.

Sometime after that encounter in Sedona, I was back home and sat to do a reading at the request of Gary Schwartz. The reading did not go well at first. It was as if the information coming through were somehow blocked. In frustration, I asked the client who he had hoped to hear from. He told me that he was hoping to receive validation about things other mediums had told him about himself. I was surprised that Gary had asked me to do a psychic reading instead of tuning in to spirits on the other side, but I wanted to give them both what they desired.

I set the new intention of tuning in to information about the client, himself, and immediately felt an up-shift in the energy present. I recognized the presence as that of Archangel Michael. I knew him by the feel of him. He came with a message for me. He said, "It is time to get yourself out of the little box you've put yourself in." When I told my client who was present, he said, "Can you ask him if we have ever met physically in this lifetime?"

My rational mind wanted to rebel, but by this time I was in a highly expanded state of consciousness. I proceeded to share with the client details of an encounter that he later confirmed were exactly what he had experienced the night his life was saved by a stranger on a dark, country road. The client had been falling asleep at the wheel on a long trip when a man appeared, seemingly out of nowhere. I asked Michael to describe what happened, and he showed me a man dressed all in white who looked like a preacher. He was carrying nothing but a Bible. He and my client had discussed death and dying, and they exchanged a look deep into each other's eyes that was like looking into the soul.

My client confirmed all of these details. Had I not felt the highly refined energy that I recognized from that visit from Michael in Arizona, I might have thought I was simply reading my client's mind, but this was very real to me. It showed me that higher consciousness can materialize in physical form, breaking the rules of our dimension of reality if it serves a purpose. In this case, this man did not drive off the road that dark night, but went on to do very good works for humanity.

What good do these kinds of readings serve? What good is tapping into the higher realms if the result is not growth or service to the Whole? Is it useful? In that reading for the client, Michael said the following:

Any effort that you can make to raise consciousness through the awareness of the basic essence of all life, which is love, is well worth the effort. Continue with all diligence your efforts to bring more awareness of the basic fact of life that all is one ... that love is all that matters.

To me, that reading was very useful. I went on to follow his advice. I took the lid off the box from that day forward and allowed those in spirit to get through whatever they knew was in the best interest of all concerned. This willingness took my readings to a whole new level. I know now that Spirit always knows what the client needs, whether that be hearing from deceased loved ones or hearing guidance about issues in their personal lives.

The information coming through is now often channeled directly until I open my eyes and find my client staring at me with wide eyes. I'll say, "That was spot on, wasn't it?" and they'll nod their heads. I can take no credit for any of it. I only had to get out of the way and allow Spirit to work through me.

How am I able to do this? Because a medium's antenna—their energy field—is just a bit more highly tuned than others. The challenge is that until you have a personal experience of these finer frequencies, it is easy to think that this physical world is all there is.

I have been going out on a limb here, talking about communing with spirits, with Jesus, and with archangels who manifest on dark, country roads. This is real "outside the box" thinking, isn't it? But what is real? Is anyone squirming yet? Ah, but we're not finished yet.

As I mentioned, I sit to meditate daily. I receive messages daily from Sanaya. One day I had a new visitor. It was male, and he had a long white beard. He looked a bit like Moses. I said, "Who are you?" and he replied, "Odin." This took me aback. I knew nothing about Odin. I did not know what he looked like, who he was, or even if he had been a real person. There's that word "real" again.

He showed me a flying horse and said, "We are showing you how to fly, to soar." I felt an actual physical pain in my side as if I had been pierced. I heard, "Odin comes to teach you the secrets of the runes. There is much wisdom there. See the one shaped like a lightning bolt. It has great meaning for you." I asked, "Is there one?" and he replied, "What do you think?"

The first thing I did when I came out of meditation was to google "Odin." Wikipedia showed me that he is a major god in Germanic mythology, especially in Norse mythology. He was considered the Allfather of the gods ... pretty high up there! Every photo I came across showed him looking like an image of Moses with a white beard. I found it particularly interesting in light of my latest book, *Wolf's Message*, that Odin was usually depicted with two wolves at his side.

The rune connection was prominent in *Wolf's Message*. In this alleged visit with Odin he had said, "Odin comes to teach you the secrets of the runes." I had never heard of runes until I heard from Wolf, who painted their symbols quite often. I discovered that morning that Odin is, in fact, credited with discovering runes. According to the myths, he discovered them when he hung from a tree upside down for nine days, pierced in the side by his own sword, just as I had felt the piercing sensation in my own side.

I looked to see if there was a rune with a lightning bolt as Odin had advised me, and he was correct: there was one. It is called "Odin's Rune." This is quite appropriate in light of how my stepdaughter and Wolf were killed, and it became even more appropriate as I read of its meaning. Odin's Rune—the lightning bolt—is the rune of messages, prophecy, and wisdom. He had said he came to teach me the secrets of the runes because there is much *wisdom* there. All of this did, indeed, have much meaning for me, as he said it would, especially when I found out that yes, Odin had a flying horse.

May I remind you of my background? Former aide to the Chairman of the Joint Chiefs, a commanding officer, and now I am being visited by Norse gods. So, I went back into meditation and asked him to appear again. He did. I asked him to tell me more. He told me much, much more, but we need to conclude this presentation. I will get to the point. In that second visit with Odin I asked, "Are you REAL?" And he replied, "As real as you are, but not human." I asked, "But you are a myth," and he replied without missing a beat, "YOU are a myth. Nothing is real."

What purpose does a myth serve? The myths that recur throughout history are attempts to answer universal questions about life. Odin answered some of my questions about life quite clearly. He stated:

"You must stop differentiating between real and unreal. Do you not know now that angels and archetypes are real? All archetypes are groupings of consciousness at different levels of vibration. Anything that you can create in consciousness is real and can convey truth, messages, information, learning, healing, and growth. All is not as it seems. You are just another part of me."

I had asked Odin, "Are you real?" and he replied, *"As real as you are."* So I ask all of you: What is real?

How do you explain flying horses, feeling physically pierced in the side, runes shaped like lightning bolts? Was he a myth? From the soul's point of view, the only question that matters is, "What purpose did his visit serve?" It helped me to understand even more that All That Is is Consciousness expressing itself in all forms and without form.

Remember: the thinking mind is only one aspect of our wholeness. The thinking mind actually interferes with our perception of life as a dynamic, interrelated, unfolding whole. The thinking mind says that all of these stories are B.S.!

If I had dismissed Odin's visits as "not real," I would have denied myself his third and most recent visit. I hadn't thought of Odin in months, but there I was meditating and he made his presence known. We chatted for a bit, then he said, *"Who was my son?"* I thought for just a moment, and then I recalled learning this when first researching Odin.

I replied, "Your son was Thor, the Norse god associated with lightning." There was that lightning connection yet again.

Then Odin asked, *"And who was Susan's dog? Think of the puppy on the couch. Get the photo."* This, for me, was a true, "Oh my God" moment. I instantly recalled one of the last photos taken of our Susan nine years ago, just a few months before she was struck and killed by lightning. She is lying on the couch with her new puppy who she had named none other than *Thor*.

Until that moment just a few months ago in Odin's third visit, no one had made the connection with the dog's name and how Susan was killed. She bought him and named him after a god of lightning just a few weeks before she was killed by lightning. Sitting that morning at the breakfast table, I wondered, "What was her other dog's name?" At first I couldn't remember, then it was dropped into my thoughts: *Her other dog was Loki.*

Ty immediately looked up Loki on the Internet, and we discovered that Loki is considered by some to be the son of Odin.

Wolf knew when, where, and how he was going to die. He left proof in his final prophetic poem. Did Susan's soul also know? From talking to thousands of souls and experiencing countless miracles, I know that the soul is aware of far more than our conscious human minds are. Why? Because the soul walks in both worlds at once, and the two worlds are intricately connected like a giant web.

I picture the greater reality like the fabled Indra's Net—a vast web with a jewel at each juncture. Each jewel represents an individual life form, atom, cell or unit of consciousness, and each reflects all the other jewels in a cosmic matrix.

This evening I have tried to set the stage for the rest of this conference by redefining reality and opening your minds to all possibilities. I have tried to show you that we cannot put consciousness ... spirit ... reality in a box. All of the stories I have shared with you are evidence of one divine mind. Some might call that "God"—but to me, that term is too restrictive to describe "All That Is."

Remember ... we are talking about different realities combined. Taken all together, they represent oneness, wholeness, "that beyond which there is nothing more." My friend, retired professor James E. Royster, author of the book *Have This Mind*, has coined an inclusive term for that *"indescribable/indefinable force beyond which there is nothing more."* He calls it "Ultimacy."

I like this term much better than "the Absolute." With the definite article "the" you are inferring something that is definite, and "Ultimacy" is not anything that can be defined, therefore no 'the.' Also, unlike "the Absolute" there is no term indicating anything opposite to Ultimacy. Since Ultimacy is all there is, there can be nothing opposite.

What is real? The only true "real" is Ultimacy.

But let's not get wrapped around semantics. That would be like the woman who approached Thomas Edison and asked, "Mr. Edison, what is electricity?" And Edison replied, "Madame, electricity IS. Use it."

So, ladies and gentlemen, whether you call it *God, Mind, Ultimacy, Consciousness,* or *Whatever* ... use it!

This is the start of what is going to be a mind-expanding conference entitled "Aspects of Consciousness," where we get to explore aspects of all that is. If "all that is" is "Ultimacy" ... then anything is possible.

May we open our minds to the web of all possibilities this weekend and beyond, without defining things as "real" or "unreal." If we can do that, then we will experience first-hand what it is like to experience miracles in our lives as we enjoy the limitless gifts of simply "being."

Author Bio

Suzanne Giesemann, M.A.

Hay House author Suzanne Giesemann is a retired U.S. Navy Commander with a Master's Degree in Public Administration who served as a Commanding Officer and as aide-de-camp to the Chairman of the Joint Chiefs of Staff on 9/11. The author of eleven books, today former-commander Giesemann is a mystic, spiritual teacher, and practicing evidence-based medium focusing on self-transformation and spiritual awareness. In her presentations and workshops, she shares ancient spiritual wisdom blended with modern discoveries in science and consciousness. She backs up her teachings with verifiable evidence received during over a thousand one-on-one sessions with clients and through daily personal experience with higher levels of consciousness. For more about Suzanne, visit www.SuzanneGiesemann.com.

Bibliography:

Giesemann, Suzanne: www.LoveAtTheCenter.com
Giesemann, Suzanne (1998). *Conquer your Cravi*ngs. McGraw Hill
Giesemann, Suzanne (2007). *It's Your Boat Too.* Paradise Cay Publications
Giesemann, Suzanne (2008). *Living a Dream.* Paradise Cay Publications
Giesemann, Suzanne (2009). *The Priest and the Medium.* Hay House
Giesemann, Suzanne (2012). *The Real Alzheimer's: A Guide for Caregivers That Tells It Like It Is.* One Mind Books
Giesemann, Suzanne (2011). *Through the Darkness.* (ghost written for Janet Nohavec) Aventine Press
Giesemann, Suzanne (2011). *Where Two Worlds Meet.* (ghost written for Janet Nohavec) Aventine Press
Giesemann, Suzanne (2011). *Messages of Hope: The Metaphysical Memoir of a Most Unexpected Medium.* One Mind Books
Giesemann, Suzanne (2012). *Love Beyond Words*
Giesemann, Suzanne (2013). *In the Silence: 365 Days of Inspiration from Spirit*
Giesemann, Suzanne (2014). *Wolf's Message*

EFT and ADC for Physical Manifestations of Grief

Larry Burk, MD, CEHP

Abstract

Unresolved grief can manifest in the body as persistent physical symptoms, particularly involving the lungs and sinuses as an imbalance in the metal element according to Chinese five element theory. Chronic sinusitis, postnasal drip and recurrent bronchitis are common examples of grief-related afflictions. Once the psychosomatic origins of the symptoms are recognized, effective treatment can be facilitated using acupuncture, Emotional Freedom Techniques (EFT) and hypnosis. Dreamwork can then be used to introduce the concept of after-death communication (ADC) as an additional method of resolving grief.

Unresolved grief can manifest in the body as persistent physical symptoms, particularly involving the lungs and sinuses as an imbalance in the metal element, according to Chinese five element theory.[1] Chronic sinusitis, postnasal drip and recurrent bronchitis are common examples of grief-related afflictions. Psychoneuroimmunological mechanisms can explain the connection between stress and the development of chronic illnesses, but do not provide a complete explanation for the occurrence of metaphorical symptom complexes.[2] These symbolic diseases are often invisible to conventional physicians who attempt to treat such conditions with surgery and pharmaceuticals.

Medical exploration of the emotional roots of symbolic diseases has been pioneered by clinical immunologist/psychiatrist Brian Broom, who established a Mind-Body Programme in New Zealand to teach clinicians how to think symbolically in evaluating patients with somatization. An example of unresolved grief in his practice involved a 48-year-old male with a 10-year history of congestion, sneezing, and "cold, wet eyes." The symptoms that he described as "crying, without crying," began after he left his wife. During intensive psychotherapy he expressed a sense of sadness and failure at losing her. His symptoms resolved when he let go of longing for restoration of the relationship.[3]

The concept of symptoms as metaphors from an intuitive perspective has been popularized by Louise Hay.[4] She provides possible metaphysical causes for a variety of grief-related conditions. Post-nasal drip relates to "inner crying and childish tears." Sinusitis relates to "irritation to someone close." Lung problems relate to "depression and grief." Pneumonia relates to "emotional wounds that are not allowed to heal." While these symbolic meanings often seem like oversimplified generalizations, there is quite often a nugget of truth. She recently collaborated with psychiatrist/medical intuitive Mona Lisa Schulz in correlating the symbolic diseases of the chakras with references from the psychiatric literature.[5]

Once the psychosomatic origins of the symptoms are recognized, rapid treatment can be facilitated using hypnosis,[6] acupuncture[7] and Emotional Freedom Techniques (EFT).[8] EFT is moving more into the mainstream with the recent publication of a systematic review of 18 randomized controlled trials.[9] EFT tapping can be combined with breathwork and shaking in the EDANVIR protocol.[10] Once the body memory of the grief experience has been neutralized and reconsolidated with EFT, hypnotic reframing of the loss can be more easily accomplished. Dreamwork can then be used to introduce the concept of after-death communication (ADC) as an additional method of resolving grief.

Simply acknowledging that there might be a connection between lung and sinus disease and unresolved grief is enough to start the process of healing. After opening this possibility for the client it is likely that a variety of approaches that the practitioner is already trained in can be used to work with the emotional issues underlying the physical metaphor. The following introduction to EFT is sufficient to allow the incorporation of tapping into the therapeutic process using the EDANVIR protocol (Energize, Desensitize, Awfulize, Neutralize, Visualize, Internalize and Revitalize). Like self-hypnosis, EFT is a self-healing technique that can be taught in groups to clients to use between therapy sessions.[11]

The Energize step begins with the client rubbing on the sore spot on their chest while repeating a paradoxical affirmation summarizing their grief experience that includes a tapping reminder phrase. The Desensitize step involves sequential self-tapping on nine acupoints on the face and chest while repeating the reminder phrase. The Awfulize step expands the phrase to include deeper aspects of the issue. The Neutralize step adds positive phrases every other acupoint, balanced with the negative phrases. The Visualize step shifts to all positive phrases becoming self-hypnosis. The Internalize step includes brief hyperventilation with breathing in a healing color and then breathing out a color associated with grief.

The Revitalize step involves shaking the arms and legs to release any remaining body memories associated with the loss and to bring in new energy. These seven steps are followed by imagery work in a safe preferred place. First, any remaining grief is drained into a healing object and let go in a ceremonial fashion. Then the deceased is invited to come with them on a time travel journey back to positive memories of the past. After this ego strengthening task the client is given the option of revisiting any remaining grief memories and rescripting the outcome to restructure the memory. Finally, future progression is used to redefine the relationship with the deceased from a metaphysical perspective.

These hypnotic approaches can be useful in metaphysical relationship restructuring, where the connection to the deceased is maintained on a non-physical, spiritual level.[12] Practitioners may enhance this discussion with clients by asking whether any dreams of the deceased have occurred since death, as this form of ADC is relatively common in the general population.[13] Encouraging clients to keep dream diaries can be a valuable supplement to EFT and hypnosis, especially when suggestions are given to facilitate dream incubation of an ongoing connection to the deceased. It provides an opportunity to redefine the relationship from one of mourning and loss to one of meaning and transformation.

This combined approach was particularly useful in the case of a psychotherapist who self-referred, following a discussion about symbolic diseases in an EFT workshop, for treatment of chronic sinusitis and recurrent pneumonia nine months after the death of her husband.[14] She wanted to explore the symbolic nature of her symptoms in hopes of avoiding sinus surgery. ADCs from her husband in dreams provided the basis for imagery work during the EFT sessions, which in combination with acupuncture resulted in rapid clearing of her sinuses in time to cope effectively with the anniversary of his death. She canceled the scheduled surgery and subsequently referred other clients with similar grief-related symptoms.

Endnotes

[1] Jarrett, L. S. (2001). *Nourishing Destiny: The Inner Tradition of Chinese Medicine.* Stockbridge, MA: Spirit Path Press.

[2] Broom, B. C., Booth, R. J., & Schubert, C. (2012). Symbolic diseases and "mindbody" co-emergence. A challenge for psychoneuroimmunology. *Explore.* 8(1):16-25.

[3] Broom, B. (1997). *Somatic illness and the patient's other story: A practical integrative mind/body approach to disease for doctors and psychotherapists.* London: Free Association Books.

[4] Hay, L. L. (1988). *Heal your body: The mental causes for physical illness and the metaphysical way to overcome them.* Santa Monica, CA: Hay House.

[5] Hay, L. L. & Schulz, M. L. (2013). *All is Well: Heal Your Body with Medicine, Affirmations and Intuition.* Carlsbad, CA: Hay House.

[6] Elkins, G. R. (2000). Hypnosis, grief, and mourning. *Australian Journal of Clinical and Experimental Hypnosis,* 28(1):61–73.

[7] Suh, J. D., Wu, W. A., Taw, M. B., Nguyen, C., & Wang, M. B. (2012). Treatment of recalcitrant chronic rhinosinusitis with integrative East-West medicine: A pilot study. *Archives of Otolaryngology and Head and Neck Surgery,* 138(3):294-300.

[8] Burk, L. (2010). Single session EFT (Emotional Freedom Techniques) for stress-related symptoms after motor vehicle accidents. *Energy Psychology: Theory, Research and Treatment,* 2(1): 65-71.

[9] Feinstein, D. (2013). Acupoint stimulation in treating psychological disorders: Evidence of efficacy. *Review of General Psychology,* 16:364-380.

[10] Burk, L. (2012). *Let magic happen: Adventures in healing with a holistic radiologist.* Durham, NC: Healing Imager Press, 311-314.

[11] Church, D., De Asis, M., & Brooks, A. J. (2012). Brief group intervention using EFT (Emotional Freedom Techniques) for depression in college students: A randomized controlled trial. *Depression Research & Treatment,* 2012, Article ID 257172, 7 pages.

[12] Gravitz, M. A. (2001). Perceptual reconstruction in the treatment of inordinate grief. *American Journal of Clinical Hypnosis,* 44(1):51-55.

[13] Daggett, L. M. (2005). Continued encounters: The experience of after-death communication. *JHN,* 23(2):191-207.

[14] Burk, L. (2013). EFT for Physical Symptoms of Grief. *RealitySandwich.com.* http://realitysandwich.com/177896/eft_physical_symptoms_grie/

Author Bio

Larry Burk, MD, CEHP

Dr. Larry Burk is a holistic physician specializing in acupuncture, EFT, dreamwork and hypnosis. He was an Associate

Professor of Radiology at Duke University Medical Center until 2004, when he started Healing Imager, P.C. He was co-founder of Duke Integrative Medicine and former board president of the Rhine Research Center. Dr. Burk is a Certified Energy Health Practitioner and is also certified in clinical hypnosis. His book *Let Magic Happen: Adventures in Healing with a Holistic Radiologist* was published in 2012. His blogs, newsletters and other publications can be found at www.larryburkmd.com.

Energy Psychology
A Brief Introduction

David Feinstein, Ph.D.

Our ability to help people overcome self-defeating emotional patterns, achieve higher levels of psychological well-being, and open their spiritual sensibilities is accelerating at an extraordinary pace. This book introduces you to a powerful development within that unfolding story.

Candace Pert, Ph.D.,
In her Foreword to *The Promise of Energy Psychology*

Energy Psychology has been called "acupressure for the emotions." It is a therapeutic approach and a self-empowerment tool that draws from ancient spiritual practices and healing traditions. It provides simple methods for shifting brain patterns that maintain unwanted thoughts, actions, and emotions, such as fear, anger, anxiety, jealousy, shame, and depression. By tapping energy points on the surface of the skin while focusing the mind on specific psychological problems or goals, the brain's electrochemistry can be shifted to quickly help

- Overcome fear, guilt, shame, jealousy, anger, or anxiety.
- Change unwanted habits and behaviors.
- Enhance the ability to love, succeed, and enjoy life.

The approach offers powerful tools for the clinician as well as potent back-home tools for the client. This class is a hands-on introduction that will teach you the basic principles and enough technique that you can immediately begin using Energy

Psychology in your own life and make informed choices about how it might be integrated into your practice if you are a clinician.

Energy Psychology combines tools from conventional psychotherapy, such as focused imagination, with tools from healing and spiritual practices that understand the "vital energies" that are at the foundation of physical and mental health. It works by stimulating energy points on the surface of the skin which, when paired with specific psychological procedures, send signals to the brain that may impact stress chemicals such as cortisol and DHEA, deactivate limbic system arousal, and rapidly alter neural pathways. In brief, undesired responses can rapidly be uncoupled from their triggers, providing you with greater ease and freedom to live your life more effectively and joyfully.

Energy Psychology is still a controversial development within the mental health field. The techniques look quite strange, are adopted from foreign ancient cultures, and the claims of a growing number of practitioners seem almost too good to be true, but evidence is mounting that these techniques are significant, powerful tools for both self-help and clinical treatment.

Energy Psychology Fact Sheet

What It Is:

Energy Psychology is both a clinical technique and a self-help approach that provides simple methods for shifting brain patterns that lead to unwanted thoughts, actions, and emotions. It draws from ancient healing traditions, such as acupuncture and yoga, and uses them in thoroughly modern ways.

The Essential Principle:

Recent research shows that the brain's ability to alter neural pathways that are the source of many psychological disorders is far more extensive than previously believed ("neural plasticity").

How It Does It:

Tapping on acupuncture points (along with related techniques) while an anxiety-evoking memory or thought is brought to mind sends signals to the brain that turn off the anxious response in the moment and rapidly alters the brain chemistry that maintained that response.

The Conditions It Helps:

Variations of this strategy also appear to shift, for the person's benefit, the brain's coding of irrational anger, jealousy, guilt, shame, unremitting grief, compulsive behaviors, phobias, PTSD, depression, addictions, and chronic pain. The method has also been shown to promote peak performance and to help in attaining personal goals.

Who Practices It?

Both licensed mental health professionals—such as psychologists, psychiatrists, and social workers—and life coaches who do not treat mental disorders use the methods of Energy Psychology with their clients. Energy Psychology also offers back-home techniques for clients as well as potent self-help tools for those not in counseling. Variations include EFT (Emotional Freedom Techniques), TFT (Thought Field Therapy), and TAT (Tapas Acupuncture Technique), among numerous other formats.

What Does It Do to the Brain?

Energy Psychology works by stimulating energy points on the surface of the skin which, when paired with various psychological procedures, send signals to the brain that may impact stress chemicals such as cortisol and DHEA, deactivate limbic system arousal, and rapidly alter neural pathways.

Has Its Effectiveness Been Established?

Evidence is mounting that Energy Psychology is a significant, powerful tool for both self-help and clinical treatment. A literature review found 51 of 51 peer-reviewed outcome reports to show that the method was effective with a range of populations and conditions (Feinstein, 2012, *Review of General Psychology*). Also see *http://www.eftuniverse.com* and click "Research" in the sidebar. Links to some 300 articles can also be found in The EFT & Energy Psychology Article Library at *http://www.eft-articles.com*.

A Basic Energy Psychology Protocol on a Page

Preliminaries: Energy balancing, select memory or problem, rate distress from 0 to 10, formulate "Reminder Phrase."

Part 1: Acceptance Phrase. Rub the arm attachment area or tap the Karate Chop points while saying "Even though [name problem]" and then place hands over center of chest while saying "I deeply love and accept myself." Repeat three times.

Part 2: Tap the points (see below) while saying your Reminder Phrase out loud.

Part 3: Integration Sequence. Tap the indented area beneath the point where your ring finger and little finger meet on the back of your hand as you: 1) close your eyes, 2) open your eyes, 3) look down to the right, 4) look down to the left, 5) circle your eyes, 6) circle your eyes in the opposite direction, 7) hum a bar of a song, 8) count to five, 9) hum again. Optionally, end by sweeping your eyes out and up, sending energy through them.

Part 4: Repeat Part 2.

Repeat this sequence (Parts 1 through 4) as needed, until you can rate the memory or problem as 0 or near 0. Challenge the results by trying to invoke the disturbing feeling.

If the Problem Is Not Responding, identify and address other aspects of the problem, psychological reversals, scrambled energies, or energy toxins.

The Tapping Points:
- Inside of eyebrows
- Outside of eyes
- Under eyes
- Under nose
- Under lower lip

Collarbone points (K 27)
"Arm Attachment" points (optional)
Over thymus (optional)
Spleen points (4 inches below underarms)
Side of legs between hip and knee (optional)
Karate Chop points
    Triple Warmer point above knuckles between 4th & 5th fingers

Psychological Reversals

Psychological reversals might be based in

- conflicted *desire* about reaching the goal
- a sense of *not deserving* to reach the goal
- a feeling that it is *not safe* or *not possible* to reach the goal
- that reaching the goal is not compatible with the person's *identity*

    For instance, a person who wants to lose weight may have no difficulty with the thought, "I *want* to lose weight." But an energy disruption might appear with the related thought "I *deserve* to lose weight" or "It is *safe* to lose weight" or "It is *possible* for me to lose weight" or "I will do what's necessary to" or "I would no longer *be me* if I lost weight" or "If lose weight, men will start hitting on me."

    Useful themes to explore when identifying whether or not a psychological reversal is at play include:

I want to

I deserve to

It is safe for me to

It is possible for me to   } *reach this goal.*

I will feel deprived if I

I will do what's necessary to

I would still be me if I

To temporarily neutralize the energy that maintains a psychological reversal—long enough for the tapping rounds to work—massage the Central Meridian Lymphatic Points (where the arm attaches to the shoulders) while repeating an Acceptance Statement three times.

The format for the Acceptance Statement can be based on the above wordings. For instance, if the psychological reversal is "It is not safe for me to overcome my fear of driving," the Acceptance Statement would be

"Even though it is not safe for me to overcome my fear of driving . . . I deeply love and appreciate myself."

Author Bio

David Feinstein, Ph.D.

David Feinstein, Ph.D., is a clinical psychologist who has served on the faculties of The Johns Hopkins University School of Medicine, Antioch College, and the California School of Professional Psychology. Author of eight books and more than eighty professional articles, he has been a pioneer in the areas of Energy Psychology and Energy Medicine. His books have won nine national awards, including the *U.S. Book News* Best Psychology/Mental Health Book in 2007 (for *Personal Mythology*) and an *Indies* Best Books Award (for *The Promise of Energy Psychology*)

An Experiential Approach to Survival of Death
Extracts from EVP and ITC Images

Nandini Sinha Kapur, Ph.D., JNU

Abstract

Literature and laboratory findings have debated and proved the survival of human spirit/soul after physical death. This brief paper is based on the presenter's personal experience of actually experiencing her late husband's presence in her life and house. Initially, my husband, Prof. Vijay Kapur, who died of sudden cardiac arrest in his Delhi University office on 31 May, 2013, made his presence felt through a lot of noise, sweet fragrance, and taking water from the glass of water kept for him in front of his photo (July 2013-August 2014).

Recorded conversations with Vijay began in January 2014. These have yielded wonderful results, proving that Vijay has survived by his personality, memory, consciousness and even exact voice. Water ITC indicates his willingness and mission to announce to the world that Vijay has survived.

This is a preliminary note based on the author's personal experiences. This narrative is supported by a few EVP recordings and water ITC images to prove survival of bodily death. This essay opens with a quote from Ian Stevenson's observations.

Ian Stevenson argued for the importance of studying spontaneous experiences in physical research. To those who dismiss such cases as mere "anecdotes" and the study of them as "unscientific," Ian called attention to "the revolution accomplished within our generation in ago as mere 'bird watchers,' they have shaken the dogmas of men who were content to study animals only in laboratories. Those of us who study spontaneous cases are the ethologists. Scorned thirty years were content to study spontaneous cases are the ethologists of parapsychology" (Steven son, 1971, p. 123).

Ian was the premier modern "ethologist of parapsychology." He did more than perhaps anyone else in the 20th century to identify, investigate, and report what he called "major paranormal phenomena." Although in the course of his long career he investigated nearly every kind of such phenomena, he concentrated on those especially relevant to the question whether human personality survives the death of the body. As he and others have pointed out, the phenomena of psychical research in general, suggesting as they do that consciousness can operate beyond the confines of ordinary sensorimotor processes, could be said to support the survival of consciousness beyond the death of the physical body.

It is reasonable to suppose that, whatever aspect of a living mind mediates, it may survive the death of the body with which it is associated. However, evidence of extrasensory perception is only indirect evidence pointing to the possibility of survival after death; and when we discuss the question of survival after death, we usually mean to consider direct evidence that a particular personality survived it.[1]

The author is a career academic without any background in paranormal experience. The death of my revered husband, Prof. Vijay Kapur, in a sudden cardiac arrest in his office in FMS, Delhi University on 31 May 2013, in front of our eight-year-old son, Aditya, was the turning point in my life. It marked the beginning of paranormal experiences. On the very night of his death, I was intrigued by the auto-adjustment of time in Vijay's Airtel Mobile. We left for the Hindu Pilgrimage Centre, Haridwar (foothill of the Himalaya, located on the Ganges) a son 5 June 2013, to immerse the sacred bones into the Holy Ganges as every Hindu does one way to Haridwar. I discovered that someone had made a call from Vijay's mobile to a Delhi University landline number on that morning. I was very surprised as we were very busy that morning hurrying for Haridwar. I called that number and found it was the examination branch in Delhi University. Vijay was busy preparing project results for his MBA students of Delhi University as grade sheets had to be issued. He had submitted all grade sheets in May 2013. This phone call kept me wondering, but I was indeed too grieved to ponder over it. The entire month of June was spent in death-rituals. There may have been other signs of Vijay's survival of bodily death but I was too distressed to note. It all began in July 2013. Here was the "subliminal self" of Vijay.

In the first week of July 2013, on my way to Aditya's school one afternoon (travelling in Vijay's car), I and my driver for the first time smelled such a sweet fragrance of flowers in the midst of a traffic jam that we did not doubt the presence of Vijay. I was later told by the Indian Paranormal Society that this "spirit-manifestation" repeated itself in March 2014 and August 2014, among other occasions. Vijay made his presence felt many times by making noises such as crashing utensils in front of me and my attendant, the sound of someone walking in Sandals heard by Aditya once (June, 2014), opening doors heard by driver, and I heard many times the drawing of curtains. Vijay demonstrated his presence in the house after his physical death: very important.

Another dimension was his expression through writing and mobile telephones. In January 2014, we discovered two "I" like words on two walls facing each other in Vikram's room (Vijay's brother) in pinkish-paint. We had an animated discussion as to whose work it was at that height on the wall. All concluded that Aditya, 9 years old then, could not have done it, since he could not reach that height. Aditya denied doing it and we know that Aditya was not in the habit of scribbling on wall. It is still a mystery about what kind of ink or paint was used. Now those two pinkish letters have worn off and the paint has come off. I still wonder how Vijay mastered that "paint." He was actually practicing writing that he had done all his life. He proved it on 25

February 2014 when we discovered a legend on the glass-mirror in my bathroom—"love you"—clearly written. We tried hard to photograph the legend, which was difficult because the legend was on a mirror.

Vijay also made his presence felt through mobile telephones. I received two blank SMSs in my in-box from Vijay's mobile on 1and 2 August 2013. I immediately checked the "sent box" in Vijay's mobile. There was no SMSs sent on 1 and 2 August, 2013. My investigation stirred a hornet's nest in my extended family, warning against a stranger's closing my husband's mobile connection. When I met the president of the Indian Paranormal Society (New Delhi) for the first time in late September 2013, I was told that those two blank SMSs from Vijay could indicate significant news that was about to happen. I came to know on 3 August 2013 that one of Vijay's close senior colleagues, Prof. Bhalla, from FMS, DU, had passed away in a sudden cardiac arrest in his house on the night of 2 August 2013. Prof. R.S. Maan died on 1 September 2013.

The second incident happened on 5 November 2013. I had a faint idea that my maternal uncle was ported for a cataract surgery in November, 2013. I usually don't scroll-down the menu. But I started scrolling down and stopped at "reminder." I was surprised to read "remembers Mama" (mater not uncle). I realized Vijay's instructions and immediately I called up my uncle next day morning. He needed some small help from me on the day of his surgery, 15 November 2015. This message stayed in my "Reminder" box for months and disappeared. The message that still remains in my "Reminder" box came on the night of 23 September 2014. I went for a new Honda Amaze car in late September 2014. It is a significant point that I first booked the base model of a Honda Amaze on 5 May 2013, exactly twenty-five days before Vijay physically passed away on 31 May 2013. On the night of 23 September 2014 I was stopped for a second time to open my "Reminder" box. I was pleasantly surprised to read the legend, "New Amaze," with the date of 28 September 2014, exactly the day of delivery (Sunday, 28 September 2014). We all realized that Vijay was closely watching each and every development in his family's life.

The above narrative of our experience of Vijay's survival of bodily death certainly proves the concept of Frederick W.H. Myers's "**subliminal** self." In Myers' well-known publication, *Human Personality and Its Survival of Bodily Death*," he explains that the soul of man is capable of existing independent of the body in some super-terrestrial or extraterrestrial realm. He perceived that the soul could only partially manifest itself through the human brain and material world. Much of the life of the soul fails to find expression in our conscious and organic life through its interactions with this very inadequate material mechanism beneath the threshold of consciousness that is said to constitute the subliminal self (From Wiki source 1911 Encyclopedia Britannica based on F.W.H. Myers, *Human Personality and Its Survival of Bodily Death*, 1st ed. London, 1903., 2nd ed. Abridged and edited by L. H. Myers, London, 1907., Morton Prince. *The Dissociation of a Person*, London, 1907, J. Jastrow, *The Subconscious*, London, 1906).

However, we may contest one of the premises in this survival thesis that the personality which survives the "death of body" is not the normal self-conscious personality of a man as is known and valued by his friends but a "stunted distorted fragment" (F.W.H. Myers, *Human Personality and Its Survival of Bodily Death*, Wiki source).

Some of the EVPs with Vijay recorded between October 2014 and March 2015 prove that Vijay "has mind of his own" and "living consciousness" (Gary Schwartz, *The Sacred Promise*, pp. 38-39). Some EVPs have yielded a conversational mode in which Vijay greeted in response to greetings (December 2014). Prof. Gary E. Schwartz, in *The Sacred Promise: How Science is Discovering Spirit's Collaboration with Us in Our Daily Lives*" (New York-London-Toronto, 2011), forcefully argues a very pertinent point: that these people who regularly took charge in life continue to take charge in the afterlife. "People who asserted themselves on this side continue to assert themselves on the other side."

Schwartz rightly point out that the deceased have minds of their own and demonstrate intention, assertion, decision making, self-control, disagreement, and stubbornness—characteristics people showed in life that continued after they died (*The Sacred Promise*, pp. 41.44).

Some of my best recorded EVPs with Vijay contradict such a perception of a "stunted-personality" and prove that the personality after physical death has retained consciousness and memory and responds to questions depending on the availability of energy, lunar cycles, geo-magnetic forces, and an emotional quotient. It is indeed interesting that the concept of a subliminal-self was also well understood and read by one of India's greatest recent philosophers, Rishi Shri Aurobindo (earlier Aurobindo Ghosh, a militant freedom-fighter during the Indian free struggle against the British—Raj/British Colonial Empire). In his famous work, *Life Divine*, he dealt with the concept of a subliminal-self in the chapter titled "The order of the Worlds" (*The life Divine*. Pondicherry, 1943, pp. 795-822).

While discussing different planes or systems co-existing with the physical universe, Aurobindo opined that there is a secret, continuous action of the higher powers and principles from their planes upon terrestrial beings and nature through the subliminal self, which is a projection from these planes into the world of the sub-conscious. It must have effect and significance (*The Life Divine*, p. 821). In this context, Aurobindo quotes one of the ancient, most sacred books of the East, Taittiriya Upanishad: "He passes in his departure from the world to the physical self; he passes to the self of life; he passes to the self of mind; he passes to self of knowledge; he passes to the self of bliss; he moves through these worlds at will" (Quoted in the chapter titled "Rebirth and other Worlds; Karma, the soul and immortality," *The life Divine*, p. 821). I quote Shri Aurobindo: "It is the soul-person, the psychic being, that survives and carries mind and life with it on its journey, and it is the subtle body which we know to be the characteristic case or sheath and the proper subtle-physical support of the inner being . . . it is in the subtle body that it passes out of its material lodging . . . But a transference to planes of mind existence or life existence implies also a mind and life sufficiently formed and developed to pass without disintegration and exist for a time on these higher levels. If these conditions were satisfied, a sufficiently developed psychic personality and subtle body and a sufficiently developed mental and vital personality, survival of the soul-person without an immediate new birth would be secured and the pull of the worlds would became operative. . . . For this discarding of the old and preparation of new forms the soul must dwell for some time between two births somewhere else than on the entirely material plane. . . ." (*The Life Divine*, p. 829).

The concept of survival of human personality, consciousness and memory after bodily death has been objectively proved by electronic voice phenomena (EVP). Friedrich Jorgensen and Konstantin Raudive are well-known pioneers in EVP. As the above narrative amply proves, I was convinced by July and August 2014 of Vijay's survival of bodily death. I was frantically looking for someone or some organization to help me in connecting to Vijay's soul/spirit-being. Unfortunately, this subject is still not believed by the so-called educated and elite Indians. I searched and crossed paths with the Indian Paranormal Society with its head office in New Delhi.

I got an appointment with its president, Revered Gourav Tiwari for the end of September 2013 while he was shooting in Australia for "Haunting Australia." Revered Gourav turned out to be very human, encouraging, and supportive at a time when my close relatives thought I had gone crazy due to grief over the sudden death of my husband. He refused to do a séance, but advised me to connect with my husband using any tape recorder. I purchased a new mobile telephone for this purpose and started recording my brief conversations with Vijay by the end of September 2013. We were delighted to hear the recording on 25 September 2013. On that day, Aditya suffered a hairline fracture while playing on a tennis-court and had to yield. Similarly, Aditya reported seeing his father after a year again on the afternoon of 15

September 2014 in the corridor of our house. He reported that a "Papa-like figure with a flowing white garment, turned his head with open mouth toward me as if to talk to me." I checked with my house maid separately and she reported that Aditya had walked out of the bedroom into the inner-corridor around 3 p.m. on 15 September 2014. Hence, both the appearance of Vijay on 28 September 2013 and 15 September 2014 reminded us of Gary Schwartz's observations on spirit's willful intent: "I can surprise you with an unexpected visit."[2] It is important to note that there was a huge (X-class) solar flare between 10-11 September 2014. It is conjectured that the solar flare and magnetic storms help paranormal events.

I initially thought that was simply the sound of breathing, but the Indian Paranormal Society found it as Vijay's voice saying, "Hello Nandini. Love You." It was our first-experience of hearing Vijay's voice and it was obviously difficult to control our emotions. However, subsequent night recordings yielded little; I stopped regular recordings and searched for other signs of Vijay's presence in the house. Occasional noises and drawing of curtains continued to manifest his presence. I was presented with a small DVR by the President of the Indian Paranormal Society at the end of January, 2014. I regularly conversed with Vijay from late January 2014 onwards. This was a turning point in my life using EVP and proving survival of Vijay after his bodily death. Initially, Vijay kept saying, "Nandini" often and his son's name "Adi" by March 2014. I must share with enlightened readers that I recorded Vijay's breathing, yawning, and surprisingly, even the sound of coughing on 31 March 2014.

I had a doubly pleasant surprise on 31 March 2014. We held a prayer meeting in my mother's house, because it was her death anniversary. I was depressed and recorded a conversation with my mother. But what I heard was not my mother's voice or response; it was all Vijay's responses.

Some of the best EVPs I presented at the 40th annual ASCS conference can be categorized in two categories. Although there were many examples, one EVP recorded on the afternoon of 28

October 2014 is extremely informative and educating. Vijay introduced us to the world of the afterlife. We were lucky to get some information directly from Vijay. The second category presented here relates more to conversational style. Vijay responded well to my greetings and questions. I present the following sample.

Recd. 4 - 28/10/2014—Vijay answered my question on water ITC images, but spoke at 2 minutes 50 seconds: "Don't you worry. . . life and death." Between 4 minutes 5 seconds and 5.50 /6.50: "Many are there" as we got images of two ladies as well. What Vijay meant was that there were other near relatives along with him who were keen to show their images. And that is what he meant by IRMA (we hear it as) or "Us Maa" meaning "your mother." Please note that my beloved mother Mrs. Dipali Sinha died on 24/03/2012. She had been gone a year before my husband's death.

Recd. 44 (23/12/2014) Vijay said at 1 minute 38 seconds: "Nandini" 2.30—2.40, and at 3.10 "Happy birthday" as I reminded him that my birthday was on 27 December.

Recd. 45 (25/12/2015): Vijay greets "good morning" in response to my greeting "good morning." At 3 plus minute, Vijay says "yes" when I ask him "have you accepted Merry Christmas cake"? I always offer him whatever food I am having with my family in front of his photo.

These above recordings clearly demonstrate that Vijay and I have had conversational sessions just like between two people on the earth plane.

Anabela Cardoso, in her famous work, *Electronic Voices: Contact with Another Dimension,*[3] makes a very pertinent observation evident in the above EVP recordings: "I have to say that to the best of my knowledge there are no examples of real ITC communications (i.e., communications containing a meaningful interchange of ideas) arising solely from a request by the experimenter and without any previous relationship between him or her and the communicators, although such connection does not have to necessarily go back to Earth time together. . . . In my opinion, affinity between the two sides is an indispensable condition for the contacts to happen. It is difficult to define with precision which expression such relationship may assume but we have already spoken about the Group Soul and that is the best way to look at it. The will and the desire to effect communications and a deep longing for the contact from both sides are other conditions that offer a good basis to think about this important issue.

Finally but not the least, Aditya and I were very keen to see Vijay in his spirit /ethereal being. The Indian Paranormal Society conducted the first session of Water ITC images on 10 October 2014 in our drawing room. Vijay did his best by imprinting his name Vijay on water. Some other photos of human-bodies came, both male and female. It was clear from the EVP of 28 October that one female possibly was my mother's spirit-photo. I conclude this brief narrative with some the best water ITC photos of 6 December 2014, 8 January 2015, 6 February 2015 and 4 May 2015.

Finally but not the least , perhaps the most important lesson to be learnt from the experiential approach is that "there is a large body of empirical observations relevant to the question of survival, and that no one should come down firmly on either side of the issue without considering that evidence seriously."[4] As Ian himself put it, "the only improper stance are denial that there is any evidence worth looking at or assertion that what we have will suffice."[5]

Endnotes

[1] Stevenson, 1982, p. 116.
[2] Schwartz, Gary E. (2011). *The Sacred Promise: How Science is Discovering Spirit's Collaboration with us in our daily lives,* New York-London-Toronto. p 44.
[3] Cardoso, A. (2010). *Electronic Voices: Contact with Another Dimension.* Washington and Winchester, UK: 6th Books.
[4] Stevenson, 1982, p. 120.
[5] Stevenson, 1982, p. 120.

Author Bio

Nandini Sinha Kapur, Ph.D.

Dr. Kapur is a historian with nearly two decades of teaching experience in the University of Delhi. She joined SOITS in 2009. Dr. Kapur has several research publications to her credit and is the author of three books: *State Formation in Rajasthan: Mewar During 7th -15th Centuries, Reconstructing Identities: Tribes, Agro-Pastoralists and Environment in Western India* (AD-7th -20th Century), and *Environmental History of Early India* published by Oxford University Press, 2011 and 2nd reprint to this book came out in 2012. She is the recipient of the prestigious Homi Bhabha fellowship and has been a visiting Scholar at Harvard, Chicago, Columbia, London and Leiden Universities.

Energy Medicine and Regression

Donna Eden and David Feinstein, Ph.D.

Abstract

This paper defines regression and energy medicine. It then answers three questions: (1) How is energy medicine practiced? (2) How does energy medicine work? and (3) Is energy medicine spiritual? The paper ends with comments on healing the past with energy medicine.

Regression is the process of energetically and psychologically returning to the time and place where core issues in our present lives became established. This may involve loss, betrayal, illness, injury, or other forms of trauma, and it may be from an earlier point in this lifetime or may be experienced as having occurred in a past life. When we have intractable physical, emotional, or energetic difficulties that seem to have no clear physical cause-and-effect relationships, a Regression session can illuminate how and when these patterns were created. In the energetic field of that earlier time, balancing and restoring disrupted energies using energy medicine techniques can be deeply healing.

Energy Medicine is the art and science of assessing and harmonizing the body's energies to maximize one's own or another's well-being. The body's energies include the electrical, electromagnetic, and electrochemical energies that are recognized by science as being involved in every bodily function, and they also include the more subtle energies (such as "chakras" and "meridians") recognized by time-honored healing and spiritual traditions as providing the animating force of the physical body as well as its invisible infrastructure. Conventional medicine, at its foundation, focuses on the biochemistry of cells, tissue, and organs. Energy Medicine, at its foundation, focuses on the energy fields of the body that organize and control the growth and repair of cells, tissue, and organs. Changing impaired energy patterns may be the most efficient, least invasive way to improve the vitality of organs, cells, and psyche.

1. How is Energy Medicine Practiced?

Energy Medicine utilizes techniques from time-honored traditions such as acupuncture, yoga, kinesiology, and qi gong. Flow, balance, and harmony can be non-invasively restored and maintained within an energy system by tapping, massaging, pinching, twisting, or connecting specific energy points (acupoints) on the skin; by tracing or swirling the hand over the skin along specific energy pathways; through exercises or postures designed for specific energetic effects; by focused use of the mind to move specific energies; and/or by surrounding an area with healing energies.

Donna Crossing Her Energies

2. How Does Energy Medicine Work?

Energy Medicine recognizes energy as a vital, living, moving force that determines much about health and happiness. To maintain vibrant health, the body needs its energies to

- Move and have space to continue to move. Energies may become blocked due to toxins, muscular or other constriction, prolonged stress, or interference from other energies.
- Move in specific patterns generally in harmony with the physical structures and functions that the energies animate and support. "Flow follows function."
- Cross over at all levels, from the microlevel of the double helix of DNA, extending to the macrolevel where the left side of the brain controls the right side of the body and the right side controls the left.
- Maintain a balance with other energies. The energies may lose their natural balance due to prolonged stress or other conditions that keep specific energy systems in a survival mode.
- Conversely, when the body is not healthy, corresponding disturbances in its energies can be identified and treated.

3. Is Energy Medicine Spiritual?

Entering the world of your body's subtle energies is a bridge into the domain of your deepest spiritual callings and your eternal essence. While no particular belief system, allegiance, or religious affiliation is associated with Energy Medicine, many people find that energy work touches into the realms of soul and spirit.

Healing the Past with Energy Medicine

Physical and psychological challenges are often rooted in earlier experiences. By combining energy medicine with basic regression techniques, the energetic patterns that were locked in at the time of the earlier trauma or other formative experience can be freed, balanced, and harmonized. In the process, the earlier experience is "healed" so it is no longer causing thoughts, emotions, and behavioral patterns tied to the earlier period. This can be a large step beyond simply *experiencing* the earlier event.

Author Bios

Donna Eden is among the world's most sought, most joyous, and most authoritative spokespersons for Energy Medicine. She has been able to clairvoyantly "see" the body's energies since childhood, and her abilities as a healer are legendary. Her best-selling book, *Energy Medicine,* is the textbook in hundreds of healing classes. Available in 18 languages, it won golds in both the *U.S. Book News* and Nautilus competitions. www.LearnEnergyMedicine.com.

David Feinstein, Ph.D., is a clinical psychologist who has been a pioneer in developing innovative therapeutic approaches, leading to nine national awards for his books on consciousness and energy healing. He was the recipient of the *U.S. Book News* Best Psychology/Mental Health Book Award of 2007. He has served on the faculties of The Johns Hopkins University School of Medicine and Antioch College. www.EnergyPsychEd.com.

Dreaming the Future
Evidence for a Holistic Connecting Principle

Dale E. Graff, M.S.

Abstract

This presentation reviews a variety of psi and precognitive dreams for personal and experimental situations. Controlled experimental psi dream projects were for pictures in sealed envelopes, on a specific page in a future newspaper or on a random selected page in an unopened magazine. Some of the psi dream projects were for targets at long distances, including deep sea and European locations. These projects provide insight into some of the cognitive aspects of psi perception and how psi information is accessed and interpreted prior to or after its emergence into the dream. They also illustrate the independence of distance on the psi process. Some precognitive dreams were of future news headlines; others provided warnings of approaching events to be better prepared when they occurred a few days after the dreams. One precognitive dream related to the health situation of someone over a thousand miles away. A precognitive dream that occurred during wilderness travel led to the prevention of a dangerous situation. Precognitive dreams occurred during an overseas assignment when involved in the search for a hostage. A precognitive dream that linked with synchronicity illustrates the precise timing of approaching future events. Various concepts that may have relevance to psi and precognitive dreaming are reviewed, including associations with holograms, non-local quantum physics phenomena and a speculative quantum physics perspective involving energy and how reality may be a projection into space-time and is not imbedded in it. I conclude with perspectives on the significance of psi and psi dreaming, especially precognition and on the holistic principle that they imply.

Background

The occurrence of psi phenomena such as extra-sensory perception (ESP), precognition, telepathy, remote viewing and some forms of intuition provide evidence for the vastness of our conscious-subconscious abilities. Conventional sciences do not accept these as valid since statistical proof is considered elusive or insufficient. Those who have studied the psi field can accept the reality of the phenomena. The ESP research by J. B. Rhine at the Duke University parapsychology laboratory in the 1930s–1960s and numerous others since then provide a valid scientific basis for psi as experienced under controlled conditions. However, these effects do not represent the richness or full potential of psi experienced spontaneously by a variety of people as reported in case studies (Rhine, 1961, 1981; Feather, 2005; Ryback, 1988). Research based on Dream State Psi (DSP), referred to as dream telepathy at the Maimonides Medical Center in Brooklyn, NY, in the 1960s–1970s, provided additional statistical validation of psi, as did the research by the Stanford Research Institute (SRI), International Conscious State Psi (CSP), research referred to as remote viewing (RV) in the 1970s–1990s (Ullman/Krippner/Vaughn, 1974; Puthoff/Targ, 1976). Most individuals may experience a few spontaneous psi events over the years. Some incidents may be compelling, others may be subtle and overlooked as being of psi origin. Psi research and evidence from spontaneous events indicates that psi is ubiquitous and potentially available to anyone (Graff, 1998).

My interest in psi resulted from spontaneous instances involving intuitions of future incidents and occasional precognitive dreams. The research published in *Dream Telepathy* by Ullman/Krippner/Vaughn indicated that the dream state was probably the most convenient mode for experiencing and systematically studying psi on a personal level. It seemed the only requirement was to set the intention to dream about an objective (the target) and recall the resulting dreams. Consequently, I began a systematic investigation of Dream State Psi (DSP) using pictorial material consistent with the dream telepathy approach to see to what extent I could experience psi dreams for possible insight into the psi dream process, how psi imagery is created and the degree of accuracy obtainable. Evaluation was based on a direct comparison of dream content to the target picture's imagery. I explored two types of pictorial targets: those that existed but were unknown and those that did not yet exist anywhere at the time of the psi dreams.

The Maimonides Slide Targets

I organized a local area study group with people having similar interests and developed procedures for data and target control that simulated formal psi experimentation. I had obtained a complete set of a target pool used during the Maimonides dream telepathy research and we used these targets for our psi dream investigations. This target pool consisted of a complex set of 1,024 slides organized according to ten information categories. The number of slides resulted from their binary evaluation method. This huge diversity of pictorial material was ideal for exploring the nature of psi dream perception since the content could not be anticipated and the effect of target pool construction on psi data quality could be evaluated.

Four of these psi dream experiments were controlled and monitored by colleagues. Two psi dreamers were involved, a colleague and myself. Our primary objective was to determine how closely our dreams would correlate with the content of the concealed target slide. We also wanted to see if combining the results of two dreams for the same psi target picture would provide a more complete representation of the unknown picture than the dreams of one individual could provide. Previous successful investigations indicated that the dreamer usually did not perceive the entire target picture but only had key elements in their dreams. Our psi dreams were presented as sketches and written narratives to the target slide control person before the slide was removed from the opaque envelope for evaluation. Our projects were double blind projects; we did not use a target picture observer. No one knew the target picture's identity at the time of the psi dream. The psi dreams were scheduled for every other night in order to maintain focus on the psi dream investigations.

The first slide target had overlapping imagery with unusual context: a foot in a red stocking, a red apple with a key inserted, a cartoon figure diving into an area that resembled water. My colleague did not provide a sketch, but presented this written narrative ... *I come to a river, jump in and start swimming, trying to get out of the current....* This correlated with the dynamics implied by the cartoon figure. I had two dreams and combined the imagery into one sketch. It provided a detailed representation of the forms and shapes on the target but presented them as a *real mountain and stream.* My dream was accurate in composition, but did not present the correct meaning of the slide images. The apparent river in the slide is not a river, but a strip of turf that resembles water.

The second slide was a composite of several diverse images: a field with golden flowers, a zebra and a large tree that had the face of an owl imbedded in its roots. Small animals were on the tree. My colleague had dreams with a *fear or terror theme, imagery of flames, a baby in the dirt, a man on a horse and the face of an animal.* I had a dream with *threatening content involving a struggle with a shrouded figure* and another dream with a *grotesque face.* Prior to sleep, a visual occurred that resembled a *skull.*

The owl face in the slide appeared in my pre-sleep image and dominated our dreams, invoking the sense of something *threatening.* The golden flowers in the field probably invoked the flame imagery in my colleague's dream. I did not perceive the obvious zebra, but may have sensed only a portion of it. The front half and its unusual face probably became a *shrouded figure wearing a striped robe* in the dream. My colleague did perceive a large animal (horse) but not a zebra. Our subconscious minds interpreted the slide from a threat perspective, probably a result of how the psi information entered our brain's perceptual system.

The third slide only had two elements: a close-up view of a golden corncob section with a large square of melting butter on top. Our dreams had no emotional element but had a variety of images. We both had *food and plant-like imagery with emphasis on repeated shapes, including large squares that were presented as slices of bread.* We considered our results to be only a partial success. Some of the shapes correlated but not in the larger context of the target.

Prior to the fourth and last slide target, we agreed to focus on having a dream that contained most if not all of the target picture's elements in one integrated presentation. As a result, we did have similar, even mutual, dreams. The target slide had a dominant blue-tinted surrealistic landscape. A large building with many columns was in the central distance. The terrain was covered with rocks of various shapes and gullies cut through the foreground. Both of our dreams had *surrealistic blue-toned dream landscape with dominant rocky features and unusual geometric structures in the distant center.* We also had dream images of *unusual creatures, with a frog, fish and lizard appearance.* In my dream, *the lizard shapes were creeping from left to right over the rocky dream landscape.* My colleague's dream presented the blue landscape as *snow-covered;* my dream presented it as *bathed in moonlight.* No animals are in the target picture. However, the rock formations and scratches in the slide have contours that could invoke animal or face-like imagery. Our intention for experiencing dreams that presented an integrated representation of the target picture was successful.

Implications from the Psi Dream Investigations

From these controlled experiments, we concluded that the psi dream process for double blind pictorial targets closely tracks ordinary vision. The specific imagery in the dreams, regardless of how the image was interpreted, correlated with known visual responses related to edge detection, contour following and contrast sensitivity. When image boundaries overlapped or contrast was poor, the dream imagery was inaccurate. Some of the target elements provided "attractors," depending on the dreamer's personal interests or background. We noted that color identification in the target picture was highly reliable. One of the dreams presented imagery that correlated with scratches on the slide's emulsion! However, when shapes and forms are in the pictures that are not easily recognized, a perceptual process occurs that defaults to a primitive fight-flight-freeze response (Goleman, 1994). The dreams for imagery that could be troubling may be presented as a threat or a potential threat.

As the investigations progressed through the four targets, it became apparent that our dreams reproduced the forms or shapes in the slide correctly. However, their meaning, their context, was usually incorrect unless the imagery was self-evident and of personal significance and meaning. These results made us aware of the evaluation difficulties for formal psi experiments if the data is only presented in writing with emphasis on perceived meaning. Sketches of dream imagery keeps evaluation on a form correlation basis, consistent with how psi functions for this type of psi investigation.

These initial investigations, and many since that time, provide evidence for how dreams or other forms of mental imagery may be constructed. Elementary building blocks of perception may be hard-wired in our perceptual system that is assembled to create an image. These pre-images occasionally appear prior to or after a dream and can resemble small geometric shapes. These shapes are usually static but can be dynamic and moving. Sometimes color elements without form appear. Usually the small geometric forms are similar to tiny pixels. Some of these are referred to as form constants (Cytowic, 2002). Vision theorists also consider pre-existing vision templates, such as cylindrical shapes, as being part of the vision image construction process (Goldstein, 2007).

Target Pictures in Magazines and Other Sources

These include pictures on randomly selected pages in unopened magazines and pictures chosen by colleagues located thousands of miles distant. Some of the pictorial psi targets chosen by colleagues involved target observer protocols and were for both Conscious State Psi and Dream State Psi projects. One of the psi targets, a page in an unopened magazine, provides additional insight into the psi process. The picture on the target page showed swirling contours on the surface of a lake. However, when the picture was held at a bright light, the reverse side of the page could be seen. This reverse side had a raft-like shape on a swimming pool. The dream that occurred was unusually dynamic, *presenting a raft being drawn into turbulent water and submerged.* This suggests that the act of future observation may have been the psi source; i.e., the psi process was one of precognition and not real time access of the intended picture that was on a page in an unopened magazine in a dark room.

Psi Targets at Distant Locations

A few long-distance psi projects were performed to see if differences between them and the local area psi projects could be detected. These include a Conscious State Psi (CSP) or Remote Viewing (RV) project with a colleague located 1,000 miles distant and a Dream State Psi (DSP) project with a colleague in Austria, 7,000 miles distant.

The RV target picture showed a boat made of reeds floating on a lake in South America. A boatman is guiding the boat. A mountain range is in the distance. The sketch provided by the remote viewer was a near *exact replication of the boat* in the picture. However, it was perceived in a context associated with Egypt. Results of the RV and the psi dream projects were similar to those for the local and slide targets, demonstrating independency of distance. The psi data correlated well in pattern matching but not in interpretation, as previously observed for the slide target pictures.

The target picture chosen by my colleague in Austria showed several dancers, whirling dervishes, performing a dynamic routine of spinning and twisting. The central dancer wore a brilliant yellow gown. The setting was on a low stage inside a large room. For this psi dream project, a target observer protocol was used. The dream that occurred presented *a room full of dancers*. This dream was *extremely dynamic*, consistent with the implied dynamics of the whirling dervish dancers in the target picture. The dominant *yellow color* of the central dancer's dress in the dream also correlated with the color of the gown worn by the dervish. The dream setting of *a stage and background structures* also correlated with the target picture's elements. However, a variation in the dream dynamics and its interpretation occurred during the dream. Initially, the dream presented *a chaotic scene with people in Western outfits fighting one another*. At mid dream it shifted suddenly to *gentle dancers leaping upon a low stage to begin a swirling dance routine*. This transition in the dream context could suggest that the intention of the target picture observer may have entered into the dream scene to provide a correct interpretation.

The target picture observer in Austria did occasionally visualize dynamic whirling dervishes during the night. Perhaps her intention led to a shift in the dream from fighting to the correct dancing scene. If so, this would suggest that a mind-to-mind connection occurred, not only a form-only access typical of double blind protocols.

For another long-distance psi dream project, the targets were pictures in sealed envelopes located in a deep diving submersible 1,000 feet deep and 500 miles distant from the dreamer. One of the target pictures showed a complex room scene with a blanket that had complex geometric designs along its border. The resulting dream presented *a sheet of linoleum with complex designs* similar to those in the target picture. Similar to the other psi dream projects, the forms and shapes were perceived accurately but not the specific interpretation. In this case, the distance, the extra shielding of salt water and a steel-hulled vessel did not affect the psi data quality. This is another indication of a possible precognitive source for psi dreams.

This psi dream may have resulted from precognition of the time several days later, when I received feedback after I correctly selected this picture as the likely target from a set of six possibilities. If so, then precognition could be the operative mode of psi perception for many other psi projects. The psi projects reviewed in this presentation could be a result of real-time psi access of the target or precognition. When an observer is present, that person's knowledge may also have a role in the psi process, especially as it relates to interpretation.

Lucid Psi Dreams

Sometimes dreams are lucid (Waggoner, 2009). The dreamers know when they are in a dream and dreaming. Awake state consciousness and awareness enters into the dream. Lucid dreams may occur spontaneously or when desired. A lucid dream involving a psi target picture had highly accurate results. The target was a randomly selected page in an unopened magazine. The black and white picture showed a man lying in a field on a blanket. The field and surrounding area had few other features except for a long pole that seems to be pressed on his head. When the spontaneous lucid dream began, *I begin to think about the psi target in that unopened magazine. Instantly I become aware of walking in a field, where I see a man lying down. His head is facing away from me. I see a long thin pole, pick it up, walk toward him and tap him on the head! He does not respond, I am puzzled and shift my attention to another scene.*

This portion of the lucid dream had no color, consistent with the black and white picture. The lucid dream presented all of the target picture's elements correctly. This suggests that achieving lucidity in dreams has the potential for improving the over-all quality of the psi dream and perceiving the intended picture, or any other psi objective, in its proper context.

Psi Targets in the Future

Psi projects can be developed that specifically explore precognition. Typical precognitive projects are targets selected from several possibilities after the psi session or psi dream. One of these was a part of a controlled psi dream project. The target picture was on a page selected randomly from a large art book three days after the scheduled psi dream event. The target picture was the cover for the book, *Uncle Tom's Cabin*. The content included a woman in a blue sweater running toward an ice-covered stream. Her face is obscured. She is carrying an infant. Ice floes are on the stream and animal tracks are in the surrounding snow. Large dogs are dimly visible in the background.

Several dreams occurred that had most of the target picture's elements. One dream presented *a woman with indistinct features. She is wearing a blue blouse and holding something.* Another dream presents *an ice rimmed stream, snow with animal tracks and a vague sense of animals in the dim background.* My winter outdoors activities probably led to the accurate perception of the ice-covered stream and snow in the target picture. The complex arrangement of elements in the picture required several dreams for accurate picture reproduction. My sketches for this target picture were based on the endings of these dreams. In previous experiments I discovered that the dream's ending has the most accurate data.

Another precognitive target option is to seek dreams about photographs that will appear in future newspapers. This provides the opportunity for convenient independent precognitive investigations. It can also provide psi target pictures that do not even exist at the time of the psi dream. Psi dreams for future photographs are more reliable than future printed material and more feasible to evaluate.

Recent newspaper photographs were psi dream projects. The objective was to dream about the photograph that will be on a certain page in a specific newspaper section three days in the future. For one of these precognitive dream projects, the photograph in that newspaper section showed Queen Elizabeth looking through a large window at a scene of London. The resulting dream was brief but presented a *complex scene filled with city buildings*. The sketch correlated well with the actual scene; however, the location was not perceived.

In another precognitive dream, the photograph in that newspaper section was a close-up of the black box recovered from the Germanwings airplane crash in the European mountain. The resulting dream was brief, *presenting a large square object perceived to be a cast iron stove*. The shape in the dream correlated with the appearance of the black box but not the interpretation. Captions to these photographs explained the picture. However, their meaning did not enter into the dreams. Those photographs were taken 1-2 days after the dreams; i.e., they did not exist at the time of the dream.

The first future news psi dream project I participated in with others occurred in 1980. The psi dream material was documented and independently verified 5 days in advance of the future event. For this psi dream experiment, the objective was to experience a psi dream that would present any significant event published on the first page of the area newspaper within a week. On the night of the intended psi dream, a dramatic dream occurred *involving a large commercial airplane crash*. I made a sketch of the dream's ending that illustrated the *airplane flying over a runway and then diving straight down into the ground at the runway's edge*. Six days after the dream, a tragic airline crash occurred near Warsaw, Poland. There were no survivors. Many details of the dream correlated with the actual event. The plane lost control close to the end of the airport runway and dove straight into the ground. The dream setting, *a flat area near an old military facility*, matched the actual location. The airplane in the dream was large but not exactly like the Russian-built IL-62 that crashed. The dream provided *information about the cause of the accident; something broke or tore the rudder controls at the rear of the airplane*. Ten weeks after the crash, the news reported the cause: turbine disks blew apart and cut into the rear of the fuselage, severing the control lines. Although I have experienced other accurate precognitive dreams about future airplane crashes, this incident was the only one documented in advance of the incident.

Psi During Travel

When we travel, we are usually more relaxed and open to unexpected experiences than when in our usual environment and routines. These can include intuitions, psi dreams or synchronicities. Sometimes our safety may be of concern, as a spontaneous experience during a remote river journey illustrates. A dramatic psi dream led to a potentially lifesaving response when a companion slipped into the icy water of an Arctic river. Awakened *by the troubling nature* of the dream and its association with one of my canoe companions, I immediately went to the river in time to help him out of the water. Other intentional and spontaneous psi dreams occurred during an overseas assignment involving the search for a hostage. The dreams presented accurate information on the hostage's location, in a *second floor room above a grocery store*, and the general *city area in North Italy*. Precognitive dreams also occurred that indicated the individual's rescue *would be successful*. These dreams were indirect but associated with the actual event.

Health and Safety

Several excellent sources exist that provide a variety of spontaneous psi experiences related to health and safety. Some of these psi experiences provided alerts to emerging physical situations prior to the occurrence of symptoms (Ryback, 1988). *Healing Dreams* (Barasch, 2000) is an account of a dream forewarning of a cancer that the author took seriously and consequently avoided major medical issues. I facilitated an informal medical diagnostics experiment with Marc Barasch that proved to be accurate. The resulting psi dream illustrated how the sensation of pain felt by others can be sensed at long distances.

In the dream, I *become aware of a filling that has come out of a tooth. The pain builds up, becomes intense* and I wake up. When I examine my mouth, I can find nothing wrong; I have no more pain. Suspecting that this experience related to Marc, I sent him an email describing the loose filling and tooth pain dream. Shortly after, he replied confirming a significant dental emergency had just occurred that required immediate medical attention. He had been in a lot of pain.

Other sources (Feather, 2005) are available that show how psi dreams can alert individuals to approaching dangerous situations. Some of these warnings could be avoided or prevented; others could not. L.E. Rhine provides statistics on the types of spontaneous precognitive dreams in her studies of 3,000 spontaneous incidents (Rhine, 1981). About two-thirds of these dreams related to the dreams of the dreamer or close family members, the others to acquaintances or strangers. Some of these precognitive warnings led to avoidance or prevention of the emerging event. Sometimes the only option when such dreams occur is to be better prepared. Most of these psi dreams were precognitive, indicating the primary future seeing nature of psi.

Synchronicity

Sometimes experiences labeled as coincidences are not totally random occurrences, as is commonly suspected. These are usually referred to as meaningful coincidences, or synchronicities, a term originated by the eminent psychologist and dream pioneer, Carl G. Jung, a contemporary of Sigmund Freud. Jung's publications (Jung, 1969; Jung, 1961) provide synchronicities that he and others experienced. Other accounts of synchronicities exist (Graff, 1998; Hopcke, 1997). I recently experienced a synchronicity that was preceded by a precognitive dream. Subsequent actions led to the dream becoming reality later that day. I refer to this synchronicity as the "Incident at Harrisonburg, VA." This incident is unusual since I have a photograph of the accident published in the Harrisonburg, VA, newspaper.

This dream occurred prior to the start of a long road trip from my home in Pennsylvania to the Rhine Research Center (RRC) in Durham, NC. I was scheduled to facilitate a psi dream workshop that weekend. The night before the trip began I set the intention to experience a dream with any information relating to the drive. At 4:00 AM, I woke from a *troubling dream about a horrific accident scene*. I made a sketch showing the position *of a large truck and a smashed car in the median strip*. I left the house at 6:00 AM and in a few hours came to a sign alerting drivers to traffic congestion ahead. Deciding to avoid this slowdown, I detoured to a parallel road. However, due to an error in reading the traffic alert sign I returned to the Interstate behind the congestion. Two hours later I came to the accident scene at Harrisonburg, VA. The scene closely resembled the dream's ending. Upon my return a few days later I bought a copy of the area newspaper that had a photograph of the accident taken from the same perspective that I had seen in the dream. The accident occurred at 6:00 AM, two hours after my dream. Had I not made a mistake in reading the traffic alert, I would have bypassed the incident and not seen it. This seems to be an example of precognition and synchronicity. Actually seeing the future accident scene was a meaningful event since I had been hoping for a new psi dream to include as an illustration in my workshop.

Psi Sources

One of the difficulties that conventional science has with psi is that the phenomena are independent of space and time, and therefore violate conventional understanding of the physical universe. This viewpoint is, however, coming into question since certain effects in quantum physics, quantum coupling, also occur that are instantaneous, regardless of the distance between the coupled particles (Radin, 2006). Another issue is what or where is the source of the psi obtained information, especially the future-seeing, precognitive aspect? I consider several perspectives on the sources of psi that include hypothetical information domains that can be given various labels similar to holographic concepts, but with a future projection feature to account for precognition. A theoretical quantum physics concept based on a quantum physics formulation developed by Schommers (Schommers, 1995) considers that energy is an abstract concept and reality is not imbedded into space-time but is projected into it. The reality of precognition, however, is not easy to accommodate in any quantum model. Perhaps all of psi is essentially precognition where the experiencer accesses the future –his or her own future experience–what or wherever it is.

Summary

A review of psi and psi dream experiences from independent investigations, and of spontaneous psi incidents, indicates that psi is a fundamental phenomenon regardless of in what mental state the effects are experienced and brought to conscious awareness. No difference is observed in results of psi experiments performed for targets at varying distances, including those at transcontinental locations from the psi experiencer, and for those with psi targets that do not yet exist, such as those in future newspapers photographs. The psi process for pictorial projects seems to initially enter the older regions of the brain's perceptual networks, where basic survival instincts reside. The actual image construction and recognition process is primarily pattern matching with patterns already in or similar to those in memory. Image construction may evolve from small imagery templates to larger forms until the image can be recognized subconsciously. However, direct mind-to-mind connections may also occur, such as evident in medical- or health-related situations. One or the most intriguing psi related experiences, synchronicity, suggests that an orchestrating effect can occur that coordinates subconscious actions in order for the meaningful coincidences to become manifest. There seems to be something inherently holistic about psi and synchronicity, perhaps something archetypal that connects the personal with global or universal aspects of reality. Perhaps at deep subconscious levels our essence can or does extend to other realities within the cosmos, the multi-universe or spiritual domains.

I suggest that the psi effects, or the principle behind them, are a holistic pattern-seeking and future-oriented process that had, and still has, a role in our evolution. Through continued explorations of our deeper conscious/subconscious nature, we can come to better understand our role as participants and co-creators from a global, universal and spiritual perspective.

Bibliography

Barasch, Marc. (2000). *Healing Dreams*. New York, NY: Penguin Putnam.
Cytowic, Richard. (2002). *Synesthesia*. Cambridge, MA: MIT Press.
Feather, Sally Rhine & Schmicker, M. (2005). *The Gift: ESP, The Extraordinary Experiences of Ordinary People*. New York, NY: St. Martin's Press.
Goldstein, Bruce. (2007). *Sensation & Perception*. Belmont, CA: Thompson-Wadsworth.
Goleman, Daniel. (1994). *Emotional Intelligence*. New York, NY: Bantum.
Graff, Dale E. (1998). *Tracks in the Psychic Wilderness*. Boston, MA: Element Books.
Graff, Dale E. (2000). *RIVER DREAMS*. Boston, MA: Element Books.
Hopcke, Robert. (1996). *There are no Accidents: Synchronicity and the Stories of our Lives*. New York, NY: Riverhead Books.
Jung, Carl. (1961). *Memories, Dreams, Reflections*. New York, NY: Vintage Books.
Jung, Carl. (1969). *Synchronicity: An Accusal Connecting Principle*. Princeton, NJ: University Press.
Puthoff, Harold & Targ, Russell. (1977). *Mind Reach*. Delecorte Press.
Radin, Dean. (2006). *Entangled Minds*. New York, NY: Paraview Books.
Rhine, Joseph B. (1964/1973). *Extra-Sensory Perception*. Boston, MA: Brandon Press.
Rhine, Louisa E. (1961). *Hidden Channels of the Mind*. New York, NY: Wm. Morrow Co.
Rhine, Louisa E. (1981). *The Invisible Picture: A Study of Psychic Experiences*. Jefferson, NC: McFarland & company.
Ryback, David & /Sweitzer, Lelitia. (1988). *Dreams that Come True*. New York, NY: Doubleday.

Schommers, Wolfram. (1995). *Symbols, Pictures and Quantum Reality.* Singapore: World Scientific Pub.

Ullman, M., Krippner, S., Vaughan, A. (1974). *Dream Telepathy.* New York, NY: Penguin Books.

Waggoner, Robert. (2009). *Lucid Dreaming.* Needham, MA: Moment Point Press.

Author Bio

Dale E. Graff, M.S.

Dale E. Graff is a researcher, writer, and speaker internationally known for his insights into the processes of the mind. He was a director of STARGATE, the government's program for research and applications of remote viewing—an aspect of extrasensory perception (ESP). He coined the name STARGATE to symbolize an innovative effort of exploration that expanded the range of human potential. He is recognized for his understanding of our natural psi talents as being a spectrum available while awake, Conscious State Psi (CSP), and while asleep and dreaming, Dream State Psi (DSP). His books, *Tracks in the Psychic Wilderness* and *RIVER DREAMS* have brought him international recognition as he describes his personal evolution from scientific doubter—degrees in aeronautical engineering and physics—to that of accepting the reality of psi abilities. His books discuss remote viewing, psi dreaming and synchronicity and present psychic experiences in a neutral perspective, free of dogma and belief systems. He facilitates workshops on psi and psi dream topics and performs independent research on precognitive dreaming.

Nightmares
Urgent Messages from the Guiding Self

Howard W. Tyas, Jr.

Abstract

For Jung there is an older, wiser part of the psyche, the Self, which desires both the well-being of the ego and the establishment of a dialectic relationship between the ego and the deep recesses of the unconscious. It is in the context of this dialogue that one's true personality is hammered out through the process Jung referred to as individuation. Dreams offer singular and therapeutic perspectives initiated by the unconscious. They are designed to maintain a psychological balance in the moment, while also beckoning us toward a life felt to be authentic. When we lose sight of or stray from that authentic personality, the Guiding Self will often resort to nightmares to redirect our attention—the more nightmarish the dream, the more urgent the call. Nightmares attend to those wounds we carry that are in need of healing; they help us address the fears and anxieties life so often brings; and they call us to focus on issues hindering us from living a creative and meaningful life.

This paper begins the exploration of nightmares by examining the personal and psychological context out of which nightmares arise, namely, the self-regulatory nature of the psyche and the ongoing process of individuation. It briefly addresses understandings of the nightmare expressed in art, then the phenomenon of the nightmare as experienced in film. A majority of the paper is devoted to looking at various dreams that are nightmarish in quality, with an eye toward trying to understand both their urgent message and their timely meaning.

This paper explores nightmares that occur in response to a traumatizing event or experience, and the truth behind them. Nightmares can result from a complex formation of military combat or PTSD, natural disasters, intentional acts of violence and violation, and the death of a loved one. Dr. Tyas explains how nightmares can be a transition to healing.

I want to thank you for your warm welcome and the opportunity to share some thoughts with you about nightmares. Most people tend not to remember their dreams. However, the dreams we do tend to remember are either those "big dreams" that evoke a sense of awe and wonder or those nightmares that provoke a sense of fear and terror. That second category of dreams will be the one we'll be addressing this evening. And I would invite you now, here at the very beginning, to recall a nightmare that still lingers, and just hold it in your imaginary hand through the course of the evening, perhaps taking a peek at it from time to time to see if it looks different now from how it has looked in the past. Hopefully, you may see some meaning in the madness.

One of the pillars on which Jung's thought and work rests is the developmental life process he called individuation. For Jung it was a natural process, a universal process, one in which we are all engaged, whether we realize it or not. It is a process that involves moving towards the embodiment of what we might call our "true personality." That true personality, or that sense of our authentic self, is that which makes each of us unique; that special sense about ourselves we may have been aware of, or others may have observed unfolding in us, from our earliest years. Jolande Jacobi describes this process quite well in her book, *The Way of Individuation*.

> Like a seed growing into a tree, life unfolds stage by stage. Triumphant ascent, collapse, crises, failures, and new beginnings strew the way. It is the path trodden by the great majority of humankind, as a rule unreflectingly, unconsciously, unsuspectingly, following its labyrinthine windings from birth to death in hope and longing. It is hedged about with struggle and suffering, joy and sorrow, guilt and error, and nowhere is there security from catastrophe. For as soon as a person tries to escape every risk and prefers to experience life only in his head, in the form of ideas and fantasies, as soon as he surrenders to opinions of 'how it ought to be' and, in order not to make a false step, imitates others whenever possible, he forfeits the chance of his own independent development. Only if one treads the path bravely and flings himself into life, fearing no struggle and no exertion and fighting shy of no experience, will that person mature their personality more fully than the one who is ever trying to keep to the safe side of the road.
>
> <div align="right">Jolande Jacobi, <i>The Way of Individuation</i>, p. 16</div>

Our tendency, as human beings, is precisely to keep to the safe side of the road. Few of us intentionally, excitedly seek out those kinds of experiences in life that challenge our self-assumptions, make us uncomfortable, or lead us in directions that carry the possibility of catastrophe, even if that seeming catastrophe might ultimately lead to our own growth, development and maturity. As Jacobi observes, we would rather escape the possibility of risk and failure, content ourselves with the security of a self-reassuring world-view, be guided primarily by personal ideas and fantasies, opinions of "how it ought to be," or the imitation of others. That is life, as the majority of humankind knows and lives it. But apparently, there is something within the psyche that won't settle for that. There appears to be something in the psyche that keeps pushing the envelope—something intent on introducing us to situations, whether inner or outer, that upset us, disturb us, and maybe even torment us—in an effort to engage us in this individuation process. Individuation involves our discovering and choosing that true personality each of us embodies.

This urge toward developing a more balanced life, a more authentic personality is felt and experienced in different ways. In our outer, our waking life, it may take the form of a yearning, an attraction, or a kind of "falling in love" with someone or something that beckons us, presses us in directions we had not thought of going. In our inner life, our dream life, this urge toward a more developed personality usually takes the form of "big dreams." These are the kinds of dreams that rock the ego's world, overwhelm us with images, words, experiences, encounters, feelings designed to move us forward. They may address wounds, long buried, that are now in need of healing. They may address fears and anxieties that render us paralyzed and unable to tread bravely onto the path toward our own completeness. These dreams may address perceptions and behaviors that are not consistent with this unique process unfolding within us, a process designed to mature our personality with creativity and meaning. For Jung, it is the Self, or what I will be referring to as the Guiding Self, that orchestrates this transformational process.

In what is referred to as the Houston Films, a series of interviews with Jung done by a professor of psychology from the University of Houston in the late 1950s, Jung describes the Self as 'merely a term that designates the whole personality.' [Second Interview, disc 6] In his "Definitions" in Volume 6 of the Collected Works, he says, "The Self is not only the center, but also the whole circumference which embraces both conscious and unconscious; it is the center of this totality, just as the ego is the center of consciousness." [CW, Volume 6, par. 789] Whether awake or asleep, this Guiding Self, this overarching archetypal pattern operating within the psyche, seemingly, is working on behalf of the personality—to help maintain a certain psychological balance in the moment and to move both the ego, as well as the whole personality, forward in its unfolding.

One of the other pillars on which Jung's thought and work rests, especially for our purposes tonight, is Jung's observation that the psyche contains a self-regulatory quality or nature. This self-regulatory quality is quite natural. It is a given. It is a part of every person's psychological makeup, present at birth. Jung writes,

> The psyche is a self-regulating system that maintains its equilibrium just as the body does. Every process that goes too far immediately and inevitably calls forth compensations, and without these there would be neither a normal metabolism nor a normal psyche. In this sense we can take the theory of compensation as a basic law of psychic behavior. Too little on one side results in too much on the other. [1]

He goes on to write,

> As a rule, the unconscious content contrasts strikingly with the conscious material, particularly when the conscious attitude tends too exclusively in a direction that would threaten the vital needs of the individual. The more one-sided his conscious attitude is, and the further it deviates from the optimum, the greater becomes the possibility that vivid dreams with a strongly contrasting but purposive content will appear as an expression of the self-regulation of the psyche.

Jungian analyst Marie Louise von Franz was once asked about nightmares and this was her response:

> Well, nightmares are substantial, vitally important dreams. They wake us up with a cry; they are the electroshock Nature uses on us when Nature wants to wake us up. The word *nightmare* comes from *mare*, and the idea was that an evil ghost in the form of a black horse was riding you in the night, and so you woke up with a cry, completely exhausted.

The waking-up point of the dream means the bang with which the unconscious says, 'Now, that is it, now attend to that!' And so the nightmare is really shock therapy. It wants to shock us out of a deep, unconscious sleepiness about some dangerous situation. When we have nightmares, it means we are in a psychological danger of some sort and much too sleepy and unaware of it. Then we have a nightmare to wake us up. The nightmare has a characteristic of a certain urgency, as if the unconscious would say, "Look here, that problem is urgent!"[2]

So there is something about the very nature of how our psyches have been formed and how they function that involves this self-regulation. It is often compensatory. We go too far in one direction or we get off our path, the psyche endeavors to compensate by employing images, symbols, experiences, feelings, dreams designed to bring the ego back to a middle path, back to an attitude, an action, a self-perception that reflects the entire personality's notion of what constitutes our authentic self, our true personality, or perhaps even the nature of our life's opus or work. Again, it does this naturally. It does this autonomously. It does this automatically. It does this without the least consternation as to whether this compensation will make us feel comfortable or uncomfortable, or extremely uncomfortable. To a large extent, it does not care about your personal values or society's social norms. It is simply sending us a message. The more off-course we are, the stronger the message, the more nightmarish the content, the more disturbing the affect. And hence, the title of this presentation—"Nightmares—Urgent Messages from the Guiding Self."

The term "nightmare" has been used almost exclusively, at least since 1829, to refer to a type of really bad dream that suddenly awakens the dreamer with a start. But before then the word reflected the belief that at night a "mare," not a female horse, but a "mare," would sometimes pay dreamers a visit. **Mare** was the Scandinavian word for a goblin, an evil spirit, an incubus (or a male demon) or a succubus (a female demon), who would visit those who sleep, and especially those who sleep alone. The Oxford English Dictionary defines nightmare as "a [female] spirit or monster supposed to beset people and animals by night, settling upon them when they are asleep and producing a feeling of suffocation by their weight." A second and related definition reads, "A feeling of suffocation or great distress felt during sleep, from which the sleeper vainly endeavors to free himself; a bad dream producing these or similar sensations." There is, however, a later reference to nightmares, reflecting Germanic stories, where a demon or a witch visits the dreamer in the form of a horse or a mare, and then rides the dreamer into a state of frenzy, anxiety and exhaustion. You may be familiar with the very famous painting of Henry Fuseli, the Swiss-Anglo artist, entitled "The Nightmare."

Now we could spend a considerable amount of time exploring what this painting may have represented for Fuseli himself, which some have conjectured involved an unrequited love, obsession, and a predilection toward the macabre. But we will not. Many interpreters have projected various sexual meanings upon the characters in the painting, and I am not saying they could not be there. It is just a rabbit hole we are not going to have time to go down tonight. And it is interesting, if not mysterious, to note that Fuseli himself provided absolutely no commentary on this painting.

So let us just say that this painting exhibits some of the period beliefs and images associated with the experience of having a nightmare.

First, there is the dreamer, who is asleep in a very unconscious, outstretched, vulnerable position. We really do not know what she may be experiencing while asleep.

Then there is the goblin, the male incubus, the evil spirit, sitting on her abdomen, no doubt making it hard to breathe, perhaps representing the common feeling of suffocation, trying to catch one's breath. The imp, with its semi-human face, pointed ears and glaring eyes, is looking straight at us, the audience. It sees us. There is nowhere to hide. And it is wearing no clothes, no persona. It is naked; it is what it is.

And finally, from behind the curtain or veil, the ghostly head of a horse appears, with its blank, vacant, rather haunting eyes, and an open mouth. It is said that this horse's head was not in Fuseli's original drawings and only appeared later, perhaps to convey the popular belief at the time that nightmares were also demons or witches disguised as a female horse.

And what might we make of the table and its contents in the left foreground? Again, we do not really know. Like everything else in the painting, another opportunity for projection. They could be perfumes, medicines, or perhaps laudanum, a narcotic mixture of alcohol and opium, which was widely used in Fuseli's time. If it was laudanum, it might account for the nightmare itself, and the visitation of such frightening guests. This is Fuseli's "The Nightmare."

Now let us see if we can make a transition from this artistic portrayal of a nightmare to the actual experience of a nightmare. What does the phenomenon of a nightmare entail? What happens to us, not just psychologically, but physiologically, when we experience a nightmare? I could ask you to close your eyes and remember or relive an actual nightmare you have dreamt. Or, we could watch one. This is a nightmare taken from the film Dreamscape that came out in 1984, starring Dennis Quaid. While rather tame by today's standard for special effects, I think you will get the gist.

What did you notice happening to you physiologically, in your body, while you were watching that clip? What kind of feelings or reactions did you experience? *[Shallowness of breathing, fear, rapid heart rate, surprise, shock, a "fight, flight, freeze" response, anxiety, paralysis, jittery feet/legs/fingers, discomfort, flashbacks, panic?]* I wonder if the experience would have been different if we had left the lights on. This little exercise may seem a little silly, but it has everything to do with why we have nightmares and the message they are trying to convey. They take a form, they tell a story that is meant to make us uncomfortable—not just up here in our heads, but also down here in our guts, at a feeling level. We can always play head games, we can engage in mental gymnastics with thoughts and words we don't like, but it is hard to ignore a feeling, especially a feeling that terrorizes us. It is that heaviness in our chest, that shallowness in our breathing, that paralysis in our movement that conjures up images in our imagination of something otherworldly, something frightening, like a goblin, or a demon, an incubus or a succubus, sitting on our chest.

Sometimes we actively feel threatened by something in our nightmares. At other times it is simply the passive presence of someone or some "thing" that causes us to be terrorized—like the vacant stare of a pale horse from behind a curtain, or the eyes of a ventriloquist's dummy that follow us across a room, or that three-foot-long spider resting motionless at the other end of the couch. The physical feelings and reactions we have during the nightmares we dream are not just the understandable responses to a frightening situation. They are also a means the Guiding Self uses to get our attention about an issue that is very, very important.

The nightmares we suffer do not come arbitrarily. They come with intention and purpose. As I mentioned earlier, they are a reflection of the psyche's self-regulatory nature and thus a natural response to something that has happened or may happen in a person's life.

Now, that "something" may be traceable to an actual event in outer life, along with our response to that event, such as a wounding, a shock, a disappointment, a failure, a loss, an abuse or a threat. However, that something could just as easily be an inner, intra-psychic issue that begs to be addressed, such as a fear, a developmental step not taken, an important decision hanging in the balance, a self-perception that does not reflect our authentic personality, or a serious misjudgment that is simply inaccurate. But it is important to understand that these issues, whether inner or outer, whether past or present, these issues that precipitate nightmares do not always have to be negative or a lack of something. It is quite possible that the issue or event could be quite positive and life-serving in nature. It could be an unexpected success, an opportunity of great magnitude, a transformative awakening, a sudden recognition, a monetary windfall, or a dream come true. It is the fact that we do not perceive it, in that way, that leads to the creation of a nightmare meant to wake us up, to command our attention.

There are those outer events that are so overwhelming and horrific that they produce exceptionally disturbing feelings that the ego simply cannot understand or withstand. When that event is suffered early in life it can overwhelm a somewhat delicate ego still developing. Powerful feelings can arise. The ego can feel overwhelmed by an intense sense of danger. When this happens, the psyche, as a natural response, can protect the integrity of that young ego, as well as the safety of the whole personality, by dissociating; that is, sending the affect as well as the memory of that event into the unconscious. It is what is frequently called a defense mechanism. Examples include children who experience emotional, physical, or sexual abuse; a young person who witnesses or suffers the horrors of violence; an adolescent who is victimized by incessant bullying; a sensitive young person who is confronted with the reality of death. All these situations can be experienced as traumatic, where the child or young person is overwhelmed by spontaneous, intense feelings, unable to make sense of what has just happened, what they just witnessed. These kinds of experiences often produce nightmares, even though those nightmares may not surface for months or even years after the traumatic event, simply because the ego, at the time, was not ready to deal with it.

However, traumatic events are not confined to childhood. Anything can be experienced as a trauma at any time in one's life: being robbed at gunpoint, surviving a natural disaster, being involved in a car accident, suffering sexual violence, losing your 401K or your job, the sudden death of a loved one, the end of a significant relationship, being told you have a terminal illness, having to move from your home unexpectedly, forced retirement, our men and women having come home from Iraq and Afghanistan. The list can go on and on. Anything can be one straw too many. When the ego is severely compromised, when it is cruelly wounded, nightmares often arise as a natural response.

It is important to understand that most nightmares coming in response to a traumatic event come not to further the trauma, but to help the ego process it, even when at times such nightmares feel re-traumatizing. They come for a natural, necessary reason. I was at a party one evening where I knew very few people. While everyone was milling around, a man and I struck up a conversation. You know some of the most dangerous words heard at a party? "What do you do for a living?" I told him I was a Jungian analyst, that I worked a lot with dreams. And he said, "Let me tell you a story about some dreams I had." He was a helicopter pilot during Viet Nam. He would fly into battle situations and pick up wounded soldiers, taking them back to the M.A.S.H. unit. He told me that during those flights he never had any difficulty. He did what he had to do, what he was trained to do, what was expected. When he came back Stateside, after his service was over, he never had a problem. Then all of a sudden he started having these recurring nightmares of flying his helicopter in to pick up wounded soldiers, but then having to leave that last wounded soldier behind. This repetitive nightmare was really tearing him up. But, he said, he never sought out any kind of counseling or psychotherapy.

Then, he went on, "One day, when I was in Washington, D.C., I decided to visit the Viet Nam Memorial. I walked the length of that memorial from one end to the other. I looked at the names of all the soldiers who died, all the soldiers who did not come back alive. And it was the strangest thing. After doing that, I never had those nightmares again. They just stopped."

It's an amazing story. We did not go into why that was. It did not seem appropriate in the moment. Afterwards, I fantasized about the meaning of that symbolic act—how, when you look at the names etched into that memorial, you not only see the names of all those soldiers who never came back alive, but you also see your own reflection in the highly-polished stone. Maybe he was just now dealing with a sense of survivor's guilt, or maybe trying to process the intense feelings of fear, the sense of danger, or the bloody horrors of war that he could not allow himself to acknowledge or examine at the time. Maybe it had something to do with entering the second half of life, where one attempts to pull the pieces of one's life together into one fabric, to take stock of one's life in a search for meaning. I do not know. But what I do know is that the psyche was doing precisely what it is designed to do: to protect the integrity of the ego and to eventually process our wounding experiences. Hopefully, that processing will bring some measure of healing, allowing a person to continue their life and the pursuit of his or her true personality. Nightmares are a natural part of the healing process, the individuation process. They are just very urgent messages designed to get our attention.

Sometimes these nightmarish dreams are a reliving of the trauma itself, with all the accompanying feelings and sensations. Sometimes they are a little more veiled and must be worked with therapeutically to understand their message.

There is a parallel between these traumatic nightmares and what we often refer to as "recurring dreams." The similarity is simply the fact that they both recur. But whereas traumatic dreams come in response to a particular traumatic event that is now being worked through, recurring dreams are addressing a very important issue that needs to be dealt with. They may not arise in response to a specific traumatic incident at all. The visual picture I have about what is going on in recurring dreams is this: there, in the center of the room, is the issue that needs to be addressed. The Guiding Self, in a sense, sends a dream and we are given an opportunity to see and feel that issue from this particular perspective. Maybe we pick up on it, maybe we do not. If we do not, then sometime later the Guiding Self sends another dream. It is not exactly the same dream, but there is a recurring theme, or character, or situation, or predicament, or feeling; and we are given another opportunity to see the issue, and hopefully, to do something about it. Now if we do not see it or do not want to see it, then the Guiding Self continues to circumambulate, to walk us around that central issue in the hope that we will eventually get the message, sooner rather than later. And if that central issue is really critical, if it is important that we see it, then the Guiding Self may begin to turn up the heat as the dreams come. That often leads to these recurring dreams becoming more and more nightmarish in quality. But as I am contending, these nightmares are not being sent to torment us, but to wake us up, to invite us to see what we not seeing, and to deal with that central issue that may very well be holding us back from moving forward on our individuation journey or providing us with a much needed psychological balance.

The nightmares we have almost always come in response to something in our life that needs attention. Nightmares are a natural part of how the psyche has evolved and how it functions, psychologically and otherwise. And again, it is important to realize that nightmares come to help; they are designed to promote life, to facilitate healing, and to foster growth in the individual.

As I have shown, there are nightmares that come in response to a specific traumatic event, which can vary in intensity. At other times, however, nightmares may address other issues, feelings, situations, or perhaps an aspect of ourselves that we are not aware of or are not dealing with, but desperately need to. Nightmares are not capricious. They may be an onerous blossom, but they arise from our own psychic soil.

The story lines that nightmares present are varied and unique. I do not think I have ever seen two that are exactly alike. The images and situations are limited only by the psyche's imagination. Here are some of the manifestations that people have found to be nightmarish in quality. You could perhaps add your own variation to the list.

- Being menaced or pursued by persons, animals, monsters, or demons (very popular)

- Realizing that one is the victim of a conspiracy or sinister plot
- Experiencing helplessness as intruders try to break into the house
- Fearing a fall from great heights (on the edge of a drop-off, or while flying)
- Being in a car or other vehicle that is running out of control (no brakes)
- Suffering physical injury (a poisonous bite, wound, dismemberment)
- Death (being killed in a dream)
- Combat situations: hand-to-hand combat, shooting, terrorism or war
- Natural disasters: earthquakes, fires, floods, tornadoes, hurricanes
- Helpless/abandoned/crying babies (or small animals)
- Realizing one has committed a terrible crime
- Having feelings of "craziness," dissociation, unreality
- Losing something deemed to be of immense value
- Intense anxiety about being inadequate or having failed
- Being frightened and unable to determine if one is awake or asleep
- Confronting or being enveloped by a dark void

It is not unusual for more than one of these motifs to appear in any single nightmare. We are going to examine a couple of nightmares now to see if we can get a sense of what these urgent messages might be, given the life situation of the dreamer. Some of the rest, and more, we'll try to examine tomorrow at the workshop.

This first dream is from a 32-year-old man who has just begun analysis. We will call him Jack. Jack was a young man, very much the intellectual—good education, a thinking type. The reason he gave for seeking out analysis was he had read some of

Jung's work and was fascinated by the theory. He did not have any particular problem or issue, at least that he was aware of, that could account for this sudden interest in the Jungian approach.

People come in for analysis for all kinds of reasons. Often there is a crisis one can identify as the precipitating event—relationship problems, a failure or disappointment, maybe an old wound that just has not healed. Sometimes people are suffering from a general malaise or listlessness. Still others are confronted with a difficult decision or a situation where they feel stuck, not knowing what to do or which way to turn. Jack was coming in through yet another door, using the typological strength with which he was most familiar and comfortable—his thinking. And he could not wait to get started. Journaling, dream interpretation, archetypal associations, active imagination—he was ready to jump in. Then he brought in this dream, or rather this nightmare.

> I have been in a motel-type setting with many rooms. It seems I am going to school there. I go down to the pool and am enticed by three young women to go in and try the ice-cold water. I decline and leave. I walk back to my room, hoping to get something to eat. I pass two members of my church that I like a lot, as well as a man I know from somewhere who I do not trust. We pass. As I approach my room, I realize that there are a number of people waiting to capture me and others like me. I begin to run, trying to get away. I feel overwhelmed. I pass other groups of people who are likewise lying in wait. I reach a certain point where I am confronted by a group of people holding syringes. I am afraid, terrorized, and panic-stricken. I want to get out, but there's no way out. A couple of people throw their syringes at me and I try to duck, falling down, as though I've been hit, hoping they will leave me. But then I realize that I was hit, in the back of the neck, and I am beginning to feel the effects. I cannot move. I am paralyzed and helpless. As I lay there outstretched, a man puts a needle into my arm. It's

sodium pentothal. As I feel a certain numbness beginning to spread through my body, the man says, "We're going to figure out why you came here."

As we began to work with the dream, Jack associated motels to places where one stays when they are far from home, in unfamiliar territory. The fact that he seemed to be going to school reflected what he was expecting of these analytic sessions—he was hoping to learn something, to further his education. He did not know what to make of the three young women. He was not interested in going into the pool of ice-cold water. He felt reassured seeing the friends from church. But then there was that one unknown man that he knew from somewhere, whom he did not trust. After that, he was off and running, so to speak. And he described the chase as terrifying. There were so many people. And it just kept escalating. He confessed he was deathly afraid of needles. He had never felt so powerless, vulnerable, and out of control. He wondered about those last words spoken by the man who put the needle into his arm, "We're going to figure out why you came here." What did he mean?

This was definitely a nightmare. "Afraid, terrorized, panic-stricken." His words. We worked through it with the usual back and forth, give and take. Dreams are inexhaustible in meaning, containing many issues and perspectives worth considering. But oftentimes one particular message will present itself as the most pressing. And this is where we ended up—this dream, this nightmare was addressing his attitude toward the analysis itself. The unconscious is a far-away place, especially for someone not acquainted with the territory. It is good to have a safe place to stay, like a motel, a home away from home. And, yes, there is much to be learned from listening to the unconscious in the multiple ways it can speak to us. But it is a different kind of learning. Advanced degrees do not guarantee safety. Being a strong thinking type may not be enough. Too cavalier or naïve an attitude may not get you very far. This is serious business. The unconscious has its own wisdom, its own way of compensating an attitude that lacks respect, or perhaps is a little too enthusiastic.

When you look at the overall structure of the dream, you can see that it is the dreamer's refusal to go into the ice-cold pool of water that soon leads to all hell breaking loose. Entering such a pool is often a necessary and ritualized step, a step usually taken <u>before</u> one enters the Other World. In the Asclepian dream temples of ancient Greece the suffering supplicant would undergo a ritualized bath before entering the *abaton*, that special room designed for dreaming and hopefully for meeting Asclepius, one of the Greek gods associated with healing. Native Americans are bathed in the intense steam of the Sweat Lodge before beginning their Vision Quest. Christians are baptized with the waters of penitence, absolution and inclusion before beginning their new life. In so many rituals around the world, there is almost always a period of preparation, in whatever form that may take. Before one enters that liminal space to meet the powerful forces of the Other World, it is helpful, it is advised, and it is wise to move into the dream world slowly and respectfully.

And it is not as if the Guiding Self in Jack's dream was not proactive. It did send three young women to beckon him. But Jack declined. He would rather go back to his room where it is comfortable. It is interesting that in doing so he passes two people from his church. Edward Edinger, a Jungian analyst, uses an insightful image, I think, when talking about how people engage the powerful, archetypal forces of the unconscious. He compares these numinous, instinctual archetypal patterns in the psyche to wild animals. He suggests that those in the church do indeed spend time with these wild animals in the context of their particular religious faith. But, it is more like going to the zoo, where the wildness is safely contained behind the bars or the retaining walls of their beliefs and practices. On the other hand, he says, those who meet and engage these wild animals by working with their dreams and who consciously participate in their individuation process resemble more those who are on safari, where there is always the possibility of being eaten.

Passing the two people from his church who are going in the opposite direction may represent the dreamer's passing the protected comfort of his intellect to now stare directly into the abyss.

Here, the Guiding Self seems intent on addressing the issue of how one engages the unconscious, saying in effect, "Well, if you don't want to go the prescribed way, that is, undergoing a ritual of preparation, symbolized by taking a dip in the pool of water, then how about a baptism by fire? These are some of the things you may encounter. Are you prepared? Are you ready?" What then follows is literally his worst nightmare. As someone who lived primarily in his head, he is being thrown into the depths of feeling and emotion. And for him, it is a frightening, terrifying experience. The unconscious could not have chosen a more threatening weapon of choice to make its point than the threat of needles and syringes. Look at the words he uses: overwhelmed, afraid, terrorized, panic-stricken, paralyzed, helpless, numb. And consider that very last statement, "We're going to figure out why you came here," even if it takes truth serum to do so.

Sometimes, as in this case, nightmares appear to perform the function of a sentry; that is, someone who stands guard, who protects the treasure, who confronts anyone who may not be ready, prepared, or respectful. In the Far East, there are demons that guard the doors of the temple, who ward off and keep out those who are unprepared or have no business entering that sacred space where the numinous mysteries of life might be experienced. This nightmare might also be seen as an attempt on the part of the Guiding Self to test the dreamer. "So you want to do analytic work? Are you prepared for what you may find? Do you know what might be standing behind those doors to the unconscious? Well, we are going to figure that out."

Perhaps you remember in Dante's *Divine Comedy* the words sitting over the Gates of Hell—"Abandon hope, all ye who enter here." And yet, as the story goes, one must pass through the darkness and the shadows of Hell before making one's way to

Paradise. It may have been a scary awakening, but a necessary one, before Jack began his work in earnest.

The nightmare now of a 41-year-old married woman, the mother of two small boys. We will call her Jill.

> I am in Russia. A war is going on. Men are setting up cannons. Two sides—ready to fire. My two sons and husband are going to stay and fight. I decide to leave. There is no way I want to be a part of war. I see a man getting ready to light his cannon. They are about to fire. I start walking away and join others who are leaving. We walk fast. There is a sound of a cannon firing. I am holding a woman's hand and then someone fires at me with a gun. The woman and I have been talking in English and I realize we look like Americans, who are the enemy. So I drop her hand and we keep walking and pretend we are Russian (even speaking Russian). She says she knows somewhere we can go and stay for safety. An Evil Café. I am not sure I want to go and I worry about the boys. Will we ever be united? (The final question changed as she later wrote the dream down, "Will I ever be united?")

Jill was a very bright, talented woman; however, her presentation was marked by anxiety and tearfulness. Her father and mother were both very driven individuals. The father built a very successful business; the mother was very bright and well-educated, but gave up her dream of having a career to become a successful homemaker. Her mother tended to be rather critical of both her husband and Jill, so much so that her father spent most of his time at the office, leaving Jill to fend for herself. Jill said she felt abandoned by her father.

She wasn't even sure she wanted to be in analysis, not because she could not afford it, but because she felt she did not deserve it and was also afraid of what she might discover or do as a result. Her frequent fantasy involved leaving her husband and children, going off to California to live the Bohemian lifestyle of an artist. She was very gifted, artistically and otherwise. After graduating from college, she gave up a career as a newspaper journalist to become a wife and mother.

These were her associations to the dream. **Russia** reminded her of how she had decided to major in Russian literature while in college, a decision her parents could not understand. She said she felt "called" to it. She loved the passion, the aliveness, the intrigue, the poignant human issues dealt with. **War** was a man's thing; that's how they settle issues; too much testosterone, machismo. **Cannons** were seen as loud, destructive, and phallic; able to kill or wound from a great distance. **Regarding her family**, she basically had a good relationship with her husband, although he had his issues, which he was reluctant to deal with. She found caring for and mothering her two sons often more than she could handle. So often she wished she could abandon them and go off to do her own thing. **The other woman** in the dream she saw as a sympathetic person with whom she felt a genuine relationship and someone who cared for her personally. There was nothing overtly sexual about their holding hands, she said. She just felt connected to her in a good way. The **Evil Café** brought back memories of her eating disorder, developed during college, which really got her father's attention when the school called to inform him about her illness. She still wrestled with feelings of guilt after eating sweets. **The closing question(s)**: she was aware that something was split or at war within her. The issue of "wholeness" came up repeatedly, in her family, in herself, and in her self-perception.

It is said by Russian literary critics that there are two recurrent themes in Russian literature: suffering as a means of redemption and unsuccessful love affairs. In this nightmare, set in Russia, there is a war going on, a conflict between two sides, between two values, between two yearnings, between two self-perceptions. This war might have its roots in the relationship between her mother and father, which could account for the mother's critical attitude as an expression of anger arising from her giving up a promising career to become a mother, which she found burdensome. It may also account for why the father spent so much time at the office, and, as a result, why the business was so successful. To a large extent Jill could be seen as a casualty of this war, an orphan constantly criticized by her mother, abandoned by her father. This war can also be seen in the tension between two yearnings: that of being a wife and mother on the one hand, and that of being a professional woman, an artist, on the other. This same war may very well have raged within Jill's mother when she was a young woman. And then there is the internal war raging around whether she was a valuable person, someone worthy of enjoying the goodness of life and the development of her true personality.

She had been fighting this war for some time, trying to be heroic, fighting the good fight, while being completely surrounded by Y-chromosomes. But the war within, and seemingly without, was incessant. And understandably, she was tired. "I don't want to be a part of war," she says. And yet the war continues. Cannons are firing, inflicting damage from a great distance. But then it becomes personal; someone fires a gun directly at her. This was the nightmare for her—being unable to escape a conflict that had depleted her energy, her ability to make necessary choices, and her hope for a future that was creative and self-expressive. Her nightmare is showing her the gravity of the situation as it is. It has the potential to overwhelm her and to cause her great harm.

But in the dream she finds she has a friend, a woman, with whom she can connect by holding hands. They are moving away from the war zone, but she is still in danger. She is speaking the language of the enemy, English. And she looks like the enemy, American. In a real sense, from all outward appearances, she was living the American dream—a beautiful house in the right zip code, a husband who loved her and was an excellent provider, two young boys who were great kids, given the fact that they were typical little boys. But inside there was a war raging. In fear, she drops this other woman's hand, but they continue walking together. Then her friend suddenly remarks that she knows a place where they can go for safety—an Evil Café. It doesn't sound like a safe place to Jill. And she's worried about her boys, still so young. Will the split ever be healed, united? In the midst of this ongoing war, this nightmarish conflict, it is hard to imagine that safety could be found in something as ominous as an Evil Café.

Nightmares have a way of leaving us hanging, leaving issues unresolved. When a nightmare wakes us up with a start, it has already performed its main function: to alert us, to startle us, to draw our attention to a critical life issue. But it rarely gives us the solution full blown. More often we just get the wakeup call. What we do with the issue once we have a sense of what it is, is left up to us. We still have to play our part in the healing process. But sometimes, the nightmare can give us a clue.

Jill was fearful, yet curious about this Evil Café. But how could an Evil Café hold the promise of safety, an escape from this war raging outside? In addition to dream interpretation, Jung also valued the technique of active imagination, where a dreamer lowers the threshold of consciousness by entering a semi-meditative state and then entertains conversations with dream figures. To a very large extent, that is what Jung's *Red Book* contains. But active imagination can also be used to "dream a dream forward," especially with those dreams that end without a solution or result. I asked Jill if she would be willing to try active imagination—to cross over that threshold and step inside this Evil Café. She said she was. She went back into the dream and at the end of it, she walked through the front door of the café and in her mind's eye, this is what she saw.

There were round tables set up toward the front window where couples of men and women were seated, pleasantly talking. Toward the back of the café was a stage where women were dancing, something, she thought, that resembled the Can-Can. And then back toward the front of the café was a large table laden with all the most delicious desserts she could imagine. She tried one of the desserts—a piece of chocolate cake—and it was so delicious. When she slowly came back to full "awakeness," we discussed what she had seen and felt. This was not at all what she had envisioned when her woman friend in the dream had suggested the Evil Cafe as a place of safety. But something had been stirred up.

A week later, when she came in for her next appointment, she entered carrying a three-dimensional diorama of this Evil Café. There was something about this dream image that captured her imagination and she decided to use her creative skills to reproduce it. Everything was there: the couples at their round tables, the stage of dancers, and the large table of desserts; even the name of the café on wax paper in the front window. That is when she made the discovery. The Guiding Self sometimes likes to play word games.

Something suddenly clicked for her. What had, from one perspective appeared to be "evil," from another perspective read "live." What Jill saw inside the café contained "life." But she never would have known it if she had not gone into what she feared, what she distrusted, what she disparaged—in effect, what she considered "evil." Her friend in the dream, what we might refer to as a very positive shadow figure, knew something very important. This unknown female figure most probably represents something of the archetypal, nurturing mother. Not only would this Evil Café prove to provide safety from the war that was raging, but also healing. But she would first have to step inside that café before she could see and live out what that café had to offer.

This dream, this nightmare, made a huge impression. It was a dream, and an active imagination, she would come back to again and again. Engaging in the war, choosing sides, adopting a fighting spirit, battling what she perceived to be the enemy, would not bring about a sense of peace within her. Seeing and understanding that this war might be better addressed by caring for herself, mothering herself, giving expression to this yearning for wholeness, maybe even indulging herself at times, these represented a new direction, a new direction that came from within her. But it was only a beginning.

It took some time, but I sensed something was shifting when she traded in her mini-van for a Volvo station wagon, where she could carry her art work in the back; when she rented a "studio with a view" in the art district, where she could go to work on her art at any time of the day or night; and when she used some of her financial resources to go back to school to work toward an art therapy degree. These were all things suggested in her active imagination; that is, relating to that masculine principle within her, symbolized by the couples conversing at the round tables (the round shape itself being a symbol of wholeness, perhaps a more feminine expression of wholeness); expressing her own creativity through the arts, symbolized by the high energy dancing on the stage; and indulging herself in the good things life may offer, symbolized by the tasting of a dessert from a full table. These were all actions, arising from her own psyche, designed to lessen the fear and anxiety produced by the war raging within her and to provide an opening toward individuation. And this all began in response to a nightmare that got her attention in a way nothing had before.

Now experientially, a nightmare may get our attention. It may press us hard to attend to something, but the usual reaction to a nightmare is to try not to think about it, to just be thankful it is "not real," and to hope we never have such a dream again. The problem with that reaction is the unconscious does not give up easily, especially with issues that are critical to our development or our psychological balance or are a matter of life and death. The Guiding Self is simply doing what it does naturally. And it is a master at weaving stories designed to command our attention with terrifying images. I want to close, however, with an encouraging proposition.

When a person cultivates a dialectic relationship with the Guiding Self (that is, a give-and-take dialogue between the ego and the unconscious); when we are consciously involved in the process of addressing old wounds, traumatic or otherwise; when we are engaging split-off parts of our own personality—it is possible to experience a nightmare, even a terrifying nightmare, and respond to it with a certain amount of equanimity. You will still feel the shock, you will still be jolted by the feeling of fear or terror as you awake, but it won't paralyze you or produce a sense of dread that dominates the rest of the day if you find the courage to appreciate why that nightmare arose. You may not comprehend completely what it means or what issue it is addressing. Its lingering feeling may accompany you throughout the day. But just knowing it has come in your service, for the purpose of your health, your healing or your wholeness, may be enough to change a spontaneous response of avoidance into one of curiosity. It is possible to awaken from a nightmare with a "Whoa!" followed shortly by "I wonder what that's all about?"

Endnotes

[1] "The Practical Use of Dream Analysis." *CW 16: The Practice of Psychotherapy*. Par.330.
[2] Marie Louise von Franz. "The Devouring Mother," *The Way of the Dream*, 1994. Page 88.

Author Bio

Howard W. Tyas, Jr., D. Min.

Howard W. Tyas is a certified Jungian analyst and a licensed Pastoral Counselor. He currently has a private practice in Charlotte, North Carolina, working primarily with adults in individual analysis, making use of dream material and expressive techniques. He also lectures, leads dream groups, and conducts monthly seminars focusing on dream work and various images which reflect what C.G. Jung referred to as the individuation process.

Dr. Tyas has a Doctor of Ministry degree from Austin Presbyterian Theological Seminary in Texas. In 1991, Dr. Tyas traveled to Zürich, Switzerland, to study at the C.G. Jung Institute, where he graduated with the Diploma in Analytical Psychology in 1996. Dr. Tyas is a member of the International Association for Analytical Psychology and the Association of Graduate Analytical

Psychologists (Zürich). He is a charter member of the North Carolina Society of Jungian Analysts.

Your Soul Is Your Real Self & How EMDR & the Vagal Nerve System Cleanse Your Soul

Karen E. Herrick, Ph.D.

The wings that form the butterfly lie folded in the worm.

Abstract

Your individual pattern is your soul, which separates from your physical body and becomes your structure in the etheric world. While you are on earth, you add positive and negative experiences to your soul. It has been said that once on the "other side" people sometimes take a "soul shower" in order to dispel unhappy experiences from this life. If this is true, which part or parts of our physical body do you think we take to the other side? And what types of therapy here on earth could soothe and shower this part of you before you return "home"? We in the therapeutic field are learning that neurobiology can be synthesized with our therapeutic concepts, providing new treatment interventions.

June Beltzer in her psychic dictionary (1986) gives one definition of a soul as "A set of predisposing factors which affect how each individual pattern relates to all the rest; the pattern is a soul and it separates from the rest and has a unique set of predisposing characteristics." It is the part of you that lives forever. Every religion states that we have a soul; however, in our religious education(s) we are not taught about the purpose of our soul. In fact, we have a built-in amnesia regarding knowing about it.

Your soul begins to become visible during your life when you sometimes realize you have extrasensory or synchronistic experiences. Your soul is touched by these experiences and you feel the *touching*. Spirits (guides, ancestors, angels) also send images and flashes of inspiration to you through your soul. Your will deepens with the crises of everyday life when you are looking for answers to what is happening to you. As we go through the pain and awe of experiences in life, we are opened to another dimension *if* we use these experiences for growth. Sometimes you then start to realize that there is a spirit part of you that *knows*. These "aha" moments let us have a glimpse of our soul. If you begin to know your soul, you will learn to be more self-reliant.

Your soul is the highest center of wisdom and perspective. Where is it located? According to Carl Jung, the Swiss psychologist, it is located in the fifth layer of your unconscious. Your soul comes to earth to learn and it is developed from stories that have happened to you. How did you come to be? Who were your parents, grandparents and other ancestors? What messages were you given as you were growing up?

Your soul contains your possibilities, your talents, and your unrealized potential. It also contains your past, present and future. It holds your personality and many other personalities that have come from your past lives. It also contains your imagination, and through the use of your imagination you may be able to find out more stories about yourself from other time periods. Remember, Plato said we all know more than we think we know. And, Plato believed in souls.

When we chose our parents, we chose what culture, what country and what area of the world we will live in. Our lives have themes. We set goals and we're supposed to follow them through. What themes did you choose for your soul to work with? Maybe you came to earth to be a parent, or to be a daughter or a son? Maybe you are here to be a strong member of a community and to lead? Maybe you came here to take risks and to be "different?"

Maybe you came here to be a better male or female or to make up for some past lives where you didn't make very good decisions?

We all start our soul journey in a family. What emotions were stirred in you in this family? What emotions do you hide? What role models did or didn't you have? How did you learn to express yourself? Or maybe you don't express yourself; instead, you keep things closed and inside of you? Maybe in this life you are supposed to speak out? If you came here to overcome closed-off emotions, what is it that you would be afraid to say? <u>Your soul is integrated by your thoughts.</u> What type of thoughts usually direct your day?

Developing a conscience is the soul's job. You are here to learn right from wrong. Were you taught to have a connection to God or a Higher Power as you developed your soul? Do you believe in a God or a Higher Power or that there is this spirit part of you called a soul?

Sometimes a person doesn't connect to their soul unless they become "dead." When you die, the soul leaves your body out through the top of your head "Something" pulls you out of your physical body. Your body then looks wispy and ethereal. Your soul feels wonderful when it is released from your brain and your body! It feels FREE! Leaving your body is like shedding your skin or like peeling a banana. Your body simply has been the vehicle that you needed on earth to aid in your soul's growth. Your body is like your car. It moved you all around while you were on earth. All souls are held accountable for their conduct in the bodies that they have occupied.

You have guides, angels and positive ancestors who help you on your soul's journey. Guides chose you and no two guides are the same. The two themes we all need to deal with on earth are to be separate and isolated. We come into this world alone and we leave alone. It's important to remember when we're feeling separate and isolated that there is an unseen world all around us where spirits, guides and ancestors are helping us. Perhaps if you don't believe you have guides, you could "act as if" and see for a period of time what happens. Guides are more parental than dictators. They suggest, they prod, they remind and they send people to do the same to us. It's important that we wake up eventually and hear and see these signs so we can *know*.

One of our jobs here on earth is to develop trust. If you are now confused in life, this is good. Confusion means you are working through something big and new opportunities await you. Be curious during your confusion. Another job we have is to go "beyond your ego." Your ego is anything you would say after "I am…" Your ego probably says you have no spiritual guides. In this area, we need not listen to our ego. It doesn't know everything.

Another purpose of your soul is to make you human. As you address and overcome pain and frustration, you will connect to who you really are. Pain opens you to other dimensions. Your soul, being honest and sincere, is driven by integrity. Integrity has to do with what you do when no one is watching you. Hurt people mistreat other people in order to get even. They create negative karma for themselves. Perpetrators of harm to others will do penance by setting themselves up as victims of this harm in their next life.

Also, it is good to remember that along with learning our own lessons we come to earth to play a part in the drama of others' lessons as well. We picked a "group" of people to come into this life with and we all play different parts. Eyes are the windows to the soul. No other physical attribute has more impact when soul mates meet on earth than the eyes. There is a familiarity when you meet a soul mate—a *knowing*.

We come into this world to learn to know what we are feeling. To really know how you feel and then trust that feeling teaches you to trust in yourself. Once you can trust your feelings, your job is to create and transform things in your life. What would you like to create in the future?

It is important again to remember that your soul contains your past, your future and your unrealized potential. It also contains your God-Image and what spirit means to you. Your soul regulates, governs and matures your personality by giving you situations to work through. Your soul often appears in dreams as the ideal personality. This personality will give you hints as to what it is you're supposed to be working on now.

Another purpose of your soul is that through experiences and the decisions you make you are supposed to mature based on overcoming your many difficult body assignments during your task-oriented life. You are energy in an energy field. You generate energy every day. How you use your energy depends on your experiences in life and what you choose daily to keep experiencing. You can generate more energy to work on your soul's purpose to get what you want now. Remember, when you pass over to the other side, when you so-called "die" and this life flashes before you, please make sure it is worth seeing.

Your soul never quits completely the body with which it is united. Time is very limiting. This is why your soul is timeless.

Appendix

The field of psychology doesn't recognize the existence of a soul. In fact, one of the first formal acknowledgments of non-ordinary experiences published by the American Psychological Association (APA) in the year 2000 was entitled *Varieties of Anomalous Experience Examining the Scientific Evidence.* An anomalous experience "is irregular in that it differs from common experiences, is uneven in that it is not the same as experiences that are even and ordinary" (Cardena et al., 2000, p. 4). These experiences are not an indicator of psychopathology. These anomalous, extrasensory and/or paranormal experiences are sometimes the beginning of when a person's soul begins to become visible during a person's life. Your soul is touched by these experiences and one feels the *touching*. However, the study of these experiences or this book is not a practice that is normal in the field of psychology.

The APA *Diagnostic and Statistical Manual of Mental Disorders (DSM)* is a textbook that reflects the official categories of mental illness that are seen and written about by some mental health professionals in the United States. Different editions are published when the APA feels there are enough changes being seen in therapists' offices to warrant a newer publication. In 1994, for the DSM-IV edition, a new diagnostic category was published entitled V-Code 62.89 "Religious or Spiritual Problem." This was proposed, written and supported by statistics for two non-ordinary experiences—Mystical Experiences and Near-Death Experiences (NDEs). This diagnosis was written to help explain distressing anomalous experiences of a spiritual nature but was shown in the DSM-IV and written by the APA as if it related only to religious and faith issues. The DSM now currently in use is the DSM-V.

In 1980, the APA added Post Traumatic Stress Disorder (PTSD) to the third edition of the DSM. It took Army invasions and the lobbying of veterans and feminist activists in the area of family violence to bring this diagnosis to the forefront in psychology. The PTSD concept ushered in a significant change since the agent that caused PTSD symptoms came from outside the individual rather than an inherent individual weakness inside of the person. These soldiers were exposed to trauma due to surviving the horrible situations of war. The WWII soldiers returned with cardiology and gastro intestinal issues but the Viet Nam veterans returned with PTSD. This diagnosis has grown to include many other traumatic situations that people experience, such as sexual abuse and domestic violence cases.

One psychotherapy approach that is being used now for PTSD is Eye Movement Desensitization and Reprocessing (EMDR), which is a memory processing system as well as being helpful in affect regulation. A research theory is *The Polyvagal Theory Neurophysiological Foundations of Emotions, Attachment Communication, Self-Regulation* (2011) by Dr. Stephen Porges. Polyvagal is a theory for visceral neurological processing. While both utilize the neuro-system in some way, they do not act in the same way.

EMDR is a comprehensive, integrative psychotherapy approach. It contains elements of many effective psychotherapies in structured protocols that are designed to maximize treatment effects. These include psychodynamic, cognitive behavioral, interpersonal experiential and body-centered therapies. (www.emdr.com/general).

EMDR is a therapy that works for PTSD because we hold trauma in our bodies. It's a memory processing system as well as being helpful in affect regulation. If traumatic memories are unprocessed, they remain in the limbic system of the brain, which is purely sensory based. The bilateral stimulation of EMDR appears, when done safely, to allow those limbic memories to gradually be processed by the prefrontal cortex, which leads to rational thought and calmness in present day memory. No one really understands why or how this occurs physiologically, in contrast to the Polyvagal research theory, where we do.

It's also important to know that the trauma is about the entire organism. The body continues to relive the trauma as if the issue hasn't stopped. Trauma just keeps repeating itself in the body. Sounds and smells in the environment can make a body respond as if it's just happening all over again. EMDR works because it allows clients to process their memories. It has been known to work even when someone is not calm because the bilateral eye process still appears to consolidate memory.

The Polyvagal Theory is a visceral-based process where memory is not the issue. It is a "bottom-up" process from the gut up through the organs into the brain. In esoteric philosophy it is known as the "channel for the soul-mind breath" (Beltzer, 1986, p. 663), which runs from the abdomen to the heart and to the base of the brain. It controls the respiratory system in humans.

When people are assaulted by something horrendous, their body either wants to freeze, fight or flee (otherwise shown in this article as FFF). This is because during trauma a part of your frontal lobe of the brain shuts down and your limbic animal brain takes over and starts secreting hormones. When these hormones are secreted the person feels either frozen or panic and anxiety. People's bodies continue to move as if they are in any of the FFF states because their bodies continue to feel that somebody is going to or is doing something to them. This is the usual core response.

Trauma memories are disintegrated sensations regarding a story about the past. The trauma leaves residues in the body. Trauma therapy is about taking the sensations and moving through them. Many times clients continue to stay in their "animal brain" state until a therapist can help them move through it, or some clients prefer to stay in the "drama of their trauma." This is because drama has identity. One has to have an intact identity to want to release themselves from the drama of their lives.

VAGAL NERVE SYSTEM

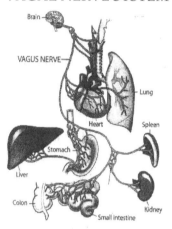

Dr. Stephen Porges (2011) states that the vagus nerve is part of the parasympathetic system of the brain and is a family of neural pathways originating in several areas of the brain stem. Approximately 80% of these pathways are "afferent"—meaning to "bring inward to a central part."(en.wikipedia.org/wiki/Vagus_nerve)

The vagus nerve is attached to both sides of the brain stem and travels from the abdomen to the brain, affecting the colon, intestines, kidney, liver, stomach, spleen, heart, and lungs. It is ubiquitous, which means it exists everywhere at the same time and has universal knowledge of the body. It is what is affected when the body is in the FFF (frozen, fright and flight) sensations of trauma.

There are three strands of the vagal nerve in Dr. Porges' theory and research. The first is the limbic or "play dead," which is the most primitive. This is where you see clients who are numbed out. The second strand is the reptile brain. This is the flight or fight strand. The third strand is the socio-receptive or balanced present state, where the vagal nerve, adrenaline and the thoughts are in balance.

Most therapy takes place in PTSD or a very anxious person in this latter strand. Here people know or can tell themselves whether the danger is real or is just being triggered. Almost all relaxation techniques calm the vagal nerve. The Polyvagal Theory only proposed a reason that they do so and explained the three-prong stages that help us account for why clients seem to act in different ways with trauma and why they often cannot incorporate the "words" of therapy. This is because they are in one of the more primitive stages. Van der Kolk of PTSD fame suggested tapping the acupressure point for a particular nerve. Tapping is an Energy Psychology method that can be used in the beginning stages of EMDR therapy.

This self-regulation nerve system can manage the body from the bottom up. During EMDR therapy, as the client is listening to music with eye movement that helps to connect the right and left sides of the brain, the vagal nerve is also calming the different parts of the body from the abdomen to the brain. Nonetheless, just using music, tapping or dance without EMDR also calms the vagal nerve. This allows the person to think more clearly as their body is calmer from the bottom up! Darwin stated that if you could change the state of your body you could change the state of your mind. This vagal system seems to send signals to the brain that it's fine to be calm now. This actually changes the state of your brain. The person now feels that they are safe.

This type of treatment helps people become more in touch with their bodies. Meditation, yoga and exercise also help people self-regulate. Meditation has shown that the more one becomes still and focuses on themselves, the more they feel in charge of their reactions. Exercise and yoga creates action with their bodies and counteracts the feelings of being trapped from the trauma, and now they have more control. They no longer feel traumatized because they are in control of the action they are practicing. They will tell you "that helpless feeling is gone from my stomach." "I don't feel that 'stuff' anymore." They begin to develop a deep sense of competency that they can now do something that will make them feel powerful again.

Freud noticed that people relived the trauma over and over again. He thought it was to rework the trauma but it really becomes more of a compulsion to repeat the trauma because it's so familiar. Apparently our mind is interested in information that we are not able to conquer. Traumatized people have a hard time taking in new information, which sometimes indicates that they won't learn from experience. This is because they are not really in the present. They're still playing out the past. People with addictions have this problem also. Their brains just aren't in any shape to develop a problem-solving strategy. This is one of the reasons why twelve-step programs many times work so well. A person can sit in meetings and develop themselves while watching more advanced people in recovery and how they behave.

Returning to PTSD, when a limbic memory triggers, it signals the vagal nerve and adrenaline rushes up the neuro pathways to the brain. The goal of the Polyvagal process, whether for trauma or plain anxiety, has nothing to do with memory, per se, but is about teaching clients how to "tap" (www.tapping.com) the vagal acupressure point on the hand without any thought or memory. This is to be done with a clear mind with taking deep breaths, staring out the window or at a candle, solely for the purpose of reducing the adrenaline back down the neural pathway to a reasonable balance

In Michael Newton's book *Journey of Souls Case Studies of Life between Lives* (1994/2013), a client of his, in describing his life between lives, told of a "soul shower" that he took once he had arrived on the other side. This was to eliminate taking the many negative things that had happened to him in his recent life onto the other side and also into a new life if he was to be reincarnated.

In dismantling the trauma from our bodies using a therapy approach such as EMDR, we can adjust and change our karmic pattern(s) of this life and of our soul to truly become more positive and more energetic. This can do nothing but help all of us become better masters of our own destinies. If by chance EMDR is not the approach for you, please gather information about other Energy Psychology methods that stimulate one or more of the human bio-energy systems, such as meridians, chakras and bio-fields.

We in the therapeutic field are learning that neurobiology can be synthesized with our therapeutic concepts. This is evidenced in the recent research of Van der Kolk, Porges, Le Doux and others, which connects trauma and anxiety issues to neurological and brain functioning as well as provides new treatment interventions to assist clients in how to de-stress physically so they can truly participate in a body, mind and soul healing.

Bibliography

A.A. World Services, Inc. (Ed.). (2001). Alcoholics Anonymous (4th Ed.). NY: AA World Services, Inc.

Alcoholics-Anonymous. www.alcoholics-anonymous.org. Al-anon, Alateen.

www.al-anon.alateen.org

Aizpurua, Jon (2013). *Fundamentals of Spiritism*. (Translation of Epsilon Book S.R.L., 2000)

Association for Research & Enlightenment. www.edgarcayce.org

Beltzer, June G. (1986). *The Donning International Encyclopedic Psychic Dictionary*. PA: Schiffer Publishing, Ltd.

www.emdr.com

Emoto, M. (2004). *The Hidden Messages in Water*. (D.A. Thayne, Trans.). OR: Beyond Words

Hogan, Craig R. PhD (Ed.) (2014). *New Developments in Afterlife Communication*, FL. Academy for Spiritual and Consciousness Studies

LeDoux, Joseph (1998). *The Emotional Brain* NY, NY Simon & Schuster

Limoges, Yvonne, Director & Editor, Spiritist Society of Florida (Est. 1982), St. Petersburg, FL.
ylimoges@aol.com Personal Conversation (2014)
Maslow, A.H. (1963). "The Creative Attitude." *The Structurist*, pp. 4-10.
Newton, Michael, PhD. (1994/2013). *Journey of Souls Case Studies of Life between Lives*. MN: Llewellyn Publications
Schwartz, Robert, PsyD, DCEP (2014). *"Tapping" into Energy Psychology Approaches for Trauma and Anxiety.* PESI, Inc. /CMI Education course.
Scotton, B. W., M.D, Chinen, A, B, MD, & Battista, J.R, MD (Eds.), (1996). *Textbook of Transpersonal Psychiatry and Psychology*. NY: Basic Books.
www.tapping.com
en.wikipedia.org/wiki/Vagus_nerve
Van der Kolk, Bessel MD (2011). *Trauma, Attachment & Neuroscience: New Psychotherapeutic Treatments.* Premier Education Solutions/CMI Education Institute course.

Author Bio

Rev. Karen E. Herrick, Ph.D., LCSW, CADC, ACMHP

Karen Herrick has shared her clinical expertise for thirty years in her private practice by lecturing throughout the United States from a Jungian perspective on dysfunctional and addictive homes, disassociation, grief, and loss. Karen is the first female President of the ASCS inthirty-seven years. Her ministry is to be actively involved in Spiritual Psychology, specifically in naming spiritual experiences and working with chronic grief using EMDR techniques. Her first book, *You're Not Finished Yet*, is available through Amazon.com, Authorhouse.com and on Kindle. Her second book, *Grandma, What is a Soul?*, is available through Amazon.com, Createspace.com and on Kindle. Her websites are www.karenherrick.com, www.spiritualexperieces.info and http://grandmawhatisasoul.com

A Case of Spontaneous Mediumship?

Stanley Krippner, Ph.D.

Abstract

In 2015 I began communicating with an events planner for the U.S. Army who shared with me a series of anomalous dreams. They were anomalous in the sense that the dreams usually contained specific names of deceased servicemen known to an assistant chaplain with whom she works. There were precursors to these dreams in her childhood, including lucid dreams, dreams about religious topics, and dreams that she felt portrayed future events. These dreams seem to be related to accounts in the mediumship literature on people who allegedly communicate with the deceased, although generally not while dreaming. Alternative explanations of these anomalous dream reports were considered but lacked explanatory value. This case of possible spontaneous mediumship presents a challenge to mainstream science but is of value as researchers attempt to understand the development and manifestation of extraordinary experiences.

The possibility of life after death has intrigued human beings for millennia. It was the impetus for the founding of the Society for Psychical Research, the oldest organization that attempts to bring a scientific perspective to the study of post-mortem survival and other issues that challenge Western paradigms (Stemman, 2005). Disciplined research on the topic, which has provoked controversy, has produced inconsistent results (e.g., O'Keefe &

Wiseman, 2005; Schouten, 1994). In the English language, the word "medium" is used to describe people who claim to possess abilities that allow them to contact and receive information from the deceased. However, there are individuals who do not refer to themselves as mediums but who have had spontaneous experiences where a deceased person allegedly has given them information that has been verified by subsequent events. One of those individuals, whom I will call "Amanda," contacted me, knowing of my research on post-mortem survival and related topics.

Amanda Fischer is an events planner for the U.S. Army, coordinating events for "relationship enrichment programs" such as retreats for both married and unmarried soldiers. In addition, she works with Army chaplains; her father was an ordained minister and she attended Protestant worship services (most of them non-denominational) in her youth. As a child, she recalled several dreams that were related to religious themes, as well as dreams that appeared to forecast future events and lucid dreams in which she realized she was dreaming (Krippner, Bogzaran, & deCarvalho, 2002). In addition, Amanda had a few dreams about deceased family members. In one of them, her grandmother (of Native American descent) told her that she understood why Amanda could not be present when she passed.

In the course of her work with the U.S. Army, she met Wink, who had been a chaplain's assistant for several years. About six months after assisting Army chaplains, Amanda began having unusual dreams and started telling them to Wink. She has not told Wink all of her dreams—only those involving what she calls a "definite compulsion" to share them with her co-worker. These dreams contained specific names and other information that could be verified.

None of Amanda's previous dreams were as vivid or powerful as those she has had over the last two years (as of this writing). Amanda contacted me early in 2015 and has given me written permission to use her dream reports in my ongoing research concerning anomalous dreams. Our correspondence has been by email, and all the names in this report are fictitious. Several other measures have been taken to preserve anonymity.

Amanda wrote me that her first anomalous dream in the series occurred about six months after she met Wink, a Native American from Arizona. His clan has an unusual language, very different from the Navajo language spoken by his father. Wink, who, as he put it, was "raised as a warrior," was told by his elders that he had been given "the gift of discernment." Recently, he held a conversation with tribal elders in which he told them about Amanda's dreams. They replied that her ability was the complementary gift to his. Wink had just begun to tell her about his military career and his overseas service when she had her first dream of the series:

Case One

I am walking across the road to see a friend's new house. Before I can return to my house, I have to go through a building. I am in an American Legion building, where I start playing bridge with two ladies. One lady is in her late 50s, and the other is her mother, about 80. I tell them I am from Kentucky, and then the daughter remarks that her mother collects business cards from the record stores she visits in Louisville. She hands me a stack of cards and in the middle is a lanyard with the name "Sanchez" on it. I recall that all of the Special Operations personnel have to wear identification lanyards while they are in their compound. I call Wink so that he can see what is in my hand. He says, "I'll be right there." I look on the other side of the lanyard and there is a picture of a rattlesnake with a knife through its tail. Wink then comes into the building, hugs the two ladies, and walks off with them. Then I wake up.

The next morning I called Wink on his way to work and told him a little about my dream. He came right over to my house. He told me that one of his friends, Jeremy Sanchez, was killed in 2004. The only surviving members of his immediate family were his mother and grandmother. Before Jeremy was killed, he was auditioning for a spot in a Special Operations unit. The symbol of the unit he wanted to be in was a rattlesnake with a sword in its tail.

Case Two

In this dream, I am arguing with Wink about the location of a venue for a special event. Then I go walking down a hallway in a property where I've coordinated events in the past. I go into a large suite where a couple of sleeping rooms share a common parlor area. As I walk into the parlor, a man is sitting on a sofa. I sit down and start talking to him about the nature of his work. I also want to share with him my connection with the Special Operations aviation world and with Wink. He hands me a manila folder and I see a name on the side. It is "Bandrews."

When I told Wink about this dream, he told me that a pilot friend of his had died on a mission. It was the first time that a manifest had been done in a way that would add the first two letters of the first name onto the soldier's last name. Britt Andrews was the pilot on that mission, but, due to the manifest change, he was listed as "Bandrews." The manifest should have read "Brandrews," but someone had made a mistake.

Case Three

This dream included several people. I hear a missile siren and dive into a nearby building. It is like an old college dormitory filled with young men. I realize it is a fraternity. I look in one room, and a bunch of guys are together playing video games and talking. I ask for someone, and they tell me his room is next door. I knock on his door, and his roommate says that he is in the gymnasium. I walk into the gym and see a group of guys standing at a desk at one end of the open gym. I ask if I can toss the football around with them, and we make small talk. One guy says his name is "Larry," another introduces himself as "Adam," and then I say I am looking for "Patrick." They say, "He's over there," and I see a guy sitting with a girl in his lap. I say "Hello," but tell them that he is not the "Patrick" I am looking for.

When I told Wink about the dream, I mentioned that I had a "Larry," an "Adam," and two "Patricks" in it. Wink was disconcerted. He told me that all of these names were the same as members of a group of Rangers he knew. "Larry" and "Adam" were both killed in IED attacks. Wink had to bring "Larry" to the hospital in two pieces. The two "Patricks" grew up in the Ranger Regiment together. The first "Patrick" went into battle and was shot. The second "Patrick" ran in to save him and was carrying him out when he was fatally shot. The first "Patrick" died of blood loss. Wink said that the first "Patrick" was his roommate in Ranger school, and that "Patrick" had pictures of him and his fiancée around his bed. Wink remembered that, in every picture, "Patrick's" fiancée was sitting on his lap.

Case Four

Wink and I are upstairs, standing in my bedroom. We are having a conversation about a new end table. He keeps trying to open the blinds, but I tell him not to, because I do not like people being able to see into my room. But then he looks down and sees someone whom he starts helping up the wall and into the window. Wink looks at me, puzzled, because he's surprised that he is seeing a man he knows is deceased. But they start talking about random things, and the man sits on the floor of my bedroom. A woman comes in and sits down and two kids start climbing on him. He says that it's time for him to go. Wink looks at him and asks me in an aside if I see the scars on his face. I hadn't until he mentioned them. Then I see scars on the right side of his face, a big one by his eye and smaller ones on his mouth and cheek. We then start walking down the stairs with him. He starts complaining that this right hip is hurting, and I give him support as we're walking and reassurance that he will be home soon. I sit him in an old chair at what would be the front door of my house. As he sits down, I take Wink by the hand and tell him that we need to leave him.

When I spoke to Wink about the details of this dream, he said that it sounded like Evan Greene, a Navy SEAL he was very close to. The SEAL, in fact, did have two children. His right eye was a glass eye, and there were scars on the right side of his face from catching shrapnel. The fight he ultimately died in was in a mountainous region of Afghanistan, when he climbed up a wall and sat as a decoy so that the rest of his team could take over the building. He was shot seventeen times. As for the front door of our house, Wink and I had blessed that door with sage so it would be the only entrance through which spirits are supposed to enter.

Case Five

I am standing in a building that looks like the repair area of a car dealership. I am about to have an altercation with a very rude man when some gentleman in uniform walks in to intervene for me. I start talking to a man wearing an old green Army uniform and immediately have the thought that he must have been in Panama or Grenada because he is an older man. He is quite a character, making jokes and giving me medical advice, telling me that my Army Ranger friend who struggles with PTSD might want to try taking "St. Jessie's wort." So I figure that his name is Jesse or Jess.

Sometime after I woke up, I told Wink that someone named Jesse visited me and wanted him to try taking St. John's wort, adding that he was from the Panama or Grenada era when there were U.S. military interventions. Wink said that there were only a few units that were involved in those conflicts. The 75th Ranger Regiment was one of them, so I looked up Rangers who were killed in action in both interventions. There was only one Jess whom I found. His name was Jess Lucas, and he was a medic who died in the invasion of Panama. Wink did not know Jess personally, but I felt compelled to share this dream with him. Wink helped me identify the correct Ranger Regiment, something I might not have been able to do on my own.

Case Six

Not all my anomalous dreams are about Wink's wartime buddies. In one dream, I am talking to Wink about a trip he is making back home to Arizona. We are looking at a map, when the name of a city jumps out at me. It is "Abuela," which I know is "grandmother" in Spanish. Later in the dream I am standing at a four-sided table with Wink's mom and an older lady. When I am standing next to her, the older lady gives me a small brown book with a white rosary tucked inside. Even though I don't understand the words in the book, I have a feeling that they are prayers. Knowing what a great honor it is to have their language shared with me, I take a quick look and then pass the book back to her.

I told Wink about this dream and texted his mother as well. She sent me a picture of an elderly lady and said it was her grandmother, the woman who had raised her. She said that her grandmother always had a prayer book with her, and she also sent a picture of her white rosary. Earlier, Wink had confirmed that the elderly lady in my dream sounded like his great-grandmother, Manzanita.

Case Seven

I woke up completely startled when my dog started howling in her sleep. I dozed back off and had a dream that I was playing laser tag with some Ranger who had a large scroll tattoo on the back of his neck. I woke up and sent Wink a message telling him about the dream at 5:45. He said that he didn't know any Rangers with scroll tattoos on the back of their neck. I went back to sleep and had another dream that I walked in on Mike in a room. He looked angry with me and came at me. He reached out for me. He looked like he was going to choke me. As he reached out for me, I told myself "You have to wake up! You're both having the same dream!" As we hit the ground, I woke up. That was around 8:30.

Wink called on his way to work and I was just telling him about the latter dream when he said, "Ummm, was that after the message you sent me about the Ranger? Because I had a dream that I was choking you when I dozed back off after your message. That was when my alarm went off about 8:30." Then he proceeded to tell me how rough the night was, especially after his younger daughter woke him up crying after having a nightmare around 2:00.

These dreams fall into a category that is often referred to as "mutual dreams" (Krippner, Bogzaran, & de Carvalho, 2002). If Amanda's report is accurate, the two dreams might signify her shared connection with Wink. The Ranger might have symbolized a call for Amanda to pay attention to her drams that night. Amanda stated, "I could write it off as coincidence" but doubted that such a simple explanation would apply.

In Retrospect

These dreams are usually about deceased persons whom Wink knew, most of them soldiers with whom he had served. He himself was actually in almost all the battles in which they died. I never see anything bloody or violent, though. The dreams take place in a casual setting. I've learned that the dreams with specific names and details that I remember after waking are the ones I should relay to Wink.

Despite the brutal and violent ways in which these soldiers died, they always appear perfectly healthy in my dreams and in good spirits. I feel that they are trying to reach out to Wink to tell him that they are fine and not in the condition in which he last saw them. Perhaps his guilt and overwhelming feelings cloud his abilities to have these dreams himself, and so they come through me.

In reading the literature on mediumship, channeling, and survival, it becomes apparent that some individuals seem to have the capacity to serve as conduits with the deceased and some do not. From this perspective, the case could be made that Amanda falls into the former category and Wink into the latter. If a deceased person wanted to contact Wink, he or she might discover that Wink was not a suitable conduit. However, that deceased person might search for a more suitable conduit, someone close to Wink who would be able to incorporate messages into nighttime dreams. Hence, Amanda could have been selected as an appropriate candidate for these messages from another dimension. This triangle seems to have worked remarkably well over the past two years.

Alternative explanations would include fraud, faulty memory, and coincidence. To rule out fraud, one would need to interview Wink to be sure that the dreams as reported by Amanda were identical to the dreams related to Wink. Even so, if there had been collusion, one could not easily determine if Amanda and Wink had concocted the dreams to fit the circumstances of the demise of Wink's buddies. The dream about Jess could have been fabricated based on research concerning the casualties of the U.S. intervention in Panama. The fraud hypothesis needs to be considered. However, the scenario is extremely convoluted. It would have been simpler for Amanda to make up the dreams without bringing in another person, one who—upon questioning—might admit complicity. One must also question the motivation. Dreaming about deceased persons is not the easiest way to garner attention in the contemporary United States. Furthermore, Amanda has made no attempt to use these dreams for commercial gain or publicity purposes.

Another alternative explanation would be faulty memory. People's dream reports never capture a dream in its entirety. Could Amanda have started to tell Wink the dream, only to have him intervene and ask, "Could this have been my buddy Hal?" Amanda could then have replied, "Yes, I believe his name was Hal or Howard." Over time, the conversation might have been forgotten and the dream report that was shared with me could have left out its evolution. Although this scenario is possible, it seems highly unlikely that this pattern would have repeated itself several times without either Amanda or Wink becoming aware of it.

The third possibility of coincidence is even more unlikely, given the specific names and details involved. However, even the most experienced dream diarist realizes that one remembers only a fraction of one's nighttime dreams. Could there be other soldiers with other messages, who contacted Amanda, who simply did not recall the dream upon awakening? Could the remembered dream be the second, third, or fourth attempt of the soldier to convey a positive message to Wink? There is no easy answer to these questions, but it appears that these dream messages provided Wink with information that helped alleviate the "survival guilt" common to veterans who returned home lamenting their buddies who did not survive. All things considered, the alternative explanations lack clear explanatory value.

The antecedents of purported mediumship have been studied; they include a variety of predisposing factors ranging from brain syndromes (Beyerstein, 1988) and childhood trauma (Kaminker, 2013) to "fantasy proneness" (Jinks, 2013) and "transliminality," the narrow boundary between the external world and one's internal states (Thalbourne, Crawley, & Houran, 2003). Amanda does not refer to herself as a "medium," even though her alleged abilities would evoke this term among many other investigators. Personally, I use the term "claimant mediums" to describe individuals who self-designate themselves as "mediums," and simply note that people like Amanda display "mediumistic qualities," without using a label that might be interpreted as pejorative. In my cross-cultural dream research, I have collected dream reports from individuals who obtain what appears to be veridical information from deceased loved ones (Krippner, Faith, & Suzuki, 2000), but have not referred to them as "mediums."

In any event, we are left with a remarkable story. If the details as presented are accurate, Amanda's collection of dream reports provides useful information relevant to what researchers call "the survival hypothesis" (Rock, 2013). The deceased persons who appear in Amanda's dreams seem motivated to contact the living for benevolent purposes. The deceased soldiers cannot do this directly, because their surviving comrade, Wink, is not a suitable conduit. However, Wink's friend Amanda is an excellent conduit, who allows them to convey their positive message quite well. Amanda's decision to share these dreams with a professional researcher rather than a reporter for a tabloid attests to her sincerity and integrity.

Discussion

Mediumship research has gained remarkable momentum in recent years but is still a controversial topic in the mainstream scientific community. Mainstream science, in general, avoids addressing several important questions: Does sentient consciousness exist external to the human's body-mind consciousness? Are spirits, ghosts, apparitions, deities, ancestor-beings, or spiritual entities real, or are they imaginary characters? If they are imaginary, what is the source of the knowledge that is attributed to them, information that has been put to practical use in advising and guiding living humans for millennia? An equally intriguing question follows: Does the human being have an internal hard-wired capacity to experience other ways of knowing, ways that are attributed to incorporeal entities? If the capacity is hard-wired, what function does the capacity serve? Is the capacity utilitarian in nature, serving an adaptive function in human evolution? Or is it a spiritually-oriented capacity that permits people to experience other ways of knowing? Or is it a combination of both possibilities?

Epistemological models have used various terms, such as exceptional experiences, anomalous experiences, psychic experiences, extraordinary experiences, numinous experiences, reincarnation experiences, near-death experiences, shamanic experiences, mediumship experiences, trance channeling, spiritualism, spiritistic practices, esoteric and faith-based practices, religious-based charismatic practices, and indigenous practices, to name a few. All of these models have been used to explore the possibility of life after death (a core belief in the mediumship practice) and each of these models has been used to examine the idea of consciousness being external to the human body-mind, at least at times. In addition, some of these models have focused on understanding and describing the mental health of individuals who have reported these experiences or on explaining the phenomenology of the experiences.

On the other hand, the future of mediumship research may take the less controversial path of describing individuals' experiences without addressing the underlying epistemological and philosophical issues, even though they are at the core of the scientific community's frequent rejection of mediumship research as a viable and worthwhile focus for serious investigation. Methodologies that focus on personality traits, lifestyles of mediums (including their values, attitudes, and interests), and the development of mediumship may all help to expand the understanding of mediumship and those who practice it. My investigation of Amanda's putative spontaneous mediumship has taken this route, focusing on her lived experience and its precursors. In addition, I have been interested in the neuroscience of mediumship and, with Harris Friedman, edited a book that attempted to pull together the sparse literature on the neurobiology of mediumship and similar extraordinary experiences (Krippner & Friedman, 2010).

However, it is questionable that these methodologies encompass a framework that would address the epistemological and philosophical issues of how to capture and study phenomena that may be external to the human body-mind consciousness. A useful strategy would be to attempt advances on both fronts: to use conventional methodologies to describe mediums and their practice of mediumship while searching for novel methodologies to address more controversial issues. Advanced brain technology might be useful to delineate how this engagement is accomplished. In the meantime, as mentioned earlier, the term "claimant medium" is a useful descriptor of men and women who claim to contact the *other*. It is non-pejorative and makes no assumptions about the reality or unreality, the integrity or lack of integrity, or the veridicality or non-veridicality of the research participant and the information that is forthcoming from a mediumistic session.

References

Beyerstein, B. L. (1988, Spring). Neuropathology and the legacy of spiritual possession. *The Skeptical Inquirer,* pp. 248-264.
Jinks, T. (2013). The psychology of belief in discarnate communication. In A. J. Rock (Ed.), *The survival hypothesis: Essays on mediumship* (pp. 90-106). Jefferson, NC: McFarland.
Kaminker, J. (2013). Mediumship and psychopathology. In A. J. Rock (Ed.), *The survival hypothesis: Essays on mediumship* (pp. 146-159). Jefferson, NC: McFarland.

Krippner, S., Bogzaran, F., & deCarvalho, A. P. (2002). *Extraordinary dreams and how to work with them.* Albany, NY: SUNY Press.

Krippner, S., & Friedman, H. (Eds.). (2010). *Mysterious minds: The neurobiology of psychics, mediums, and other extraordinary people.* Santa Barbara, CA: ABC-CLIO.

Krippner, S., Faith, L., & Suzuki, Y. (2000). National and gender differences in reports of exotic dreams. *Dream Network, 19*(1), 40-42.

O'Keefe, C., & Wiseman, R. (2005). Testing alleged mediumship: Methods and results. *British Journal of Psychology, 96,* 165-179.

Rock, A. J. (Ed.). 2013). *The survival hypothesis: Essays on mediumship.* Jefferson, NC: McFarland.

Schouten, S. A. (1994). An overview of quantitatively evaluated studies with mediums and psychics. *Journal of the American Society for Psychical Research, 88,* 221-254.

Stemman, R. (2005). *Spirit communication: A comprehensive guide to the extraordinary world of mediums, psychics and the afterlife.* London, UK: Piatkus Books.

Thalbourne, M., Crawley, S. E., & Houran, J. (2008). Temporal lobe lability in the highly transliminal mind. *Personality and Individual Differences, 1,* 180-185.

Author Bio

Stanley Krippner, Ph.D.

Stanley Krippner is Alan Watts Professor of Psychology at Saybrook University, Oakland, CA. He is the co-author of *Extraordinary Dreams and How to Use Them* and *Haunted by Combat: Understanding PTSD in Veterans,* and co-editor of *Varieties of Anomalous Experience: Examining the Scientific Evidence.*

The author expresses his gratitude to the Saybrook University Chair for the Study of Consciousness for its support of the preparation of this chapter.

Magic, Shamanism, and Technology

Michael Peter Langevin, M.S.

Abstract

Magic is not only considered *real* in much of Latin America, it's practiced as commonly as any other cultural tradition; it is integral to daily life. The farther from big cities the locals live, the more prevalent magic is to them.

Anyone who has had transcendent experiences knows the material world is but a thin slice of a much greater reality. Through such expansive perception, we join a field of knowledge that visionaries, shamans, and magic workers have occupied throughout time. Being blessed by first-hand exposure to expanded awareness assures a person beyond any doubt that they are more than their physical body. This, by extension, suggests that all reality consists of far more than meets the eye.

I came to view my spiritual path—especially my strong Latin American shamanic experiences and knowledge—as Chaos Magic, but a variety of paths can lead an explorer of consciousness on a journey of expanded awareness. The Monroe Institute, for instance, offers scientifically researched, technology-based tools that often initiate altered states. The way The Monroe Institute uses audio technology to catalyze expanded awareness demonstrates how accessible magic can actually be in people's lives. Magic is real, and we all have the inherent ability to experience it for ourselves. Many pathways lead to the mysteries and supernatural elements, which are everywhere from the Amazon Jungle to places like The Monroe Institute or your very own living room.

In shamanic societies, a shaman's ceremonies and rituals are used to heal and even to create miracles. At The Monroe Institute audio technologies are used to bring about altered states and expanded awareness. Magic exists in both places . . . and many others. The overlap, connections, and differences are fascinating, worthy of examination, and can lead to a powerful synthesis. Technology can be a distraction or even a mind-numbing risk factor, or it can be part of our path to bringing magic into our lives.

In Latin America magic is seen not only as real, but as a daily occurrence. The farther you travel from big cities, the more powerfully magic is viewed as an essential element of life. I have spent much time in Latin America, in the Andes Mountains and the Amazon Jungle. I have been blessed to witness and take part in magical experiences and shamanic rituals most people would say are impossible, from shape shifting to mind transference.

What does magic consist of? Could it be using mysterious forces and supernatural energy to alter our reality and enhance our lives? If that is the case, then what are mysterious forces and supernatural energies? In the Western world we are most often taught that reality consists only of what we can perceive with our five senses. Yet this might be an extremely limiting way of perceiving our reality. Anyone who has experienced transcendent experiences knows that the material world is but a thin slice of a much larger reality. Through such expansive perception, we join a field of knowledge that visionaries, shamans, and magic workers have occupied throughout time. When blessed by firsthand exposure to expanded states of awareness, we know without a doubt that we are more than just a physical body, and this frees us from giving our power away to limiting, or even frightening, views of reality—one important example being fear of death.

At a certain moment during one of the first ayahuasca rituals I took part in, in Latin America, I reached out my hand to the jungle and could not tell where I stopped and the jungle began. It took me a whole week to decipher the situation and realize I had been viewing reality incorrectly all my life. I do not stop where the jungle begins. None of us stops where our bodies stop; we are intricately connected and interwoven. A web of life binds everything much more closely than we are taught to believe. Once someone experiences true magic and sees expanded reality, what were earlier only nice words and spiritual concepts become a factual state. This in turn enhances every aspect of our lives. We are truly one.

My path of discovery regarding magic and shamanism was a long and winding road. But that is another article. Suffice it to say I am a son and a grandson of funeral directors, and even studied to be one myself. I went on to study witchcraft with the witches of Salem, Massachusetts. In college I began traveling to Latin America, where I had many visions and life-transforming experiences. I was also privileged to be the publisher of an international new age magazine for over twenty-five years, where I got to interview, learn from, and often become friends with many spiritual teachers, psychics, and magic workers. I came to view my spiritual path—especially my strong Latin American shamanic experiences and knowledge—as Chaos Magic. This was because they were difficult to come by in authentic form, often requiring an adventurous spirit and even great risks. Thus, they were often very messy and required getting dirty and uncomfortable. For me Chaos Magic is like a compost heap. It is messy and smelly but at the end produces great fertile soil.

In 2005 I attended a Gateway Voyage program at The Monroe Institute. Most of the experiences I had at Monroe were similar to earlier ones in various contexts. What I found very interesting and of good use was their use of technology. I was also able to get reassurance about much esoteric knowledge I had gained on my own very different path. Their approach was much more organized than I was used to. They provided a handy toolbox to draw from to explore expanded states and alternative realities. Robert Monroe, the founder of the institute, insisted on using no spiritual or new age terminology to describe what the institute does. He also worked hard to base what they offered on scientific research whenever possible. He designed their programs to be effective for a wide range of people, especially those who were just beginning to suspect that reality was more than their physical bodies and a material world. The present President and Executive Director, Nancy McMoneagle, is Robert Monroe's stepdaughter and is effectively expanding his original vision.

Many people have experienced the trance states that can be reached in drum circles. In shamanic ceremonies the shaman often sings ancient, magical chants for each stage of the progression into altered states. If a shaman has not developed this skill successfully it can ruin a ceremony, while those who are skilled can act as a catalyst to take the participants to otherwise unreachable dimensions. Throughout history people have also used dance, meditation, prayer, exercise, sex, and mind-altering substances to enter expanded states of awareness.

A year ago, I was involved in a ritual in the Andes Mountains where the shaman leading the ritual announced, "I apologize but I am a terrible singer. So I have recorded my shamanic associates singing their most powerful songs and I will play those during the ritual on my iPhone." I thought, "This will never work." As it turned out, the quality of sound from his iPhone and the songs themselves created a better sound experience than in many shamanic rituals I had been in. The songs were indeed powerful and provided a ceremony tool every bit as effective as live shamanic singing tends to be.

Certain sounds have been proven to create a frequency that generates a response in the electrical activity of the brain. An interesting example of this is the sound technology developed at The Monroe Institute, used to enhance expanded consciousness. They use an audio guidance technology referred to as Hemi-Sync® to relax people's bodies to a state of near sleep while the brain is still alert. Specific sounds are blended and sequenced to lead the brain into various states ranging from deep relaxation to profound states of expanded awareness. This audio guidance process works through complex multilayered audio signals that act together to create a resonance that is reflected in unique brain wave forms. In recent years, The Monroe Institute has also added an additional audio technology aimed at enhancing how the brain functions called Spatial Angular Modulation, or SAM for short. It involves monaural and binaural tones that—along with other various angular sound patterns in a stereophonic field—are believed to be faster than the brain can process. This is done by sending multiple sounds simultaneously through headphones. It reportedly relaxes the body while allowing the mind to explore freely. Participants in classes where SAM is used state that they are able to speak or even write at the same time as they experience expanded realities. The way The Monroe Institute uses audio technologies to act as effective catalysts for people to enter altered states is an example of how technology can be used to bring about magical developments.

I do personal rituals ceremonies and magic daily. When I need certain information to enhance my ceremonies I do not hesitate to go online and look them up. I am also in touch with magic workers I respect from Africa to Peru to compare notes via email. I often play shamanic or mind-expanding music on my computer while I meditate.

Technology is very present in most of our lives. Many of us work on computers. Most of us socialize, learn, and entertain ourselves in our down time on computers. In most homes TVs are on whenever people are there. Technology can consume and waste our lives. But it can also be used as a doorway to expand magic and increase the magic in our lives. Our challenge is to take control of our time and focus our intent to increasingly use technology as a tool of transformation. Technology is like a knife, and as any blade it can hurt or we can embrace it to increase the magic in our lives.

The term Techno-Shaman has been misused in many ways over the years. Perhaps we should instead work to become Techno-Magicians. Magic exists; we all have the ability to experience it. Many valid pathways are available to experience for ourselves the mysteries and supernatural aspects that are everywhere, from the Amazon Jungle to places like The Monroe Institute or your own living room. Used with a bit of discernment, technology can be a tool to enhance these experiences, whether it is an iPhone used by an Andean shaman or sound technology developed by The Monroe Institute to alter the frequency of our brain waves. With intent we can greatly expand the quality of our lives and fill them with magical miracles.

Author Bio

Michael Peter Langevin, M.S.

Michael Peter was the CEO of *Magical Blend Magazine.* As the publisher of what Book-of-the-Month Club calls "the most open-minded magazine in the world," he also hosted the "Magical Blend" TV show. Michael Peter has been exploring the occult and ancient mysteries his entire adult life. He first visited Peru in 1973 at age 20. He has returned to Latin America many times to deepen his shamanic studies and widen his knowledge of ancient pre-Columbian cultures. Michael Peter works as an author and lecturer in the Blue Ridge Mountains of Virginia. He also works with The Monroe Institute (www.monroeinstitue.org). Contact Michael at michaelpeterlangevin@gmail.com.

The Brain is Superfluous
Evidence from This Life and the Next

R. Craig Hogan, Ph.D.

Abstract

The explanations for how a physical brain interacts with the mind and an objective world are flawed. Evidence from the earth plane and the next plane of life demonstrates that the mind functions perfectly well without a brain. The brain is superfluous. As a result, the only components of our reality are mind and experiences. We live in an experiential reality.

Introduction

When neuroscience in the twentieth century turned to the task of understanding how the brain creates consciousness, the scientists were surprised at how difficult the task is. David Chalmers, of the Centre for the Study of Consciousness at Australia National University, called this difficulty the "hard problem" of consciousness. The reason it is hard is that when neuroscientists studied the brain to find where and how consciousness is produced, they could not find consciousness in the brain, found no means by which the brain could create consciousness, and discovered no area in which memories are stored. To date, neuroscience has made negligible progress on understanding these issues.

The reason for the failure is that consciousness is not created by the brain, and memories are not stored by or retrieved from the brain. In fact, evidence from studies and our increasing understanding of the other realms of life, including what we call the "afterlife," show that consciousness exists entirely separate from the brain.

Various interpretations have been advanced to show how the mind interacts with the brain. Most are based on the supposition that the brain, matter, and energy exist independent of mind, and the mind must affect the brain in some way to allow people to function in this objective physical world. This separation of mind and matter/energy is called dualism. Even the idealist interpretations of reality, which posit that consciousness is fundamental, contain the dualist assumption that although the mind is fundamental, it must influence the brain in some way to make mental functions possible.

This paper reviews three common explanations of the relationship between the brain and mind, showing that they do not consider everything we now know about the mind. The paper ends with a fourth explanation that considers everything we know about the mind. The fourth explanation suggests that only mind and experiences exist; there is no physical reality outside of the mind. Thus, the brain is superfluous.

I use "consciousness" and "mind" interchangeably. In some circumstances, the different connotations the words carry fit different explanations better. "Consciousness" is a more abstract, general term. "Mind" has connotations of who we are as individuals in eternity.

For more complete explanations of the information I present in this paper, I refer you to my book, *Your Eternal Self*.[1]

Sources of Information

This paper is based on the following sources of information:
- Results of studies of mind phenomena

- Statements by people on the next planes of life describing what they are experiencing on other spiritual planes
- Discoveries resulting from quantum mechanics, especially nonlocality and the observer effect

Rich bodies of literature exist today in these three areas.

Explanation 1: The Mind is an Epiphenomenon of the Brain

The first explanation of the relationship of the mind to the brain, advanced by materialists, is that the mind is an epiphenomenon of the brain. The brain secretes mind as the adrenal glands secrete adrenalin. When the brain dies, consciousness dies. The self, proponents assert, is an illusion.

However, this explanation is the least tenable of the explanations. A small sample of the evidence follows.

Neuroscientists Who Have Studied the Brain Cannot Discover How a Brain Creates the Mind

Sir John Eccles, internationally recognized brain researcher whose work has had a major influence on brain research, concluded

> . . . that the mind is a separate entity from the brain, and that mental processes cannot be reduced to neurochemical brain processes, but on the contrary direct them. And . . . a mind may conceivably exist without a brain.[2]

Another brain specialist, Wilder Penfield, was a groundbreaking neuroscientist and physician. While performing surgery on patients, he noticed that stimulating a part of the brain cortex could cause the patient to recall a memory. However, while recalling the memory, the person's conscious awareness was still active, aside from the memory, and no stimulation of any part of the brain could cause any of the actions we associate with the mind: beliefs, problem solving, decisions, or any of the other activities that happen when a person is "thinking." The mind activities went on even when he was stimulating the brain cortex, and were completely unaffected by any stimulation he applied to the brain.

He could stimulate small segments of memories, but he could not locate the mind inside the brain.

He summed up the conclusions he formed on the basis of these experiments:

> ... none of the actions that we attribute to the mind has been initiated by electrode stimulation or epileptic discharge. If there were a mechanism in the brain that could do what the mind does, one might expect that the mechanism would betray its presence in a convincing manner by some better evidence of epileptic or electrode activation.

The mind, he writes, "makes its impact on the brain" but is not in the brain.[3]

Other researchers report that efforts to find the locations of memories in the brain have proven to be equally unsuccessful. Karl Lashley, a renowned psychologist and researcher in the field of learning and memory, failed during his entire career to find the location of memory in the brain. It prompted him to write, "Memory ought to be impossible, yet it happens."[4]

The Brain Does Not Have the Capacity to Hold Memories

Pim van Lommel, a cardiologist and author of an article on consciousness in the medical journal, *The Lancet* (December 2001), concluded that the brain does not produce consciousness or store memories. He points out that American computer science expert Simon Berkovich and Dutch brain researcher Herms Romijn, working independently of one another, came to the same conclusion: it is impossible for the brain to store everything you think and experience in your life. This would require a processing speed of 1024 bits per second. Simply watching an hour of television would already be too much for our brains. "If you want to store that amount of information—along with the associative thoughts produced—your brain would be pretty much full," Van Lommel says. "Anatomically and functionally, it is simply impossible for the brain to have this level of speed."[5]

Remote Viewers See without Using the Eyes and Brain

Seeing without using the eyes and brain is very common today. Thousands of people are able to see without using their eyes. It is a very common ability called "remote viewing." The person sits quietly with his or her eyes closed and focuses on something hundreds or thousands of miles away. The remote viewer is able to see it. Not only that, but the person is often able to hear it, smell it, feel the texture, sense movement, and sense emotions involved with it. In other words, the person is doing things outside of the body while the body is sitting quietly with its eyes closed.

<u>The Government Found Remote Viewing Is Valid</u>

For several decades at the end of the twentieth century, the CIA had a remote viewing program named Operation Stargate that attempted to use remote viewers to spy on the Russians. The program had remarkable results. Below is a session by a remote viewer named Pat Price created in 1974. He was to view a mysterious, unidentified research center at Semipalatinsk, USSR, to see what was there. He sat with his eyes closed and focused on the area. On the next page is his sketch of what he saw in his mind. It had all the distinguishing marks of a gantry crane.[6]

Later, the CIA obtained satellite photos of the site. A CIA artist created the following sketch of part of the site based on photos of the actual Semipalatinsk site. It was the gantry crane displayed on the next page.

Government Verification Study: Stanford Research Institute

The government wanted to be sure that their investment in remote viewing was going into a valid enterprise, so to find out whether people can really view things from a distance using remote viewing, the government agencies commissioned the Stanford Research Institute (SRI) to perform 154 experiments with 26,000 separate trials over 16 years. At the end of that testing period, Edwin May, Ph.D., a researcher in low-energy experimental nuclear physics, headed a team of researchers that analyzed the experiments and reported to the government. They concluded that the odds against someone merely guessing what remote viewers had described when focusing on a target at a distant location was more than a billion billion to one. His only explanation was that they genuinely were seeing without using their eyes and without regard for how many miles away the target was.[7]

Government Verification Study: SAIC

Now satisfied that remote viewing existed, the government sponsors of the remote viewing activity requested a second evaluation to find out how it works. Congress and the CIA commissioned a study by the Science Applications International Corporation (SAIC). The result of the study was that Jessica Utts, professor in the Division of Statistics at the University of

California at Davis, prepared a report assessing the statistical evidence for remote viewing in U.S. government-sponsored research. She uses the term "anomalous cognition" to refer to remote viewing. This is her conclusion:

> It is clear to this author that anomalous cognition is possible and has been demonstrated. This conclusion is not based on belief, but rather on commonly accepted scientific criteria. The phenomenon has been replicated in a number of forms across laboratories and cultures. The various experiments in which it has been observed have been different enough that if some subtle methodological problems can explain the results, then there would have to be a different explanation for each type of experiment, yet the impact would have to be similar across experiments and laboratories. If fraud were responsible, similarly, it would require an equivalent amount of fraud on the part of a large number of experimenters or an even larger number of subjects. . . .
>
> I believe that it would be wasteful of valuable resources to continue to look for proof. No one who has examined all of the data across laboratories, taken as a collective whole, has been able to suggest methodological or statistical problems to explain the ever-increasing and consistent results to date. Resources should be directed to the pertinent questions about how this ability works. I am confident that the questions are no more elusive than any other questions in science dealing with small to medium sized effects, and that if appropriate resources are targeted to appropriate questions, we can have answers within the next decade.[8]

Further Research Demonstrated Remote Viewing's Validity

The Princeton Engineering Anomalies Research (PEAR) Laboratory at Princeton University began conducting its own, independent studies of remote viewing in 1978. They tested remote viewers by having a person travel to some distant location undisclosed to the remote viewer and having the remote viewer attempt to identify details about the location. The remote viewers in 334 trials were able to describe details about where the person was, with odds against guessing the details of the location of 100 billion to 1.[9]

In another study, Robert Jahn, former director of the PEAR Lab, and psychologist Brenda Dunne conducted 336 rigorous trials with 48 ordinary people who were asked to do remote viewing at distances ranging from 5 to 6,000 miles. Almost two-thirds of the results exceeded chance levels, with odds against chance being one billion to one.[10]

Russell Targ, a physicist who pioneered development of the laser, and Harold Puthoff, another physicist who wrote the widely read *Fundamentals of Quantum Electronics*, conducted experiments on remote viewing to determine whether the phenomenon was real. In their tests, they had a person whom they called a "beacon" travel to a distant site to see whether a remote viewer could receive mental impressions about the site. The beacon and remote viewer were separated by distances of several miles so there could be no communication between them, and the beacon was instructed to go to a site randomly chosen by Targ and Puthoff without the remote viewer's knowledge. The remote viewer was to then focus on the beacon trying to get impressions about where the beacon was and writing or sketching the scenes. This is a summary of their findings:

> Independent judges found that the descriptions of the sketches matched on the average 66 percent of the time the characteristics of the site that was actually seen by the beacon.[11]

These findings were far beyond chance, demonstrating that the receiver was looking at the scene where the sender was while many miles away.

Blind People Are Able to See in NDEs

Other evidence that people are able to have experiences without the brain's involvement results from near-death experiences (NDEs). Blind people, including those blind from birth who had never learned to see, can have the experience of seeing in NDEs, suggesting that their minds must be independent of their bodies, which are unable see. Kenneth Ring, Ph.D., professor emeritus of psychology at the University of Connecticut, and Sharon Cooper interviewed 31 blind and sight-impaired persons who had near-death experiences and out-of-body experiences, and found that 80 percent of them reported correctly "visual" experiences, some in detail. For example, they reported correctly actual colors and their surroundings. One patient who had become totally blind after having been sighted for at least 40 years "saw" the pattern and colors on a new tie during an out of body experience, even though everyone denied having ever described it to him. The results of the two-year research study were published in the book *Mindsight*.[12]

Dr. Larry Dossey, former chief of staff of Medical City Dallas Hospital, describes this case of a woman who had been blind from birth being able to see clearly during her near-death experience:

> The surgery had gone smoothly until the late stages of the operation. Then something happened. As her physician was closing the incision, Sarah's heart stopped beating. . . . [When she awoke, Sarah had] a clear, detailed memory of the frantic conversation of the surgeons and nurses during her cardiac arrest; the [operating room] layout; the scribbles on the surgery schedule board in the hall outside; the color of the sheets covering the operating table; the hairstyle of the head scrub nurse; the names of the surgeons in the doctors' lounge down the corridor who were waiting for her case to be concluded; and even the trivial fact that her anesthesiologist that day was wearing unmatched socks. All this she knew even though she had

been fully anesthetized and unconscious during the surgery and the cardiac arrest.

But what made Sarah's vision even more momentous was the fact that, since birth, she had been blind.[13]

It appears that Sarah's mind was seeing when her body was unable to see, both because she was unconscious and blind since birth.

Conclusion

The materialists assert that the mind is an epiphenomenon of the brain. However, the studies of brain and mind functions show that the mind is not created by the brain and is not confined to the brain. This is a small sample of the evidence:

- Neuroscientists who have studied the brain have not been able to discover how a brain creates the mind.
- The brain does not have the capacity to hold memories.
- Remote viewers see without using the eyes or brain.
- Blind people are able to see in near-death experiences.

The mind cannot be an epiphenomenon of the brain.

Explanation 2: The Brain Is like a Television Set that Receives Signals from the Mind Outside of the Brain

The second explanation for the relationship between the mind and brain is a form of dualism. In dualism, both the mind and physical realm exist, but separate from each other. In this view, the mind interacts with the physical realm by merging with the brain in some way so the brain can stimulate the body to carry out functions. The popular analogy is that the brain is like a television set. A signal comes to the television set (analogous to the mind's signal to the brain) and the television set converts the signal into sights and sounds (analogous to the brain's experiencing, thinking, making decisions, and acting). If the television set is damaged, the sights and sounds are distorted or nonexistent (analogous to brain damage, Alzheimer's, coma, and so on in the brain). However, the signal (like the mind) is whole and unblemished (as is the mind).

This explanation for the link between the brain and mind is not supported by the evidence.

There Is No Way for the Mind to Interact with the Brain

Proponents of the mind-as-signal theory to explain the relationship of the mind to the brain have not been able to explain how a mind can interact with the brain. The proponents have not been able to explain three obstacles to the signal:

- There are no orifices for the mind's signal to enter the brain. Electromagnetic waves can penetrate the skull, but people in Faraday cages, which block electromagnetic waves, still have experiences. The mind could not be conveyed by electromagnetic waves.

- No other medium to convey the mind's signal has been discovered.

- Finally, the proponents of this explanation for the mind's interaction with the brain have not demonstrated how the mind, which is immaterial, can affect the brain, which is material. In the early 1990s, theoretical physicist Roger Penrose and anesthesiologist Stuart Hameroff collaborated to produce a theory for how the brain could open itself up to the mind using quantum physics principles. Thus far, they have not demonstrated that it happens.

There are other objections to the mind-as-signal explanation of the mind's interaction with the brain.

People in Near-Death Experiences (NDEs) Can See and Hear More Acutely than Normal, but the Brain Is Not Functioning

Accounts from physicians and nurses abound about people brought back from near death who had experiences of entering a warm, loving environment where they speak with their deceased loved ones. The phenomenon was named a near-death experience (NDE) by Raymond Moody.[14] During NDEs, many people, although unconscious, see and hear what was going on as physicians and nurses worked feverishly to revive them. They recount statements made by those in the room, describe people and instruments, and even accurately restate conversations that went on in other rooms.

The International Association for Near Death Studies (IANDS), now has tens of thousands of members. Dozens of books have been written, filled with cases of people who have had near-death experiences. A Gallup and Proctor poll in 1982 estimated that 5 percent of the adult population of the United States have had near-death experiences. Other surveys put the number at 7.5 percent.[15] Near-death experiences are common.

One of the most remarkable things about NDEs is that while brain dead, without a trace of brain function, these people see and hear what is going on in the scene where their body lies unconscious, and at times in other rooms of the same building. They then remember all of the details and recount them to the astonishment of physicians, nurses, and family members.

During the near-death experience, no sensory experiences and no memory production would be possible if the mind were located in the brain. During these times, people whose brain activity is being monitored are showing absolutely no life in the brain. Dr. Peter Fenwick, a neuropsychiatrist and one of the leading authorities in Britain on near-death experiences, describes the state of the brain during a near-death experience:

> The brain isn't functioning. It's not there. It's destroyed. It's abnormal. But, yet, it can produce these very clear experiences. . . . An unconscious state is when the brain

ceases to function. For example, if you faint, you fall to the floor, you don't know what's happening and the brain isn't working. The memory systems are particularly sensitive to unconsciousness. So, you won't remember anything. But, yet, after one of these experiences [an NDE], you come out with clear, lucid memories. . . . This is a real puzzle for science. I have not yet seen any good scientific explanation which can explain that fact.[16]

A study published in the *Journal of Resuscitation* concluded that people with no brain function who describe a near-death experience in fact have lucid thought processes, reasoning, and memory during the period when their brains are not functioning. In the study, doctors at Southampton General Hospital in England interviewed 63 heart attack patients who had been evaluated to be clinically dead, but were subsequently resuscitated. To ensure that their recollections were fresh, the people were interviewed within a week of the experience. They described details and events in which they were thinking, reasoning, and consciously moving around during the period when they were unconscious, their bodies were motionless, and doctors working on them had determined their brains were not functioning.[17]

The researchers went on to collect over 3,500 similar cases of people who had been evaluated to be clinically dead., but could recall remarkable details about events during the time when they should not have been able to sense anything or remember, even if they had experienced something, because they were clinically dead.

This indicates that the brain is not necessary for people to have experiences. When the person's brain shows no activity, near-death experiences happen, with vivid visual and auditory experiences. The person is able to think and solve problems, especially when confronted with a choice to stay in the realm apart from the earth realm or return to the body and the earth realm.

Hemispherectomies Don't Disturb Mind Functions

People who have had half their brain surgically removed in a procedure called hemispherectomy function almost perfectly normally. This suggests that the mind doesn't require the whole brain to function. . The operation has been performed hundreds of times for disorders that cannot be controlled using other treatments. Even after half the brain is removed, patients retain their personalities and memories. [18] In fact, a study of children who underwent hemispherectomies found they often were able to perform even better in school.[19]

If the brain were necessary for the mind to interact with the earth plane, as a broadcast signal needs a television to convey its pictures and sound, we would expect that removing half of the brain would have the same effect as removing half of the television set: the mind would not be able to function on the earth plane. That is not the case.

People Function Normally without a Brain

A number of instances have been recorded in which a normally functioning person was found as an adult to have virtually no brain. The brain was not necessary to normal functioning or memory. This account is from a July 19, 2007, story on Reuters:

> A man with an unusually tiny brain managed to live an entirely normal life despite his condition caused by a fluid buildup in his skull, French researchers reported on Thursday.
>
> Scans of the 44-year-old man's brain showed that a huge fluid-filled chamber called a ventricle took up most of the room in his skull, leaving little more than a thin sheet of actual brain tissue.
>
> "He was a married father of two children, and worked as a civil servant," Dr. Lionel Feuillet and colleagues at the Universite de la Mediterranee in Marseille wrote in a letter

to the *Lancet* medical journal. . . . "What I find amazing to this day is how the brain can deal with something which you think should not be compatible with life," commented Dr. Max Muenke, a pediatric brain defect specialist at the National Human Genome Research Institute.[20]

That provides evidence for the suggestion that the mind does not transmit signals to the brain for normal cognitive and life functions to occur. Mind and memory function perfectly well when the person has virtually no brain tissue.

People with Dementia Spontaneously Revive

Bruce Greyson explains a remarkable phenomenon that occurs in some dying people whose mental functioning has deteriorated to an irretrievable degree at the ends of their lives. These patients have suffered from severe neurologic or psychiatric disorders, such as brain abscesses, tumors, strokes, meningitis, Alzheimer disease, dementia, schizophrenia, and mood disorders. They have long ago lost the ability for mental processing or communication. Brain scans or autopsies of many of these patients show that their brains have irreversibly deteriorated. It should be physically impossible for them to have normal brain functions.

In spite of their brains' deteriorated states, in the minutes or hours before their deaths, some spontaneously become lucid and speak normally to loved ones.[21] In a study of end-of-life experiences in the United Kingdom, 70% of caregivers in nursing homes reported that they had observed some patients with dementia becoming completely lucid in the last hours before their deaths. Greyson identified 83 cases described in the medical literature and collected additional unpublished accounts.

In one case, a 42-year-old man had a malignant, rapid-growing brain tumor. He soon became bedridden, blind in one eye, incontinent, and increasingly incoherent in his speech and bizarre in his behavior. He was unable to make sense of his surroundings, and when his family touched him, he would slap them as if he were slapping at an insect. He eventually stopped sleeping and talked deliriously throughout the night.

To the amazement of family and caregivers alike, one night after several weeks of this bizarre behavior, he suddenly became calm and spoke coherently. Afterward, he slept peacefully, without the disturbing nightly outbursts he'd had consistently until that night. The following morning, he talked with his wife calmly and coherently, discussing his imminent death for the first time. Later that day, he stopped speaking and died.

In a second case, reported by Erlendur Haraldsson, an Iceland psychologist, an 81-year-old woman living in a retirement home had been demented with Alzheimer's disease for a long time. Her family took turns visiting her, even though she did not recognize them and had not spoken to them for a year. Then one day, as her son Lydur sat at her bedside, she sat up, looked at him, and said, "My Lydur, I am going to recite a verse to you." She recited a poem clearly and loudly. She then laid back on her pillow and was again unresponsive. She remained so until she died.

If the mind were a signal coming through the physical brain, the damaged brain could not spontaneously heal itself for a short time so the person could communicate lucidly and clearly, then return to its damaged state until the transition. This phenomenon does not support the suggestion that the brain receives a signal like a television set and uses the signal to function in the physical realm.

People Who Have Transitioned Out of the Body Function Perfectly Well without the Brain

Another indication that the mind-as-signal explanation is not tenable is that people who transition off the earth plane leave the brain behind with the body, but many remain on the earth-plane vibration, seeing and hearing perfectly well. They often attend their own funerals. People who came through in the Flint séances described walking around, taking buses, riding in cars with people, and other normal activities. They could see and hear perfectly well, but no brain was involved in bringing the signals to the body.

People React to Pictures Seconds before the Brain is Involved

Dr. Dean Radin, Senior Scientist at the Institute of Noetic Sciences, performed carefully controlled studies in which people seated before a computer monitor were shown calm pictures (pastoral scenes and neutral household objects) and emotional pictures (erotic and violent scenes). The pictures were selected at random by a computer and shown in random order. Their skin conductance levels (SCL) were measured continually during the entire test. The skin conductance test is like a lie detector that shows whether the person feels stress. As you might expect, people showed stress at seeing the emotional pictures and calm when shown the calm pictures.

But remarkably, the tests consistently showed that some people reacted to the pictures with the appropriately matched calm or stress as early as six seconds before the pictures were shown, even though the computer hadn't selected them at random yet. That suggests that the people weren't using the body to learn about the pictures.[22]

The studies were replicated by Dick Bierman, a psychologist at the University of Amsterdam and Utrecht University.[23]

What this means is that the person's mind must have already been reacting to information it received before the information even existed in the physical realm for the eyes to see and brain to register. The brain is not receiving signals from the mind to cause the body to react. The body is reacting without involvement of the brain.

Conclusion

The suggestion that the brain receives consciousness as a signal to mediate between the mind and physical realm is untenable.

- There is no way for the mind to interact with the brain.

- People in near-death experiences (NDEs) can see and hear normally, but the brain is not functioning.
- Hemispherectomies don't disturb mind functions.
- People without a brain function normally.
- People with dementia and other such disorders resulting from irreversible deterioration of the brain spontaneously revive just before death.
- People who have transitioned out of the body function better than in the body.
- People react to pictures seconds before the brain is involved.

Another explanation for the relationship between the brain and mind must be found.

Explanation 3: The Mind Is in a Field Outside of the Brain and Interacts with the Brain

In an effort to explain how a physical brain interacts with the nonphysical mind, some writers have suggested that a field exists that is consciousness or that holds consciousness. Minds are linked through this pervasive field.

Writers who maintain a sense of duality between mind and brain, or at least suggest the brain must be involved in the links between minds, have found what they believe to be an ideal explanation for the links between minds in the concept of a field. A field is a region in which some force or property joins the parts embodied in the field. The earth's gravitational field holds objects on its surface and exerts a force on the moon to keep it in orbit. This field is invisible, but has an effect on the objects in its gravitational region.

The properties of a field appeal to a number of writers about consciousness. Like a field, consciousness is invisible, exerts an influence in a region beyond the focal point of an individual person, and joins all the individual parts into one whole. The appeal has resulted in a number of names for this field:

- Grand Unified field, adopted from particle physics (John Hagalen)
- Quantum field (Deepak Chopra, Mario Beauregard, Roger Penrose, Stuart Hameroff)
- Trans-dimensional Unified Field (George Ducas)
- Zero point field (Irvin Lazlo, Lynn McTaggert, Greg Braden)
- Morphogenetic field (Rupert Sheldrake)
- Etheric field (Michael Roll)
- Matrix (Max Plank)
- Hologram (David Bohm, Leonard Susskind, Michael Talbot)
- Holonomic brain (Pibram)
- Implicate order (David Bohm)
- Virtual reality (Brian Whitworth, Peter Russell)

However, no field theory has been demonstrated to be valid:

- None of these field theories has demonstrated that consciousness is in a field.
- The problem remains of not being able to explain how the brain receives the information from the field or sends information into the field to reach other minds.
- The mind functions perfectly well without the brain's assistance in near-death experiences and after the transition from using the body. If the mind were in a field linking brains, it still would not need to interact with the brain to have experiences.

The explanation that the mind is in a field joining all other brains and the universe is not tenable.

Conclusion to the Examination of the Three Explanations for the Mind's Interaction with the Brain

The conclusions we must come to are that the brain does not give rise to the mind, the mind does not come to the brain as a signal that activates the brain so the brain can control activity in the physical realm, and the mind has not been demonstrated to be in a field that activates the brain to perform in the physical realm. The mind functions perfectly well without using the brain. As a result, the brain is superfluous.

A fourth explanation explains all of the properties of the mind without involving the brain.

Explanation 4: There Are Only Mind and Experiences

Since the brain has no part in the mind's activities, all that remains for us as human beings are mind and experiences. The theory of everything must be a theory of only mind and experiences. People have experiences of seeing, hearing, touching, tasting, and smelling what we call matter and energy, but there is only the experience, not some universe outside of us that we experience and that exists when no one is present.

We have the experiences of sight and sound without an objective physical realm. For example, we have the experiences of a seeing and touching a chair, but the chair does not exist independent of our experiences. We have the experience of hearing and seeing a symphony, but the concert isn't being held outside of us; it is an experience the Source creates in our minds. What we experience we call reality or the physical realm or the earth plane. However, the physical realm is not outside of the mind. It is only experiences the mind has. We call the consistent experiences the physical realm. That seems to us to indicate that something objective must exist outside of the mind to make the experiences possible. However, the experiences occur without the presence of a brain. They exist in and of themselves, provided by the Source of Creation.

This explanation for our reality is consistent with what neuroscientists describe as our "representational reality." We cannot apprehend the world that materialists suppose is outside of us. The materialists explain that we know only the firing of neurons that give us a configuration of the neurons we have a name for, such as a sunset or a dog bark. There is no sunset or dog barking in the brain. The materialists suggest only that the neurons fire in a pattern that we call a sunset or dog barking. We experience a representation that we give a name to that we believe is in the world outside of us. However, we can never apprehend anything but the representation. Strap someone down and cause the correct configuration of neurons to fire using electrodes and the person will have the experience of being on a beach in the Bahamas; the experience will be identical to actually being there.

We know that the mind is not in the brain, but the same principle holds true for the experiences the mind has. Instead of coming from a world around us, the experiences come from the Source of Creation. They are much the same as the experiences we have in a dream that are generated by the mind. The dream has no outside world that is the source of the experiences; the mind creates our experiences of ourselves, of the people in the dream, of the scenery, and of the events. The mind has experiences with no matter or energy creating them.

People have the mistaken impression that the experiences are stimulated by a world around us because one of the distinguishing characteristics of life on this plane is that there are reasons for the experiences. This is the realm of causes and effects. To see that this is true, we can contrast this earth plane with the next plane of life, which the Theosophists and Spiritualists call Summerland, from Andrew Jackson Davis' The Great Harmonia,[24] inspired by Swedenborg.

This table contrasts the earth plane with Summerland.

Reasons on the earth plane	No reasons in Summerland
A sun gives light.	There is an ambient light with no source.
The sun provides warmth.	The temperature is always temperate, with no evident source for the heat.
Travel requires some effort, such as walking.	Travel can occur by simply intending to be somewhere.
Stars, galaxies, and background radiation show the universe is vast.	The environment the person is in is sufficient, so residents refer to no vast areas of space.
Molecules, atoms, and subatomic particles exist to show that matter is made up of something.	Buildings can be constructed through the power of thought; what is solid doesn't require that the substances be made up of tiny particles.
A brain serves as a place to believe consciousness resides because consciousness must have a natural origin.	No brain is necessary to have sensory experiences.
Organs are necessary to support the body's life and functioning.	Residents of Summerland have remarked that they don't believe they have organs.
People eat to sustain what we experience as a body.	There is no need to eat or drink. The body is sustained with no energy input.
The body must die to move from one focus or plane to the next.	Movement into different life experiences or plances occurs seamlessly, with no dead bodies.

For us to have experiences on the earth plane, we must have reasons for the experiences. The earth plane is the plane of reasons, causes and effects, histories, and beginnings and endings. However, on other planes the experiences exist without reasons, causes, histories, or beginnings and endings. That betrays the fact that the experiences exist in and of themselves, independent of what we believe is required to cause them on the earth plane. There are only mind and experiences.

The brain is just a prop to have an explanation for where the mind resides in the earth realm. Just as the sun is a prop to show where light comes from, but is not necessary for the ambient light in Summerland, the brain provides a location in which to assume the mind is housed. It is much like the wheel that spins on a computer screen in the Windows operating system when the computer is saving a document. The wheel isn't saving the document. The document would save fine without the wheel. The wheel is just a signal that the system is saving the document. The brain serves the same function, lighting up in an MRI or EEG when the person is thinking or experiencing. However, in reality the brain is superfluous. The mind has experiences independent of it.

We have the sense that an objective realm exists outside of the mind. We sense that it would continue to exist if there were no conscious beings in it. However, the realities that we create together are in our minds, not in a world that exists independent of our minds.

When we enter a meeting room and see a podium, we believe the podium is outside of us because we learned in infancy that to approach something, we must advance toward it, even though the view seems two-dimensional. There seems to be a depth or space, but the mind must provide it. When we look at something, our minds convert what we experience as sight into depth. We learned from the experience of shadows and experience of seeing the size of objects that something is close to us or far from us. We then feel we advance to it through the experience of some physical effort. That gives us the sense that the podium is in an objective space apart from us, and we are objective bodies approaching the objective podium, but it is in reality only our experience in the mind of seeing the podium and our experience of feeling we approach the podium. If we touch it, we have the experience of touching a podium, so we feel it certainly must be objective. But the reality is that we have only the experience of touching a podium. The podium is an experience in the mind.

When we leave the room after the meeting and return the next day, we experience the podium again, and the experience is the same. We believe it is an object outside of ourselves that is still hard, brown, five-feet tall, and at the head of the room because we had the experiences of hardness, the experience of the brown color, the experience of seeing its height, and the experience of seeing it in a position in every experience of a room. That gives us the impression that the podium is stable, so it must be objective, but it is just that once the experience is established, it remains consistent in our minds.

Other people come into the room and although they may not say something about the podium, they also have the experience of hardness, brown color, and so on. If they have the experience of advancing to the podium, they can have the experience of touching a hard podium. The fact that others have the same experiences also gives us the impression that the podium is an objective reality. It has to be outside of us for us all to experience the same thing.

But that's not the case. What is happening is that we are one mind. We are having the same experiences of the podium and the room just as when we bring up the memory of the room we had as children; we bring up the same memory every time. We brought it up when we were 20, when we were 30, when we were 40, and every year after. It is our single memory of that room. In the same way, each of us has the same experiences of the podium and room as everyone else because we are one mind. It is one podium and one room. The experiences remain consistent.

The analogy of the dream is common in Eastern traditions. We are in a dream. To transcend the illusion of the dream, we must wake up. In a dream, we create ourselves, the others, the scenery, and everything else that is in the dream. But what is in our dream isn't real; it's all experiences that we believe are real during the dream. The same is true of the earth plane.

Most of us believe the statement that we are creating our reality together. That is a problem for most people to understand because it's difficult to imagine that consciousness can create matter and energy as they are conceived of in a material world. However, the explanation is that we're not creating matter and energy that is in an objective realm apart from us. We are <u>experiencing</u> sights, sounds, tastes, touches, and smells individually, but our individual experiences match because we are one mind—in effect, in the same dream. Our experiences are a result of the setting that was created by others who were experiencing building the room, furnishing the room, and having people hold repeated meetings in the room. They are one with our mind also. I use "mind" with no "s" on it. We are one mind; one with each other, one with the builders, one with the furnishers, and one with the staff of the hotel that contains the meeting room.

Rather than saying we <u>create</u> a consensual reality, we should say we <u>experience</u> a consensual reality.

Within that experiential reality, we are functioning as individuals, what Tom Campbell, author of *My Big Toe*[25], calls individuated units of consciousness in the big C Consciousness. We have the impression we are separate because of the experience of our bodies. We have separate personalities and do not have free access to each other's minds. We can be saints or sociopaths, but every one of us is learning and growing toward having increasing levels of love and compassion. As we do so, our one mind is growing to have more love and compassion. When a serial-murdering sociopath kills in anger, our one mind has its light of love diminished a little. But when that serial-murdering sociopath feels a twinge of remorse and wishes he could be different, our one mind brightens just a little. Even though that sociopath has a long way to go to become a saint, he has contributed to humankind's evolution toward a loving, compassionate reality.

We must live in the consensual reality, with what Tom Campbell calls its rule set. We have the rules because we all agree to them, at the deep level of our being that isn't accessible to the conscious mind. If we all believed another rule set was correct, we would all follow it, and the physical realm (which is really just the experiences we have) would fit the rule set or belief system.

Our reality is made up of only experiences we have in the mind. There is no matter, energy, bodies, or a brain. They are all only experiences. The brain, like all the rest of what we call the physical realm, is superfluous.

Evidence that Reality Is Experiences in the Mind

The Observer Collapses the Wave Function

The Copenhagen Interpretation of Quantum Mechanics states that a conscious observer is necessary to collapse the wave of possibilities into one experience. That is called the collapse of the wave function.

What we are actually seeing is that each person journeys through time, and as he or she encounters new spaces, the spaces become experiences. If a person isn't present, there are no experiences. That is consistent with this explanation that our reality is experiences in the mind. We create the experiences moment by moment because we must have experiences to have continuity. The highest probabilities for experiences are the experiences that have consistency with previous experiences. That is consistent with quantum mechanics.

Mystics and Seers Use the Dream Analogy for Reality

A large number of mystics and seers refer to the dream analogy when describing reality:

- Chögyal Namkhai Norbu: "In a real sense, all the visions that we see in our lifetime are like a big dream."

- Swami Vivekananda: "To every one of us there must come a time when the whole universe will be found to have been a mere dream."

- Swami Krishnananda: ". . . you will see that all the objects of the world are your own universal self."

- Chuang-tzu: "There is the great awaking after which we shall know that this life was a great dream. All the while the stupid think they are awake."

- Vajracchedika Sutra of Mahayana Buddhism: "Know that the world has no self-nature, no substance of its own, and has never been born. It is like a cloud, a ring produced by a firebrand, a vision, a mirage, the moon as reflected in the ocean, and a dream."

- Jalal al-Din Rumi: "This world, which is only a dream, seems to the sleeper as a thing enduring forever. But when the morn of the last day shall dawn, the sleeper will escape from the cloud of illusion; laughter will overpower him at his own fancied griefs when he beholds his abiding home and place."

- Meher Baba: "All your pleasures and difficulties, your feelings of happiness and misery, your presence here and your listening to these explanations, are all nothing but a vacant dream on your part and mine. There is this one difference: I also consciously know the dream to be a dream, while you feel that you are awake."

- Tripura Rahasya: "This world is a mere figment of imagination ... an image on the screen of the mind ... an image on the mirror of consciousness ... a mental image."

- Sankara: "The apparent world is caused by our imagination, in its ignorance. It is not real. It is like seeing the snake in the rope. It is like a passing dream."

Suzanne Giesemann's Comments from Odin on What Is Real

Suzanne Giesemann, M.A., retired U.S. Navy Commander, author, and talented medium, described her conversation with the mythological Odin at this ASCS conference. She presents it as part of her paper in this book. Odin tells Suzanne that she must not see the physical realm as real and what is created by consciousness as unreal.

This is what Suzanne wrote:

> In that second visit with Odin I asked, "Are you REAL?" And he replied, "As real as you are, but not human." I asked, "But you are a myth," and he replied without missing a beat, "YOU are a myth. Nothing is real."

> What purpose does a myth serve? The myths that recur throughout history are attempts to answer universal questions about life. Odin answered some of my questions about life quite clearly. He stated:

> "You must stop differentiating between real and unreal. Do you not know now that angels and archetypes are real? All archetypes are groupings of consciousness at different levels of vibration. Anything that you can create in consciousness is real and can convey truth, messages, information, learning, healing, and growth. All is not as it seems. You are just another part of me." [26]

Our collective consciousness creates the experiences. The experiences are what we regard as the physical realm. We collectively experience the same reality as one mind. We are all one with each other. As Odin said to Suzanne, "You are just another part of me."

The Hundredth Monkey

Animals in separate groups are able to learn tasks more easily when another group has already learned the task, even if the groups have no contact with each other. They are one mind having experiences.

The most famous example is the example called "the hundredth monkey."[27] The monkeys involved are Japanese macaques (Macaca fuscata), which live in wild troops on several islands in Japan. They have been under observation for years. During 1952 and 1953 the primatologists began "provisioning" the troops—providing them with such foods as sweet potatoes and wheat. The food was left in open areas, often on beaches. As a result of this new economy, the monkeys developed several innovative forms of behavior. One of these was invented in 1953 by an 18-month-old female that the observers named "Imo."

Imo was a member of the troop on Koshima island. She discovered that sand and grit could be removed from the sweet potatoes by washing them in a stream or in the ocean. Imo's playmates and her mother learned this trick from Imo, and it soon spread to other members of the troop. Unlike most food customs, this innovation was learned by older monkeys from younger ones. In most other matters the children learn from their parents. The potato-washing habit spread gradually, according to Watson, up until 1958. But in the fall on 1958 a remarkable event occurred on Koshima. This event formed the basis of the "Hundredth Monkey Phenomenon."

Their one mind enabled them to learn lessons even though physically separated from one another. As one monkey learned, all the monkeys were advanced in their ability to perform the task.

The Placebo Effect: Beliefs Change the Experiences of Reality

The placebo effect is an indication that a person's beliefs change the experiences the person has, changing reality. No physical explanation for the placebo effect has been found. The changes would not be possible in a world apart from the mind because the mind, which is immaterial, cannot influence the material world. Only if reality is experiences can the world change from moment to moment.

The following placebo effect case was reported by Bruno Klopfer in 1957 in the *Journal of Projective Techniques.*[28] Dr. West was treating Mr. Wright, who had an advanced cancer called lymphosarcoma. All treatments had failed, and time was running out. Mr. Wright's neck, chest, abdomen, armpits, and groin were filled with tumors the size of oranges, his spleen and liver were enlarged, and his cancer was causing his chest to fill up with two quarts of milky fluid every day, which had to be drained in order for him to breathe. Dr. West didn't expect him to last a week.

But Mr. Wright desperately wanted to live, and he hung his hope on a promising new drug called Krebiozen. He begged his doctor to treat him with the new drug, but the drug was only being offered in clinical trials to people who were believed to have at least three months left to live. Mr. Wright was too sick to qualify.

But Mr. Wright didn't give up. Knowing the drug existed and believing the drug would be his miracle cure, he pestered his doctor until Dr. West reluctantly gave in and injected him with Krebiozen on a Friday.

To his utter shock, the following Monday, Dr. West found his patient out of bed walking around. Mr. Wright's "tumor masses had melted like snowballs on a hot stove" and were half their original size. Ten days after the first dose of Krebiozen, Mr. Wright left the hospital, apparently cancer free.

Mr. Wright was rockin' and rollin,' praising Krebiozen as a miracle drug for two months until the scientific literature began reporting that Krebiozen didn't seem to be effective. Mr. Wright, who trusted what he read in the literature, fell into a deep depression, and his cancer came back.

This time, Dr. West, who genuinely wanted to help save his patient, decided to get sneaky. He told Mr. Wright that some of the initial supplies of the drug had deteriorated during shipping, making them less effective, but that he scored a new batch of highly concentrated, ultra-pure Krebiozen, which he could give him. (Of course, this was a bold-faced lie.)

Dr. West then injected Mr. Wright with nothing but distilled water. And a seemingly miraculous thing happened—again. The tumors melted away, the fluid in his chest disappeared, and Mr. Wright was feeling great again for another two months.

Then the American Medical Association blew it by announcing that a nationwide study of Krebiozen proved that the drug was utterly worthless. This time, Mr. Wright lost all faith in his treatment. His cancer came right back, and he died two days later.

Multiple Personalities with Different Health Issues Change the Experiences that Make Up Reality

Multiple personalities have changes in their physical constituency that occur immediately when they change their belief system by changing personalities. That is an indication that their experience of themselves changes the experiences they have of themselves and others have of them. The changes could not occur in a physical world.

Anthony Robbins' *Unlimited Power*[29] describes a case of a psychiatric patient with a split personality. One of her personalities was diabetic, whereas another was not. Her blood sugars were normal when she was in her non-diabetic personality, but then when she shifted into her diabetic alter ego, her blood sugars rose, and all medical evidence demonstrated that she was diabetic. When her personality flipped back to the non-diabetic counterpart, her blood sugars normalized.

Psychiatrist Bennett Braun, author of *The Treatment of Multiple Personality Disorder*,[30] describes the case of Timmy, who also had multiple personalities. One personality was allergic to orange juice, and when this personality drank orange juice, Timmy would break into blistering hives. However, another personality was able to drink orange juice uneventfully. If the allergic personality was in the midst of an allergy attack and he shifted back to the non-allergic personality, the hives would disappear instantly.

The difference was in their beliefs. What changed when they changed their personalities was their beliefs about who they were.

When they believed they were one person, they took on that person's personality and even physical characteristics. The beliefs were in the mind; the mind created the experience of the bodies.

Dr. Emoto's Crystals[31]

Dr. Masaru Emoto demonstrated that simply taping words on bottles of tap water affects the water. When the water is frozen, the water with "You fool" on its label freezes into misshapen crystals. Water in bottles with "Love" and "Thank you" on the labels freezes into beautiful, symmetrical snowflake-like crystals. The sentiments of the writers of the labels (we assume) influenced the experiences the people involved had as they looked at the frozen water crystals.

More relevant to this discussion, water taken from a Japanese city reservoir froze into misshapen crystals. However, when a Shinto priest prayed before the reservoir, new samples of the water from the reservoir froze into beautiful, symmetrical crystals. Having a Shinto priest affect a reservoir of water by praying cannot be explained in a realm containing a physical priest and physical water. However, the realization that the minds of the people involved created the experience they all had of seeing the beautiful frozen crystals after the prayer explains the phenomenon.

The Global Consciousness Experiment

Since 1998, about 50 computers around the world have been constantly recording and analyzing white noise generated from devices much like tuning to a frequency on a radio where there is no signal. If the noise suddenly had some organization to it that was no random, we would say it was affected by something. The effect would not be audible to the human ear, but the computer can identify it and let the researchers know something happened.

These 50 or so computers measuring white noise have shown some very remarkable findings. At the time of the terrorist attacks on the World Trade Center, white noise from the computers around the world showed that something dramatic had happened.[32] More interestingly, the computers measuring changes in the white noise showed that the global consciousness had been alert at 4 a.m., five hours before the first airplane crashed (8:45) and six and a half hours before the second airplane crashed (10:30). That would have been around the time the hijackers started to put their plan into action. The events had not occurred, and whether these men were going to be successful in their plan could not have been known in any ordinary sense, but our collective minds knew what was going to happen, and our shock resulted in the experience of observing computers around the world reacting to the tragic events.[33]

The same effects on the white noise have resulted during dozens of other such incidents that affected the minds of many people, such as floods, bombings, tsunamis, house votes, acquittals of figures, earthquakes, plane crashes, and many other such events.

There is no explanation for how nonmaterial consciousness could affect physical random-number generators. However, the concept that all minds are one, and the one mind is producing the experiences such as the experience of the output of random-number generators, explains the phenomenon.

Conclusion

Our world is made up of only mind and experiences. We are one mind, so we have the same consistent experiences. We live in an experiential reality. That explanation is consistent with the data concerning the activities of the mind with no brain involved and with the realm we experience. It also explains psychic ability, remote viewing, materializations, spontaneous healing, miracles, and other such phenomena.

Endnotes

[1] Hogan, R. C. (2005). *Your Eternal Self*. Normal, IL: Greater Reality Publications.

[2] Carter, C. (n.d.). Rebuttal to Keith Augustine's attack of "Does consciousness depend on the Brain?" Retrieved May 30, 2007, from http://www.survivalafterdeath.org/articles/carter/augustine.htm.

[3] Carter, n.d.

[4] Sheldrake, R. (n.d.). Nature as alive: morphic resonance and collective memory. *Primal Spirit*. Retrieved October 2, 2007, from http://www.primalspirit.com/pr1_1sheldrake_nature_as_alive.htm

[5] Touber, T. (2007, January). Life goes on. *Ode* 29.

[6] Images from H. E. Puthoff, "CIA-Initiated Remote Viewing At Stanford Research Institute." Institute for Advanced Studies. (http://www.biomindsuperpowers.com/Pages/CIA-InitiatedRV.html).

[7] Radin, D. (1997). *The Conscious Universe: The Scientific Truth of Psychic Phenomena*. New York: HarperCollins Publishers.

[8] Utts, J. (1995). *An assessment of the evidence for psychic functioning*. Division of Statistics, University of California, Davis.

[9] Radin, 1997, p. 104.

[10] Radin, 1997, p. 105.

[11] Targ, R., & Puthoff, H. (1974). Information transmission under conditions of sensory shielding. *Nature*, 251.

[12] Ring, K., & Cooper, S. (1999). *Mindsight: Near-Death and Out-of-Body Experiences in the Blind*. Institute of Transpersonal Psychology.

[13] Dossey, L. (1989). *Recovering the Soul: A scientific and Spiritual Search*. Bantam Books.

[14] Moody, R. (2001). *Life after Life: The Investigation of a Phenomenon — Survival of Bodily Death*. HarperOne.

[15] Linzmeier, B. M. (n.d.). Attitudes toward near-death experiences. Retrieved December 6, 2006, from http://www.nderf.org/nde_attitudes.htm.

[16] Fenwick, P. (n.d.). People have NDEs while brain dead. *Near-Death Experiences and the Afterlife*. Retrieved April 1, 2007, from http://www.near-death.com/experiences/evidence01.html.

[17] Tippit, S. (n.d.). Study suggests life after death: brains of dead heart attack patients still function. Retrieved December 1, 2007, from http://neardeath.home.comcast.net/news/020629.html.

[18] Choi, C. (2007, May 24). Strange but true: When half a brain is better than a whole one," ScientificAmerican.com. Retrieved May 30, 2007, from http://www.sciam.com/article.cfm?articleId= BE96F947-E7F2-99DF-3EA94A4C4EE87581&chanId= sa013&modsrc =most_popular.

[19] Choi, 2007.

[20] Tiny-brained man's lifestyle wows doctors; He lived a normal life despite the fluid buildup in his skull. (July 19, 2007). Reuters. Retrieved July 24, 2007, from http://www.msnbc.msn.com/id/19859089/.

[21] Greyson, B. (2011). "Nature of Mind and Consciousness: Is Consciousness Produced by the Brain?" Presentation at the Cosmology & Consciousness conference, Upper T.C.V. School, Dharamsala, India, December 16-18, 2011.

[22] Radin, 1997, pp. 118-124).

[23] Bierman, D. J., & Radin, D. (1997). Anomalous anticipatory response on randomized future conditions. *Perceptual and Motor Skills*, 84, 689-690.

[24] Davis, A. J. (1852). *The Great Harmonia.* B. Marsh.

[25] Campbell, T. (2007). *My Big Toe.* Lightning Strikes Books.

[26] Giesemann, S. (2015). Getting Out of the Box: Redefining What is Real. *Aspects of Consciousness.* Normal, IL: Greater Reality Publications.

[27] Watson, L. (1987). *Lifetide.* Sceptre.

[28] Rankin, L. (2014). *Mind Over Medicine.* Carlsbad, CA: Hay House, Inc.

[29] Robbins, A. (1997). *Unlimited Power.* Free Press.

[30] Bennett, G. (1986). *The Treatment of Multiple Personality Disorder.* Arlington, Virginia: American Psychiatric Publishing.

[31] Emoto, 2005.

[32] Von Buengner, n.d.

[33] Von Buengner, n.d.

Author Bio

R. Craig Hogan, Ph.D.

Craig is director of the Center for Spiritual Understanding, devoted to helping people develop spiritual understanding through afterlife connections. He is the author of *Your Eternal Self*, presenting the scientific evidence that the mind is not confined to the brain, the afterlife is a reality, people's minds are linked, and the mind affects the physical world.

Craig co-authored *Induced After-Death Communication: A New Therapy for Healing Grief and Trauma* with Allan Botkin, Psy.D., and *Guided Afterlife Connections: They Come to Change Lives* with Rochelle Wright, M.S.

He is editor of *Afterlife Communication: 16 Proven Methods, 85 True Accounts* and *New Developments in Afterlife Communication: Proceedings of the 38th Annual ASCS Conference.*

Craig is on the boards of the Academy for Spiritual and Consciousness Studies and American Society for Standards in Mediumship and Psychical Investigation.

Muscle Testing
Communication Tool for the Unconscious and Superconscious

Larry Green

Abstract

Muscle testing (also referred to as muscle monitoring, energy testing, or energy monitoring) is a tool for accessing information often outside normal conscious awareness. With muscle testing, a practitioner (often called Kinesiologist, Applied Kinesiologist, or Energy Kinesiologist) is able to gather information on many levels about the health, function and disposition of clients. Muscle testing is widely used by doctors and practitioners for physical, bio-chemical, mental, emotional and spiritual challenges. We can use muscle testing to gather information about the function and response of a living system in relation to many internal and external environmental events. This paper will describe a brief history, current usages and possible applications of muscle testing in relation to spirituality and consciousness studies. This paper does not teach the mechanics of muscle testing. Muscle testing is both an art and a science, and is best learned in person from an experienced instructor.

In 1964 a chiropractor from Detroit, Michigan, Dr. George Goodheart, noticed his patients often did not maintain chiropractic adjustments. Looking for the cause he concluded that adjusting the spine without simultaneously resetting the supporting muscles encouraged the body to revert to the previous postural tendency and lose spinal integrity. Dr Goodheart set out to determine how to reset and change muscles and posture so as to enhance his chiropractic care. In the process he discovered a series of skills and interconnecting reflexes that helped to sustain good posture and enhance overall good health.

One of his first discoveries was that a muscle could appear strong and function well some of the time but not always maintain integrity for reasons beyond structural and anatomical considerations. A muscle's integrity could be compromised by food, environmental impacts, thoughts, emotions, and 'energies' such as those believed to comprise the acupuncture system, the bio-field and chakras. He observed that multiple influences could change a muscle's ability to perform its normal functions.

A couple of physiotherapists in the late 1940s and early 50s named Kendall and Kendall first researched the use of muscle testing as an assessment tool for injury rehabilitation. Their method of pushing very firmly on an injured limb to assess strength and function is still widely used today by physical therapists and rehabilitation specialists.

Dr. Goodheart expanded this usage by testing muscles in relation to other factors that might compromise or enhance a muscle's response. He found that food and nutrition could both strengthen or weaken a muscle's response in a very individualized manner. He discovered the relationship between acupuncture meridians and muscles, and how muscles could be used as a meridian indicator, and how strengthening a meridian could change a specific muscle's response. He connected reflexes originally discovered by Drs. Terrence Bennett and Frank Chapman for other purposes (the Chapman Reflexes and the Bennett Reflexes) and showed how they also impacted muscle and meridian response. As he developed protocols and shared them with colleagues, his discoveries grew into a program he called Applied Kinesiology (AK). To this day Applied Kinesiology is only taught to licensed physicians, primarily chiropractors, but also a few MDs and osteopaths.

Goodheart's work was popularized by Dr. John Thie, who was Goodheart's top protégé and the first president of the International College of Applied Kinesiology. Dr. Thie wrote a manual geared for lay persons in 1973. In this book, *Touch For Health,* Dr. Thie presented a systematic approach for health that anyone could learn. It used numerous muscle tests as assessment tools for health. This manual took the use of muscle testing beyond the clinical practice of chiropractors and led to the use of muscle testing by an ever-growing list of training programs and professions.

Today muscle testing is widely used for gathering information from clients and to determine effective interventions in many areas of health. Well-known protocols like Emotional Freedom Technique (EFT), Brain Gym, NAET and a large number of 'kinesiology trainings' (i.e., Professional Kinesiology, Wellness Kinesiology, Health Kinesiology, Transformational Kinesiology, Bio-Kinesiology, Educational Kinesiology, Body Talk) all grew directly out of Applied Kinesiology and Touch For Health Kinesiology. Practitioners in many fields continue to incorporate muscle testing in an ever-expanding list of applications.

The exact mechanism of how muscle testing seems to 'know' information is still speculative. Extensive reports and case studies exist showing muscle testing revealing obscure nutritional interventions that suddenly turn around chronic health conditions, uncovering very specific emotional connections that were the crux of long standing traumas, determining specific exercises for children that spontaneously adjusted brain function and change learning outcomes and more. These outcomes are regularly observed by licensed professionals far too many times and with too much consistency to be merely coincidence.

The ability to study muscle testing in the current 'gold-standard double blind' manner is not easy as at least the practitioner needs to know what is being tested. In kinesiology we state that 'energy follows intention,' and you cannot remove intention from a muscle test to satisfy a double blind test.

The reports on the use of muscle testing for physical, nutritional, emotional and mental health are widespread and can be found in books, journals, and on the internet. Less reported is the use of muscle testing as a spiritual guide and tool.

In 1995 Dr. David Hawkins wrote the book *Power Vs. Force*. Dr. Hawkins lists his credentials as both an MD and Ph.D. and as a co-author with Linus Pauling of the book *Orthomolecular Psychiatry*. In *Power Vs. Force* Dr. Hawkins asserts there is a scale of consciousness, from 0-1,000, which muscle testing can pinpoint how 'spiritual' or 'evolved' is a book, idea, country, or person. Dr. Hawkins' work popularized the idea that muscle testing can be used to determine spirituality on a linear scale. **However, most leaders in the field of Kinesiology found much of his reasoning to be suspect and his conclusions using muscle testing to be biased.** He muscle tested that his book *Power Vs. Force* calibrates higher than the Bible, which in turn he claims is more 'spiritual' than the Koran. Below is a sample of some 'calibrations' by Dr. Hawkins. The higher the number the more 'spiritual' is the person, book, organization, etc. In Hawkins' calibrations anything below 200 is considered not very 'truthful' and lacking consciousness.

Sample people calibrated by Dr. Hawkins

Jesus Christ, Buddha, Krishna, Zoroaster	1000
John, the Baptist	930
Moses	910
Abraham	850
Mahatma Gandhi	760
Mother Theresa	710
Ramakrishna	620
Confucius	590
Martin Luther	580

Dalai Lama 570

Yogananda 540

Lao Tzu 520

Alan Watts 485

Thich Naht Hanh 460

Ayn Rand .... 400+

President George W. Bush .... 400+

St. Bonaventure 385

John Wesley 360

Mother Meera 240

Maher Baba 240

John (Author of Revelations).............................. 70

Sample faiths calibrated by Dr. Hawkins

Christianity

    1st Century, "The Way" 980

    After Council of Nicea (385 AD) 485

Judaism (Modern) 530

Taoism 500

Shintoism 350

Islam (Modern) 325

Sample Christian denominations calibrated by Dr. Hawkins

Unity 540

Quakers 505

Modern Catholicism	440
Christian Science	410
Church of LDS (Mormons)	390
Amish	375
Born Again	350
Pentecostal	310
Jehovah's Witness	195
7th Day Adventist	190
Unification Church (Moonies)	150
Right Wing Fundamentalist	95

Sample books calibrated by Dr. Hawkins

Multiple books by Dr. Hawkins	990+
Bhagavad Gita	910
Torah	745
Koran	700
A Course in Miracles	600
Book of Mormon	510
Old Testament	190

Dr. Hawkins also "tested" that the U.S. invasion of Iraq was good for the world, that only 20% of humanity (but 50% of Americans) test above 200 (above 200 is the threshold for being 'conscious'), and that Wall Street, Harvard, the CIA and the American Oil Industry all test higher than YouTube, Karl Marx and Kirlian photography. Also, former President George W. Bush tests higher than The Carnegie Endowment for Peace (spiritually speaking).

In muscle testing we have learned that a bias in either the person testing or being tested can impact the outcome. For this reason when doing muscle testing both people need an unbiased, open and curious intention. Few leaders in the field of kinesiology would ascribe much usefulness to Dr. Hawkins' calibrations. The idea of using a scale for comparison is sometimes used in other ways. For example, we might test a stress response on a scale of 0-100 before and after a session as a comparison for the client's edification.

Another possible problem using a 'scale of consciousness' to test how 'spiritual' are some people and religions, is that judgments of self or others could be believed without a reasonable dose of critical insight. This could lead to damaging results to one's sense of self-worth or dismissing others wholesale because of their affiliation or beliefs.

How then might we use muscle testing to enhance consciousness and spirituality? Many systems use muscle testing in conjunction with setting goals of how an individual would like to feel or respond better in life. This can include setting goals that are considered spiritual (i.e., being more forgiving and tolerant, feeling peaceful, meditating regularly or any other goal aligned with spiritual values). Kinesiologists also use muscle testing to help find 'unconscious' thoughts, feelings and attitudes. This would be done in conjunction with helping to release any such thoughts or emotions that hold us back from living more spiritually.

One way I use muscle testing, and will in the conference demonstration, is to discover how to individually maintain good energy boundaries. Many people who would like to be of service to others find they pick up physical and emotional 'pains' from clients. Being empathic might help us serve others, but for some people it leaves them impaired by the experience and less willing to help. In the more extreme circumstance, some people are so empathetic they cannot go out in public (to the mall, to a crowded event) because they 'pick up' so many pains and emotional stresses.

I have found that often these 'overly' empathetic people have an energy boundary issue. Their energetic boundary is too porous or open. With people like this I have them first rate on a scale of 0-10 their stress about going out in public or working with others (sometimes it is specific clients or groups). I ask them to imagine themselves in that challenging situation and notice how and where they feel stress or discomfort in their system.

I then have them continue to think of this situation and test a muscle. Our experience is that when the client focuses and on a stress, the muscle will not maintain integrity and tests weak. I then have them go through a list of possible interventions and muscle test as they think of each category. When muscle testing the category that includes the specific intervention that will support them, the muscle response changes from a weak to a strong response. I next invite them to help determine the specific intervention that will help. Afterwards I invite them to now consider themselves again experiencing the stressful situation, but this time with their newfound intervention in place. The large majority of the time the experience of now thinking about that stressful event has far less pain and discomfort associated with it. Often we have not addressed the content of the stress (agoraphobia, that a certain client has disturbing energy, etc.) but only put in place something that helps protect them from the negative effects they previously experienced.

A case report: A woman reported she experienced pain and discomfort in her office, but not as soon as she left the work space. I had her think about being at work and it caused her muscle to test weak and an internal discomfort. I then asked her to think just of the physical space—the building, computers, lights, etc.—and retested her. This time the arm stayed strong. I asked her to think of her co-workers and the arm then tested weak. I asked her to name her co-workers one by one. The third person caused her arm to go weak. I asked her about this person, who worked a few cubicles down. She reported always feeling a creepy sense about him.

I asked her to think of everyone in the office all together without this one individual, and the muscle tested strong. I then had her think only about him and it went weak again. With muscle testing we had pinpointed a cause that her system felt stressed about. In this case we did not have to figure out 'the story' (although sometimes that is helpful). I had her keep thinking about this co-worker and tested her while also thinking about prayer, visualization/imagery, a guide or helping spiritual friend, and any object that could be protective for her. None tested strong, though those four broad categories often have the necessary intervention. This case was becoming interesting.

I started thinking through some other possibilities, and one that came up was a totem. I asked her if she was aware of any special totem for her, and she said, "No." I then asked her intuitively what animal might she choose as a guide and helper, and she said, "A cow." I had her image she had a cow with her at work—it could be a real cow or an image of one. She chose a small cow statue to sit on her desk. I asked her to imagine that cow statue on her desk and imagine her challenging co-worker nearby. Her arm now tested strong. I asked her to think about being at work without the cow statue and her arm tested weak. Then again with it on her desk and the arm stayed strong. Each time she imagined the cow on her desk the arm tested strong. Aside from what muscle testing had demonstrated, she could feel a definite difference in her stress and bodily discomfort when she imagined the cow on her desk.

She then told me a story. When she was in high school she took a bus home every day from school. Walking from the bus stop to her home she passed a field and every day a cow in that field waited for her near the corner of the fence and walked along the fence line with her until the other corner. She said this cow did this every day, and then she asked me if I thought that might mean something. I said, "Yes!" We then had a discussion about totems and how to connect with them and learn from them.

This is one of many ways that muscle testing can be used to enhance spirituality and consciousness. Another common way is to bring more conscious awareness to a situation by testing, in relation to an issue, through a list of emotions. This often brings into awareness a key emotion that was buried. This procedure often sheds light on the issue for the person, providing a process for the client to then connect the dots they formerly had not seen, which can lead to insight and the opportunity to respond differently.

Although there are many arenas where muscle testing can be applied, I would like to offer some cautions. As evidenced by the work of David Hawkins, muscle testing can be misapplied to reinforce previously held beliefs. I suggest always using common sense (for spiritual issues I will call this discernment) when using muscle testing.

Muscle testing can also be misused manipulatively (either consciously or unconsciously). I had a student, an orthodox Jew. She claimed that according to kosher law it is forbidden to wear clothing made of two dissimilar materials (like a cotton/wool blend). When she tested everyone about whether their clothing was 'good' for them, anyone she tested wearing a blend showed a weak response. However, when other people who did not share her belief about kosher law and clothing performed the same test, they got a different result.

Muscle testing does not predict the future, nor is it recommended for making important life decisions. It is very useful as a tool for gathering information and acting on that information in an informed and reasonable manner. This can include spiritual areas of life. Always remember to keep a clear intention for the highest good of the person being tested, and if you have any considerations that you may be biased, pay close attention.

References

Frost, Robert (2002) *Applied Kinesiology: A Training Manual and Reference Book of Basic Principles and Practice*, Berkeley, CA: North Atlantic Books

Hawkins, David (1995) *Power vs. Force: The Hidden Determinants of Human Behavior*, Sedona, AZ: Veritas Press

Krebs, Charles 1998) *A Revolutionary Way of Thinking: From a Near Fatal Accident to a New Science of Healing*, Melbourne, Australia: Hill Of Content

Thie, John (1973) *Touch For Health*, Pasadena, CA: T.H. Enterprises

Thie, John & Thie, Matthew (2005) *Touch For Health: The Complete Edition*, Camarillo, CA: DeVorss & Company

Walther, David (1988) *Applied Kinesiology*, Pueblo, CO: Systems DC

Author Bio

Larry Green

Larry is a certified kinesiology instructor and consultant. He has been teaching kinesiology for over 20 years, and other CAM modalities for over 30 years. Larry is the creator of these classes and manuals: Energy Medicine for Pets, Kinesiology for Horses and the Miracle Workers Training. Larry and his wife, Arlene Green, run the U. S. Kinesiology Training Institute in Chapel Hill, North Carolina.

Larry began meditating and doing yoga in 1971, lived for two and a half years on a mediation retreat, lived another four years as a staff member of and resident of a yoga center and has been a spiritual student all his life. He was one of the founding staff members of the Commonweal Cancer Help program in Bolinas, CA, and helped found Cornucopia Cancer Center in Durham, NC. He has been president of Cornucopia and the national Touch for Health Kinesiology Association.

Belief Systems and your Personal Power

Metaphors and Tools of *Touch for Health*® Kinesiology for Greater Self-Awareness, Clarity of Purpose, Personal Empowerment, and Physical, Mental/Emotional, and Energetic Harmony and Function.

Matthew Thie, M.Ed.

Abstract

Touch for Health® Kinesiology (TFH) is a system of balancing Posture, Attitude and Life Energy for greater fulfillment of our life purposes. This lecture/demonstration will explore the "Metaphors" (concepts and symbolism) of muscle testing and body/energy balancing together with creative dialogue and visualization for optimum holistic balance and personal meaning and satisfaction in life, with a particular emphasis on the stages/phases of cognitive and spiritual development. TFH founder, John F. Thie, DC mapped "Fowler's Phases of Faith" to the Chinese "5 Elements" or "Five Phases" of Transformation, considering our beliefs and worldview as both a linear development and a cyclical dynamic.

The Touch for Health® (TFH) Kinesiology system and concept can be seen at the core as primarily a system of developing mind/body awareness, both as a means of health enhancement and ultimately as a worthwhile end in itself. TFH derives many of its muscle/Energy balancing ideas and techniques from Chiropractic, Applied Kinesiology, and Traditional Chinese Medicine, but it is not designed for use by physicians in diagnosis and treatment of disease (finding out what's wrong and fixing it). Rather, it is meant for the use of individuals and their friends and family for their self-care, empowering them as the primary agents in the development of their own Wellness, support of their own intrinsic natural healing functions, and ultimately their own perception, appreciation, and ongoing development of their own unique purposes, and the quality of their experience of LIFE. Each of us has a continuous role in choosing where to focus our attention, energies and efforts to optimize our functions, effectiveness and satisfaction. We can use the manual muscle test as an indicator of the integrity of our physical posture, which in turn gives us powerful clues and awareness of the mental, emotional, biochemical, energetic and spiritual aspects of life that affect our health and sense of meaning and satisfaction—the symbolic "Metaphors" of our daily life. In addition to the images of the "Five Transformations" from Chinese Medicine, TFH Metaphors integrate "Fowler's Phases of Faith." We consider our Cognitive Development and conscious or unconscious Beliefs and Worldview as both a linear, hierarchical progression, and a variable, cyclical model of different modes of perception in relation to different issues, problems, purposes and life goals.

We could say that the primary Metaphor or conceptual paradigm of TFH is not finding out what's wrong and fixing it, but rather developing our awareness of the integrated body/mind whole by consciously participating in a series of activities involving **sensing-feeling-thinking, moving-balancing**, and **reintegrating**, which ultimately leads to greater postural, emotional and energetic flow and balance. This is often accompanied by release of emotional stress and tension, relief from aches, pains and symptoms, greater mental clarity and physical function and most importantly a renewal of a sense of **meaning, satisfaction, and enjoyment of LIFE.**

We start with a system that is very practical and often startlingly effective for balancing the physical posture. The method of bio-feedback through muscle testing that we use originally derives from Detroit chiropractor Dr. George Goodheart, who often said, "If your spine's in line, you'll feel fine." Yet the actual model for the *TFH workshops* and system is not Goodheart's Applied Kinesiology practice. It is the core concept of the *person-centered psychology* of Carl Rogers, and the practical workshops of *"Effective Communication"* developed by his protégé, Thomas Gordon. Rogers recognized that it is more important to focus on Wellness than on illness ("It is more important to focus on a positive goal than to 'dig out' what is wrong with you"—Dr. John Thie). Rather than analyzing, diagnosing, prescribing or advising, the most powerful thing, even in cases of physical disease, is to raise the person's own awareness of their circumstances, their feelings, their resources and their ability to take part in their self-care and make choices that will not only contribute to their healing, recovery and improvement of their Wellness, but will actually result in a more satisfying, more deeply meaningful and enjoyable LIFE. (Carl Rogers points out that in psychology, and even physical illness, ***treating problems is problematic***, and often leads to more problems, while working with the whole person in developing their mind/body awareness is efficient, more enjoyable, contributes to spontaneous transformation of perception and attitude, and also often relieves or eliminates emotional and physical problems as a side effect of the awareness process!)

Seen from this perspective, it is clear that our posture/energy balancing process becomes an elaborate means of mind/body awareness development that also facilitates the optimum balance/function of the intrinsic natural healing systems of the mind/body. The results are readily observable through changes in muscle response, spinal alignment, physical posture, neurology, energetic "Life Energy" flow, mental/emotional comfort and clarity, greater sense of personal meaning in life, etc. This is accomplished through a standard progression of education about the body/energy systems; non-judgmental, reflective dialogue to clarify personal life goals; muscle testing/balancing through touch-reflex points, such as the acupressure points from Traditional Chinese Medicine (TCM); and contemplation of possible meanings/Metaphors of our desires and our blocks/imbalances. Throughout the process we maintain the support of a gentle, "accompanying" dialogue, advocating self-awareness, empowerment and self-responsibility.

The Metaphors of TFH: Transformative Ideas and Aspects of a Mind/Body Awareness Development Process

Our book, *TFH & Chinese Five Element Metaphors*, was translated in Spain as **Metaphors of Health and LIFE** *(Metáforas para la Salud y la Vida)*. I was actually delighted by this interpretation. In TFH we might find a particular muscle is not in balance (in relation to a goal or issue) and contemplate Metaphors of the muscle itself or the related Meridian and Element from TCM. Although the Meridians have associations with physical organs, it is far more accurate and effective to contemplate the imbalances as Metaphorical, related to LIFE, rather than mistake this association as a diagnosis of a physical condition. Utilizing "Metaphorical thinking" not only allows us an alternative to the diagnostic, disease-focused approach, but also opens up a vast area of insight and Body/Mind awareness on many levels. We address your whole body, your being, in a holistic way towards improvement of your experience of LIFE rather than just fixing problems.

Metaphor Means Main Concept, Paradigm or Big Idea

When we use the word METAPHOR, we are actually working with many different interpretations or functions of metaphor. We are automatically operating on many levels, and this corresponds to the practical experience and intention of operating on many levels that is always at play in a TFH balance. One of the meanings of Metaphor (and intentions of TFH) is to see the "big picture," or main concept. Let's look at some of the main ideas of TFH so that we can appreciate how they are embodied in our balancing process. The main ideas of TFH derive from several traditions that nonetheless all resonate with the body/mind awareness process. As we increase our awareness of these concepts and their origins, we develop a **Meta-Awareness:** *Seeing the context and the interconnectedness of all aspects of a life, embodied in each moment of the balancing process.*

Health from Within

The original TFH workshop, called "Health from Within," was designed to make *communication skills AND basic skills of Goodheart's Applied Kinesiology (AK)* **accessible to lay people for home use and self-care,** to support the body's own natural healing system, that is always creating health, *from within:*

- TFH must be practical, simple, quick and effective. Hands on. No special equipment needed. For everybody. Safe without prior knowledge, and a little bit of practice. Can be done alone, but better with a friend. Standard base concepts and procedures, and open-ended for a personal exploratory journey. Immediate results that people can FEEL through practice. Increasing benefits with repetition, practice, competence, confidence, refinement and deepening of concepts and techniques.

The Person-Centered Approach

TFH draws from many practical traditions, integrated for easy use, and built upon existing structures that have repeatable results, while also harnessing and focusing our *attitude, attention, intention and awareness.*

- The Educational, Self-responsibility model: When I was a child, I believed that the purpose of following the self-responsibility model was to keep lay people without proper training from saying that they know, or treat, more than they can legally claim. With greater appreciation of the roots of

TFH and Energy Kinesiology, I realize that this model not only keeps us ethically and legally safe, the person-centered approach is perhaps the most powerful element to be preserved and respected in every aspect of the work.

- The Feedback Circle: Just sharing information is transformational. We don't necessarily have to "fix" anything. Focus on the positive goal and outcome is often immediately effective and satisfying, and also leads to greater long-term proactive choices, health development and illness prevention, rather than waiting until we're so sick that we need emergency reaction.

- Perception creates our reality: What we think and how we feel may be the most profound factor in our personal satisfaction as well as our physical health. Change in posture, effects attitude, effects perception, effects satisfaction and fulfillment in life on a day-to-day basis. And all of these factors affect each other reciprocally.

- No Man is an Island: We are social animals and TOUCH is a fundamental human need. We create a safe space for touch that is not for sex or punishment, but for health, within a clear, respectful context of informed consent and personal authority. (Oxytocin begins to flow within 7 seconds of human touch!)

Chiropractic and Applied Kinesiology

- Teach a man to fish: A true physician teaches people to know and care for themselves. Treat people, not diseases. The Holistic approach to life is most effective.

- Innate intelligence: The natural human condition is health and vitality. Misalignments or imbalances in structural, emotional or physiological aspects interfere with the communication system, within the being/environment, ultimately resulting in disease. We can help the body regain its natural balance, preventing future deterioration, and allowing the natural creative energy of the human being to flow, and every system in the body to function more efficiently.

- If your spine is in line you will feel fine: Balancing the physical posture via the muscles will influence all the organ systems of the body, as well as Life Energy flow and the overall life function of the person.

- Muscle testing is not *muscle* testing: Muscles reflect/effect muscle function, postural imbalances and neurology, brain integration, *as well as* subtle energy balance/flow in different circuits of the body related to different systems—vascular, lymphatic, spinal/nervous, energetic/emotional.

- Try it You'll Like it: A wide variety of TOUCH, with specific qualities at specific locations, including acupuncture points and meridian lines, can bring about spontaneous (reflex) change in muscle response, postural balance, etc. The practical, effective, repeatable, hands-on balancing is more important than the theory that explains the underlying mechanism of how it works.

Traditional Chinese Medicine (TCM)

Harmony in the whole system is the ultimate goal, allowing a good vibration and integration among all parts as an integrated WHOLE. Fixing problems can be helpful, but is *closing the barn door after the cows have left*. Cultivating vitality is where it's at.

- Chi is the *primary* energy: Balance of the vital energy (Chi) brings about balance and function of the whole person. Blocks in Chi or imbalances are reflected in every other aspect and eventually will lead to disease. Balancing the energy allows the internal wisdom of the body to heal itself, and we do not have to intellectually understand all of the mechanisms. Just do it. It's natural.

- The Unity Principle: Many things influence the Chi/Life-energy, including context, environment, color, sound, words and feelings. Cultivation of the SENSES, and subtle intuition, can allow us to tune into and modulate our Chi energy.

Dialogue and Metaphor

Dialogue and metaphor contextualizes, creates a specific space for balancing. Muscle biofeedback lets us find clues about where there may be an imbalance or a circuit that can be activated to improve function and overall harmony, specific to our positive focus.

- We work with WHOLE people (and not disease): The conscious intellectual thoughts and ideas, as well as the accompanying sensations, feelings, emotions, meanings, are essential to the structural and physiological function.

The LITERARY METAPHOR: Colorful, Poetic Language to EXPRESS MUCH IN LITTLE

*Rich, **expressive, symbolic words** enrich our understanding, implying more than facts or information, but also meaning and emotion. Coloring our sense of meaning in life enriches life. Finding a way **to express and understand something initially only FELT**. Intuition or "gestalt", whole body/whole world sense.*

- *Pictures/Images that resonate* on many levels creating a sense of knowing beyond words, but capturing a deeper meaning, in images that create a sensory experience, personal significance, feelings and emotions. In fact, all words are metaphors—language that represents/stands for things, ideas and feelings. When we work with Metaphors we are working with the building blocks and processes whereby human beings make, and share the meanings of the experience of life!

Metaphor: The Emotional Language

The language of Metaphor could be called "the emotional language." We are tapping into the emotional brain of the gut, where we not only do emotional processing but nutritional processing, and a huge percentage of immune function and healing/regeneration to all internal organs.

- When we work with Metaphor, we find more than the literal meanings in the words. We also find the emotional meanings.

- The Enteric system has its own "brain." All the same types of nerves, cells, neuro-chemicals as in the brain also reside in the gut (80% of serotonin is utilized in the gut!). But the language of this second brain, which also happens to be responsible for a huge amount of immune function as well as nourishment and repair, is EMOTION.

- When we communicate in the language of emotion, we communicate with the core of our being. This has a profound effect on well-being at a physiological and nutritional level, in addition to the profound shifts in feelings and sensations that are readily apparent during and after a balance.

Metaphor: How to GO DEEP FAST—Jung's Dream Language

In Germany, the *TFH Metaphors workshop* was given the subtitle "How to Go Deep Fast." Clearly, working with the emotional language of the Enteric brain has immediate, profound effects. We can go deep and have a dramatic effect via some seemingly superficial, mundane things that we choose to notice with our full attention, mind and body. Through muscle testing and metaphor, we are automatically involving and eliciting responses from our unconscious, autonomic body functions. These responses may also relate to emotions, and the subconscious—that part or our own consciousness that is not necessarily part of our waking awareness—our dream life. One way of exploring the meaning of our dreams is to consider them as a language of metaphorical imagery. There is deep meaning within your unconscious, and you can expand your waking awareness of it by working with metaphors.

Metaphor means Transformation (Karada No Fushigi)

I learned the phrase "Karada No Fushigi" from the TFH instructors in Japan. It means (Respect for) The Mystery of the Body.

- It remains a mystery how the body transforms energy into form and allows all the cells to cooperate as one self-aware BEING. Yet we can use muscle testing to better appreciate and develop awareness of the many dimensions of our being. We can notice specific movements, observing how it feels, and what ideas come into our minds based on feeling, body attitude/position or gesture suggested by the movement. We accept and respect the mystery of how the body transforms.

- Our Faculty from Japan, Kenichi Ishirmaru, tells us via *Zen Kinesiology* that each muscle test is an opportunity for a "mini-meditation" with a potential "mini-enlightenment."

- Each muscle test, and the meanings that we associate with it, can serve as a "Zen Koan"—a question that does not have a logical, rational answer, but can lead to lightning flashes of insight, *transcending the merely logical and rational, using language to reach understanding beyond language.*

- The word Metaphor can also be interpreted to mean "change" (as in the five changes of the Five Elements), new meaning, and **Transformation**. The movements of TFH activate energy flow and neurological integration. We can expand on this by bringing another metaphorical dimension to our awareness of the physical movements of the tests, and activating the body's natural transformational processes.

Metaphors of the Muscles, Meridians and Five Elements

In TFH we work with the physical muscle responses as an indicator of postural imbalance, as well as possible imbalance in the mental/emotional, biochemical, and energetic aspects of the person. We typically balance a minimum of 14 muscles (and sometimes as many as 42) as a general tune-up to the overall posture, but also choosing at least one specific muscle to represent each of the 14 major energy pathways (Meridians) from TCM, which are mostly named for their related Organs—Heart, Lung, Kidney, etc. So we might contemplate Metaphors of the muscle location, size, function, as well as symbolic associations with the Meridian/Organ and related Element from the Chinese Five Elements acupuncture model.

In TFH we use ten traditional metaphors associated with each of the Five Elements. We have the names of the Elements themselves (Wood, Fire, Earth, Metal, and Water) that are rich with associations and symbolism. We have the Seasons and Climates, representing nature both literally and figuratively. We have the five senses and five Emotions, which we frequently check to enrich our balancing process. The Emotions may resonate with our current feelings, or larger themes and patterns in life.

If we take the **Seasons to represent** *phases* **in the** *life cycle*, we create a very accessible approach to the **Power** category of the Five Elements by contemplating what might give us *personal power* at different stages in the life cycle. In the Wood Element, we have the Metaphor of **Birth**. So at this phase in life, new birth, new thoughts and expansive energy are what give us power. But if we are out of balance in our energies of Wood Element, we may be giving birth to more than we can sustain, or we may not feel the needed energy for rapid growth. In Fire we have the Metaphor of **Maturity**. One idea of Maturity is to know both your limits (fire representing danger) and your passions and full potential. As we mature, there is often a "rite of passage," which may literally be a "trial by fire." Are you in touch with your passions, but also know your limitations? Earth Element corresponds to **Decrease**. Sometimes "less is more." Unless more is more! How can decreasing something actually give you more power? In Metal Element, we come to **Balance**.

Of course, that is the main theme of TFH, finding the balance in your Posture, Attitude, and Energy, to give you the power to reach your personal goals in a more flowing, effortless way. But a totally static balance could be stagnant. Moderation in all things, *including moderation!* As we come to the Water Element, the end of the cycle, nearing the end of life, or the end of a project, we have the Metaphor of **Emphasize**. At this stage, your priority and emphasis are what give you power. When a project is nearly finished, what can you emphasize to give it the best impact? If you are in your last days of life, many previously important things are no longer the priority. If you can focus on what's most important, you can have power even in your death!

The Faith/Worldview *Metaphor Cycle*

The "11th category" that we integrate with the Five Elements is called the Faith/Worldview category. It is not drawn from Traditional Chinese Medicine but rather from studies of cognitive development and spiritual development as a parallel process to brain development and personal experience. Each of us uses a variety of different models of reality to make sense of our experience, to make decisions, to improve performance and have more personal bests. Each of these models entails certain assumptions and ideas that we believe to be true, even though we may not be conscious of these beliefs. We may not recognize our faith in the assumptions of our own worldview as faith. We might want to simply call it "Reality." We might just say, "That's just how life is." **Faith/Worldview refers to the process (largely unconscious) by which we actively construct our personal worldview, the set of beliefs that allow each of us to have meaning in our lives, a sense of what's *really* real, and make our choices accordingly.** Our faith and worldview are fundamental forces that shape our experiences, our perceptions of those experiences, our priorities, passions, enjoyment and satisfaction in life.

At least since Piaget's studies of the stages of cognitive development, we have learned about a linear, hierarchical progression of our *thinking capacity*, as we grow and have life experiences, and our brains develop. Many theorists, researchers and practitioners have built on these principles, exploring both **cognition**—the structure of human thought—and **affection**—the sensations and emotions that attend and influence what we believe that we know. James Fowler studied Piaget as well as Kohlberg's *moral* stages, Erik Erikson and Jung's *rational* and *unconscious* dynamics, and Maslow's hierarchy of needs and phases of *self-actualization,* among others.

Fowler compared these concepts to individual *spiritual development* through hundreds of interviews (Life Maps, 1978; Stages of Faith, 1981). Fowler noted that **as we develop through stages in the life cycle we develop our capacity to perceive reality**. Part of that is dependent upon the *actual development of our brain*, and our *ability to use our brain* to comprehend different aspects of reality, which is necessarily hierarchical and linear (built upon necessary prior experiences and stages). Fowler compared this pattern to **moral development or spiritual development** and found that our faith is also dependent to some extent on this same linear cognitive development.

John Thie read Fowler's books (among many others!) and said, "Fowler is talking about these developmental stages that follow a *linear model*, but it sounds to me a lot like the Chinese Five Element *cyclical model*." One name for the Five Elements is the *Five Changes* or the *Five Transformations*. So these could be the changes or **transformations of faith**. John Thie mapped Fowler's Phases of Faith to the Transformation Cycles of the Chinese Five Elements, paralleling the five seasons considered as a Life Cycle, and the five aspects of Power related to personal growth.

In that model, we normally develop through the seasons or *creation cycle* of life in a linear progression. At a particular season of life we will primarily operate in a particular stage of belief or worldview. However, at any given moment, for different issues and conditions, or goals and aspirations, we may be operating in different "belief systems." We can consider these phases as modes of perception and understanding that may or may not be effective and appropriate at different moments for different purposes. For a particular project or for a particular problem we might find ourselves effectively applying **a particular way of thinking, or getting stuck in that one perspective**.

So if the key Meridian in a Five Element pattern is Gallbladder, in Wood Element, I might want to think about the belief stage of Wood Element. Comparing our capacity for thinking and considering different perspectives (and even spiritual experiences and perceptions) with our capacity for different philosophical viewpoints yields some very valuable models for our self-awareness, and for facilitating others to enrich and expand their own perceptions of reality. We can gain insight into **our own beliefs in general, and in relation to specific life issues** and goals. Contemplating the *"Worldview" Metaphors* may broaden our perspectives and contribute to our sense of meaning, satisfaction and effectiveness in life.

As with all of the 111 TFH Metaphors of Muscles, Meridians and the Five Elements, the *"Worldview" Metaphors* often result in surprising realizations about our lives, challenges, and goals, and have been shown to balance muscles and energy with "just words." Often there is a spontaneous release of emotion. TFH balancing becomes even more holistic, profound, and effective as well as more enjoyable!

This mapping of the 5 Element Power Metaphors to the seasons of the life cycle is the model for mapping the stages of cognitive/spiritual development to the Phases of Faith.

	Fire/Summer **School Years**	
Wood/Spring **Infancy, Childhood**		Earth/Late Summer **Adolescence**
Water/Winter **Elderhood, Death**		Metal/Fall **Adulthood**

Fowler described Faith as an evolution through transformative stages in the process of composing our perception of the "ultimate environment," the highest truth, or the most comprehensive reality. An easy way to start relating to these stages is just to think in simple terms of the different *ages* **in the life cycle**.

We know right away what we associate with distinctly different times in life such as childhood, adolescence, adulthood and old age. **Wood** corresponds to infancy and **early childhood**. **Fire** Element takes us into the **school years**. **Earth** Element is associated with **adolescence**. (There may be several stages of adolescence all the way through the phases of life! This corresponds to the Earth Element property of being in the center of the other elements, and serving as the transition between the Seasons of the year and our lifetimes.)

Eventually, if you survive the school years and adolescence, in **Metal** you will arrive at something called **adulthood**. Then you get to **Water, old age, fully ripened maturity, and then death**. And some of these associations shift depending on which Five Element text you're reading. These titles don't necessarily correspond exactly to some schools of 5 Element Acupuncture. Death may come in Metal, and then there is something else between death and rebirth, some kind of transition or transformation. But all of these things can overlap each other. They are all flowing into and affecting each other through the creation and destruction cycles. And in fact, these stages are somewhat collapsed from Fowler's Phases in order to fit to the Five Elements, but the general essence corresponds well with the concept of five seasons in the life cycle.

And not everyone actually progresses through all the stages in terms of their thinking and beliefs. According to Fowler, a lot of people get stuck in the stage of the Fire Element. **You could be 80 years old and maybe never develop much beyond the "school years" attitude**. The development of your belief system isn't totally tied to your years. It's very flexible. But we have this structure to give us an idea of what are some of the **differences in perceptions of reality** at stages in life, and at any particular moment.

Season of Life: Spring, Infancy, *Early Childhood*; Phase of Faith: *Intuitive-Projective*

Beginning with the Wood Element, we have infancy and early childhood. What kind of perception of reality does an infant or small child have? At first they have no reference. Everything is new. There's no history, no basis of comparison. They experience everything on a whole body level, which we could call a purely *intuitive perception of reality*

This can also be called a *projective type of perception*, because if I have only one perception of reality, I project my perception onto everybody else. If I think or feel a certain way, my perception is that everyone else sees, perceives, and knows the same thing. Even as an adult, have you ever had that kind of feeling, where you look at another person and ask, "Why don't you already know exactly what I'm feeling and thinking? It's so real and intense for me. You're right here, why don't you see it the way I see it?

Wood Element Belief Metaphor Questions

- Do you need to use your intuition, creative vision and dream imagery to find meaning in your life and actions?

- Are you dwelling in your own personal dream world, ignoring cause and effect, and the concrete consequences of your actions?

- Are you stuck in "cognitive egocentricity," failing to consider different perspectives, or the perspectives of others? Are you paying *too much* or *too little* attention to intuition, symbols, and signs?

All of the sights, sounds, sensations, etc. of our daily experiences can resonate with meaning. Reflecting on the symbolic or metaphorical potential of events in our lives can be a powerful tool for assessing our personal balance, wholeness and wellness. Denying that our feelings and experiences have meaning leads to a meaningless existence. Yet assigning particular meaning to events or "omens," without evaluating whether this actually makes sense in the context of your life, leaves us at the mercy of superstition—beliefs that are not grounded in our self-knowledge and experience.

Season of Life: Summer, *School Years*;
Phase of Faith: *Literal/ Mythic*

Now we move on to **school years and Fire Element**. Most of us have pretty resonant associations with the school years, positive and/or negative. Or maybe we have actually blanked out those years entirely! One reason that schools are so rule-oriented is because during school age we become *able to perceive of rules*. And, actually, we kind of **cling to rules**. So we can be kind of **moralistic** at this age. If you follow the rules, you're good, and if you don't follow the rules, you're bad. It is very **literal, black and white,** and there is a tendency towards rigidity and perfectionism. With this type of literal perception, things have to be very concrete. You can see **cause and effect but it's very linear**. At this stage, the form of the dramatic story with emotional content becomes a primary mode of understanding. This is called **mythic faith**.

Fire Element Belief Metaphor Questions

- Are you hemmed in by a narrow, literal interpretation of (group) rules, morals or beliefs, or could you benefit from being conscious of conventions and not always having to "re-invent the wheel" or "go it alone"?

- Do you see yourself as excessively bad or excessively good based on your ability to strictly adhere to moral rules and attitudes that do not allow much room for mistakes? Are you trying to maintain an image of yourself as perfect, or seeing yourself as worthless if you're less than perfect?

- Do you expect precise reciprocity in your relationships, business arrangements, or with the "universe"? Are you taking the attitude that if you do "right," the result or reward must be commensurate or else you feel betrayed?

Season of Life: Late Summer—Transition, *Adolescence*;
Phase of Faith: *Conventional/Synthetic*

Earth Element corresponds to transformation between the

Elements, transition between the seasons, and the developmental stage of **adolescence**. Increasing abilities of abstract thinking allow reflection upon the self and the capacity to view one's own actions from multiple/others' perspectives. We begin to see flexibility of rules and become aware of differing **conventions**, among different groups and contexts. We see the imperfections in our own previously accepted conventions. Maybe we decide they are completely wrong. We become disillusioned with literalism and blind acceptance of authority. We reconstruct a **synthetic worldview**, in the sense of taking a little bit of everything and **synthesizing our own reality**. It's **a synthesis of disparate parts, but oftentimes it's not internally integrated**. It might be "half-baked," distorted, and not totally functional or congruent with our internal feelings.

Earth Element Belief Metaphor Questions

- Are you placing too little or too much reliance on the values of your peer group, community or culture and how you "fit in" or not?

- Are you suffering a low sense of self-worth because you are unable to live up to your own values, or the values of your family/community/group?

Season of Life: Fall, **Adulthood**; Phase of Faith: *Responsible Faith*

Hopefully, we eventually arrive at something called **Adulthood**, corresponding to the Metal Element, and we assume responsibility for our own personal lifestyle, beliefs, and attitudes. We use the term **Responsible Faith**. The word *responsible* can be heavy. People switch off! But in kinesiology, we say "**self-responsibility.**" This is the adult attitude—not that I take responsibility on my shoulders for everyone else, but I do take **responsibility for whatever I have pieced together as my reality**. I've had enough experience to see what really fits for me, **what's really true in my actual experience**. Whatever I accept as my reality, it's not because other people told me, it's because I have lived it, I have chosen it, and I feel responsible for it.

At this stage we're able to see things from **multiple perspectives**, and usually it's **more accurate** because we've lived long enough to clear up some of the distortions and we can see ourselves in different roles and different contexts. I may have some **internal contradictions** with my accepted way of living. **So polarities and contradictions continue to be a challenge**.

Metal Element Belief Metaphor Questions

- Do you take personal responsibility for your beliefs and the roles that you choose to play in different areas of your life in different contexts? Do you feel like responsibilities and roles are imposed on you by life, or family/group expectations and beliefs?

- Do your goals and your use of time and energy match what you believe are your personal values?

Season of Life: Winter, **Old Age, Elderhood, Death;** Phase of Faith: **Reintegrative/Universalizing Faith**

According to Fowler, not that many people get to the final stage of belief in the Water Element. Living a long time isn't enough to have this development. In the TFH *Instructor Training*, Maslow's Hierarchy of Needs is a topic that we consider. People usually need to have their most basic needs met before they can develop to higher orders of "self-actualization." So we need to make sure our students feel safe and comfortable, and know where the toilet is, and when they will have a chance to eat. Then they can focus on information or new skills, or even transforming their lives. But, ironically, those who have never suffered challenges and some period of difficulty meeting their basic needs often have trouble developing the level of empathy to reach the later stages of perception and belief.

People who continue to develop come to a stage that could be called **re-integrative**. At this stage we re-evaluate and re-integrate all of the parts of self and life experience. We rehabilitate all of the aspects of ourselves that have been left undeveloped, ignored, evaded, or denied. We **look at our dark side** and say, "Okay, that's part of me too." Paradoxes and polarity, yin and yang, are not seen as puzzles to be solved, but mysteries to be accepted and appreciated. Human beings are seen as BOTH good and evil; shaped by circumstances AND personally responsible for their choices. God is everywhere, but God can be present right here in this moment. God is both personal/directly knowable and abstract/beyond our comprehension.

Fully accepting internal and external contradictions, and embracing our holistic self-understanding, leads to a sense of transcendent value of faith and community among all humanity and a tendency to sacrifice the personal, individual life for the benefit of the greater good. This sense is extended in the "universalizing" stage to a fellowship among all beings and a connection with the ultimate environment or God.

Universalizing faith is where you choose to go beyond what you have decided is correct, and you start to see everything as part of the self. Personal good and bad attributes, friends and enemies, are all part of personal reality, part of "me." You really perceive a connection and value of all peoples, of all living things and the whole planet.

It's **actually a direct experience of the connection with all of creation. So you move into a new naiveté.** With all your intellectual powers, and all your experiences and wisdom, you come to a new stage where you are like a child again. Of course, we have this *idea* in Kinesiology and in energy work in general. I think most of us *think* **that's the ultimate reality, that we are all connected, we are all one**. But it is one thing to have the idea, and it's quite another **to have it as your perception** of reality, that you feel in your whole Soul. We develop a passion for the greatest good and the highest truth over lesser concerns of nation, tribe, institution, family, success, money, sexuality, etc. While we value our experience of life perhaps more than ever before, we hold it loosely, feeling less concerned for our individual survival.

Water Element Belief Metaphor Questions

- How does your sense of the Universal relate to your life and to your present goals? Is this a time for you to let go of concern for personal success, failure, contradiction, or injustice and simply concentrate on the greater good, or do you need to be proactive in your own interests?

- Is there some aspect of yourself that you need to (re)awaken to reach our goal? Are you fixating on some fault in your character, or some past regret or failure, that may need to be recognized and accepted, rather than perpetually agonizing?

Considering the Faith dimension of the Five Elements, Metaphors might contribute to your sense of meaning and purpose in life and clarify and fulfill your "Telos," your "reason for being," or purpose for which we have been created. Some phases may be consistently experienced according to our personality or time of life, while others are only experienced for fleeting moments. Still, we are capable of all of these Phases of Faith and will naturally cycle through them.

When our lives do not contain a sense of security or significance, when we are not able to love and do not feel loved, when we are holding on to life too tightly, that's an indication that we are out of balance. We can assess our posture and use muscle testing to give us an indication of where in our bodies, or in our energy systems, we are out of balance. It can be of great benefit to take a moment to do this on a day-by-day basis. Using these Metaphors of the Faith cycle in understanding ourselves and our goals can be very effective in coming into harmony with our own ultimate environment, and finding our place and purpose within it.

> Faith is an ineffable attraction towards the transcendental, but transcendental not as an abstraction but as the deepest personal love imaginable. And THAT'S what Faith is.
>
> -- Quotation from Father Helkusei, from Fowler's *Stages of Faith*

Awareness and new perspective influences and moves energy (the observer effect) at the quantum level, contributing to the overall balance and function, resulting in spontaneous transformation at physical/structural, mental/emotional, biochemical/physiological and spiritual levels. This will make balancing more profound as well as more effective, but the true power is in expanding our self-awareness and vision for our positive goals and our choices that will contribute to health, balance and enjoyment of life!

For me the most powerful aspect of the multi-factorial process of TFH Energy Balancing is the whole-being awareness that spontaneously leads to greater flow of energy/information in our body/mind, greater balance, centeredness, and integration for a more effortless, energized, creative approach to health and life, envisioning, enriching and creating the life in which we will thrive with deep satisfaction and meaning.

Belief Systems and Your Personal Power ~
Table of corresponding Metaphors

Element	Season	(Personal) Power	Age	Phase of Faith
Wood	Spring	Birth/ growth	Infancy/ Early Childhood	Intuitive-- Projective
Fire	Summer	Maturity	School Years	Literal-- Mythic
Earth	Late Summer/ Transition	Decrease	Adolescence	Conventional-- Synthetic
Metal	Fall	Balance	Adulthood	Responsible
Water	Winter	Emphasis	Elderhood/ Old Age, Death	Reintegrative-- Universal

The typical way that we access these Metaphors is during a 14-muscle/ 14-Meridian balancing session. We can balance each muscle "As you go," and for each muscle that we balance, as we massage the appropriate touch reflexes, we can mention and contemplate the Power/Belief Metaphors of the associated Meridian/Element. We might also try "just" talking about the Metaphors and rechecking the muscle. We often balance the Meridian and muscle with words!

A Shortcut would be to check Alarm Points, or Pulse Points, and consider the Metaphors of the Element of the indicated Meridians. An even simpler approach would be to check the Indicator Muscle to see which "column" and which specific Metaphors resonate (with a particular issue, affirmation, goal statement, etc.). We could balance by holding the ESR* points while visualizing and talking about the indicated Metaphors. We can also just contemplate the Belief Metaphors table as a kind of "Menu" to intuitively consider whichever Metaphor "speaks to us" in the context of the present moment, or a project or challenge in life.

Options for accessing the Belief Metaphors

1. Have in mind, or mention out loud, a particular issue, goal or affirmation statement. Measure your subjective sense of any aches, pains, tension, emotions, etc. on a scale from 0-10.

2. Check for imbalances (through self-awareness, noticing, or muscle-testing); then

    a. **Balance As You Go:** Individually check and balance each of the 14 muscles. For each unlocking muscle, contemplate one or more of the Metaphors of the Element related to the Meridian.

    b. **1-Point Balance:** Assess the pattern on the Wheel/Five Elements and choose the key Meridian to balance. Contemplate all 4 Aspects of the related Element.

    c. **Shortcut:** Check Alarm Points or Pulse Points and consider the Metaphors of the indicated Meridians.

d. **Simple "Belief" Balance with Emotional Stress Release*:** Use the Indicator Muscle and call out each "Aspect Column" from the table (Element, Season, Power, Age, Phase of Faith), or just see which column is interesting or "calls to you." For each indicated column, check the IM for each Metaphor in the column (or follow your intuition). Consider each indicated Metaphor while holding the ESR points.

3. Recheck your goal statement and any other measures from the beginning. Notice and reinforce the changes in your posture, attitude and energy!

Emotional Stress Release is a simple procedure of holding the points on the forehead between the eyes and the hairline while visualizing/contemplating any stressful event, idea or sensation, which releases the stressful charge of the experience or feelings.

Author Bio

Matthew Thie, M.Ed.

As the son of Dr. John and Carrie Thie, Matthew grew up with Touch for Health (TFH) and Effective Communication skills as part of his everyday family system. Matthew presents TFH as a learning process that anyone can be trained to use for their ongoing, day-to-day optimization of life experience. *His emphasis is on immediately putting the simple techniques into personal practice, and making the concepts and techniques personally meaningful.* From 1996 to 2005 Matthew worked extensively with TFH Founder, John F. Thie, DC, co-authoring the *TFH Pocketbook with Chinese 5 Element Metaphors* (2003) and *Touch for Health: The Complete Edition* (2005). Matthew has taught the TFH Goal-setting & Metaphor Workshop to over 1,000 students worldwide, *making TFH balancing more profound, effective, lasting, and meaningful and helping people to enjoy their own unique lives.*

Matthew continues teaching the **TFH Clinical Intensive Workshops** that John developed at Serra Retreat in Malibu, California, in addition to teaching the **TFH synthesis**, **Proficiency**, and the *advanced* **TFH Training** (Instructor Qualification).

Markers

How to Recognize Very Young Children Who May Have Had a Near-Death Experience

P. M. H. Atwater, L.H.D.

Abstract

Many children experience near-death before birth, during birth trauma, while in their mother's vagina, or as babies/toddlers. One-third in my study had pre-birth memory; half could remember their birth. Because most families ignore children's "stories," I developed a list of "markers"—how to recognize such children, even once grown.

Children of any age can have a near-death experience . . . before birth, during birth trauma, or in crisis situations when babies, toddlers, school kids, teens. What amazes everyone about child experiencers is that the majority of them remember what happened, oftentimes lifelong, in detail, and speak about it as if possessed of a more mature mind. They are usually upfront and to-the-point about God, angels, ghosts, heavenly or hellish figures, whatever they see, talk to, or feel around them . . . *that no one else can see.* If in an accident, the child can continue to interact with those who were killed, as if "the other side" were still wide open, often pointing to figures hovering about the hospital room or near the ceiling and carrying on conversations.

The behavior of children who have had near-death experiences freaks out parents and drives doctors and nurses into lengthy and prolonged states of denial, as they hastily turn to drugs for "hallucination" control. Typically, children are scooted out of hospitals prematurely if they start talking to patients who had recently died but were still "hanging around." Hospital staff find this upsetting, not to mention parents.

Since 1975, when Raymond A. Moody, Jr., MD, Ph.D., came out with his bestseller *Life After Life*, research about those who experienced life on what appeared to be the other side of death focused entirely on adults. What evolved as "the classical model" was about adults, for adults. Melvin Morse, MD, expanded research to include children in *Closer to the Light: Learning from the Near-Death Experiences of Children*. I followed using a different style, bypassing "scientific" models to let kids just be kids, describing what had happened and was still happening . . . I became as a child to see as a child. The result was *The New Children and Near-Death Experiences* and an entry in the children's section in *The Big Book of Near-Death Experiences* (the world's only encyclopedia of the phenomenon).

Research Baseline

To better understand why a list of "markers" would be helpful in identifying people who may have had a near-death experience when very young, it would be best for me to begin at the beginning—with my study of 277 child experiencers, not quite half still kids at the time, the rest adults who remembered having had such an experience when young. I targeted the years from birth to age fifteen, with the bulk of my cases occurring before the age of six.

Here's the overall percentage for 277 child experiencers:

- 60% White (U.S., Canada, France, England, Ukraine)
- 23% Latino (U.S., Mexico, Argentina, Colombia)
- 12% Black (U.S., Canada)

- 5% Asian (Malaysia, China)

NOTE: I rejected an additional 15% because the session with the child was compromised by adult interference (adult explaining/interpreting for the child). I found that fascination with "out-of-the-mouths-of-babes" reports can mislead more readily than enlighten.

Children who are at the edge of death or clinically resuscitated are more apt to have a near-death experience than adults. That means lots of kids have these. They can encounter the same range of scenario types as do adults (Initial, Hell-like or frightening, Heaven-like or comforting, Transcendent), and face the same pattern of physiological and psychological aftereffects . . . but in a different manner. Good and evil jumble together for them, and the line separating one reality from another disappears. Few children integrate their experiences; instead, they compensate, adjust, deny, or store them away on a "shelf in their mind." It's usually not until they reach adulthood that they learn about the phenomenon and begin to "connect the dots". . . why school didn't make sense when they were a kid, why they often knew what was going to happen before it did, why they healed more quickly than most and could help others heal, why they seemed to know more, see more, hear and feel more than others, and have a sense of otherworldliness and social justice that set them apart.

Imprinting and Loss of Bonding

Small children, via expressions, movements, and responses, can show signs that suggest that they may have identified with or been imprinted by the otherworldly imagery, beings, and behaviors they were exposed to during their near-death episode. Their earthly family and environs, things typical to culture and place, may seem foreign or of little interest to them afterward. Imprinting, in this regard, means to "fix firmly in the mind," and that is what I am referring to—children who fixed their sense of existing, *elsewhere*.

The temporal lobes in the brain (above the ear and around the temples) build libraries of shape, size, sound, smell, color, movement, and taste from the input they receive and are exposed to so that we know what things are and how best to respond to them. These libraries change to suit needs from the day we are born to the day we die. Yet, if a child's near-death experience was associated with birth, or occurred during the early days, months, or years of life, it is possible those budding libraries accommodate otherworldly models of identification, rather than those of earth. This imprinting can be augmented by sensory responses and intuitive knowing to the extent that the child may seem wise beyond his or her years when, in fact, the youngster is simply responding to what feels natural.

Family and friends are at a loss to understand this, of having a model of life and living at variance to their own; nor do the majority of psychologists and counselors have training in how to interpret why this might be. Hear me when I say this: *it is normal for the young to lose parent/child bonding*. This does not mean children cease to be loving and thoughtful, but it does indicate that they can become somewhat silent or distant, independent, or unusually mature and detached. Interests can change from those of the family. For preschool and school-age kids, parent/child bonding is initially quite strong and is the reason they "come back" from near-death episodes. Still, the climate of welcome or threat they are greeted with, as well as how their episode ended, directly impinges on what comes next. Bonding can be re-established for a child of any age through patience and the willingness of both child and parent to share and respect *feelings*. . . as they explore their differing worldviews.

An Adult Mind in a Child's Body

One of the criticisms I have received from publishing house editors is that my accounts of child experiencers portrayed them as much too mature for their ages. I assured them this was no exaggeration. This is how most of them really speak—as if possessed of an adult mind in a child's body. This finding broaches topics like reincarnation (the young speak of past lives as casually and confidently as they might inquire about dinner) and physical afflictions ("I knew that I was a powerful, spiritual being that chose to have a short, but marvelous, mortal existence"—a quote from DeLynn, born with cystic fibrosis).

Over half of the child experiencers in my research could remember their birth. Whenever possible I checked out these stories with parents, mostly mothers; I never found a single error. One-third had pre-birth memory—usually beginning at about six to seven months *in utero*. Medically, it has been shown that the fetus at twenty-six weeks or six months gestation experiences many sensations, including pain. This medical discovery of fetal awareness directly applies to the majority of children in my research who reported the beginnings of their memory as *a soul resident in human form* while still inside the womb. Some had recall of earlier than month six *in utero*, even of their conception, and of actively taking part as a spirit in choosing their own DNA. Most of those who spoke of remembering their conception also said they floated in and out of their mother's womb until finally "settling in" when fetal formation was more complete (around the seventh or eighth month).

It's scary what some children remember their pre-birth experience in the womb. Things like heated debates and arguments, conditions in the home, even how their mother felt about her own life—and her thoughts! Emotionally charged issues are remembered readily, especially if the child's welfare is threatened (like the possibility of an abortion or because of an accident or assault on the mother). And a missing twin—that "extra" who was never born or died at birth or was reabsorbed by the mother because of being damaged or malformed—that being can return in a near-death scenario. On occasion, the one who was aborted appears.

Soaring Intelligence and Creativity

Here are some statistics from my study of 277 child experiencers, age range from birth to fifteen years at the time of their episode:

- Faculties enhanced, altered, or experienced in multiples (synesthesia) 77%
- Mind works differently—highly creative and inventive 84%
- Significant enhancement of intellect 68%
- Mind tested at genius level with standard IQ test (with little or no genetic markers to account for scores)
    - main group (birth to fifteen years) 48%
    - subgroup (three to five years) 81%
    - subgroup (around birth to fifteen months) 96%
    - same as previous, but those who had a dark light instead of a bright light experience 100%
- Drawn to and highly proficient in math/science/history 93%
- Professionally employed when an adult in math/science/history 25%
- Unusually gifted with languages 35%
- School
    - easier after near-death experience 34%
    - harder afterward or blocked from memory 66%

I found no difference between males and females with regard to enhanced intelligence and spatial and mathematical abilities. The majority had IQ scores between 150 to 160 (past the threshold for genius), and some had IQs up to 174. Those children who had a dark light experience by fifteen months of age scored even higher on IQ tests: into the 200s. Enhancements in music were almost as high as those in math (93%). The regions for math and music in the brain are next to each other. It is as if both of these regions were enhanced together, as if they were a single unit (another argument for continuing music education in schools—if you want kids who are good in math, you must also provide music instruction).

Another note: the claim that pediatric temporal lobe epilepsy explains near-death states in the very young falls apart if you look at the facts. Peak periods when temporal lobe epilepsy is more apt to be found in boys and girls is in the range of years from six to nine. Most of the child experiencers in my research had their episode before the age of six (when science tells us that the human brain has reached 90% of its size). The age of reason begins about eight years of age.

Here's how the age clusters I found stack up via normal development:

> Birth to 15 months is when the actual wiring of the brain is determined and synapse formation increases 20-fold; utilizes twice the energy of an adult brain.
>
> Three to five years of age is the time of temporal lobe development; explore and experiment with possible roles, future patterns, and continuity of environment.
>
> Ten to 14 years of age is the time of puberty; hormone fluctuations, sexuality questioned, identity crisis.
>
> NOTE: The strongest evidence for genius with child experiencers was from birth to 15 months. Most alien, fairy, and monster sightings *with typical children* usually occur between three and five years of age (same timeframe for most of the children's cases of near-death experiences that I found).

Learning Ability Reverses

The younger the experiencer the greater the growth spurt in the brain. Most alien, fairy, and monster sightings, flying dreams, out-of-body episodes, invisible friends, and other paranormal/psychic occurrences experienced by *typical, normal children* happen between ages three and five, along with the bulk of reports of near-death states with the young. This period marks the birth of imagination, and the time when long-term memory begins and storytelling has the greatest influence. Most kids during this time are almost entirely future-oriented—temporal lobe development predominates.

Do we really understand what this implies? Temporal lobe expansion could precede temporal lobe development?

Add to the conundrum the fact that most near-death kids come back (revive) abstracting. That implies that the normal learning curve has somehow reversed. The average child learns in steps, one at a time, details built upon previously learned material. This is called "concrete" learning. For most of us, this type of education continues through the grades until we are ready for college. What I have observed with near-death kids (the younger, the more pronounced), is that they suddenly start making huge leaps of thought after their episode, clustering ideas and concepts into higher reasoning styles. They pick up answers almost before questions are asked, and they're usually point on; then they probe further, reaching for depths of thought beyond the subject at hand. If you ask them how they do it, they haven't the foggiest. This is "abstracting," where the point of focus centers on conceptual levels, sometimes even beyond thought. It's not like "seeing beyond the box." For child experiencers, the box was never there to begin with.

The ability to abstract, educators tell us, typically does not begin until the late teens, twenties, or thirties (if at all). Young experiencers who have the ability to abstract must switch or reverse their learning style to cope with the concrete methods all schools teach. The result is that far too often we lose their genius.

(Example: proficient in math/science/history, 93%; actually employed as an adult in those fields, 25%).

General Guidelines

Thanks to the success of the movie *Heaven Is for Real*, child experiencers are the rage. The movie is about Colton Burpo, a not-quite-four-year-old, who nearly died during emergency surgery. After recovering, he began to talk about seeing doctors as they worked on him and about the angels who spoke to him in the heaven world he visited, as well as his friend Jesus. Pops, too. Pops was his deceased paternal grandfather, a man he never could have possibly known, nor could he ever have heard his grandfather called by the affectionate nickname of "Pops."

What is different in the Burpo case is that the parents finally accepted as true what their son claimed, which is no small thing considering Rev. Todd Burpo's position as a minister was in jeopardy until his congregants reconsidered. Seldom do you hear such good news. Usually parents, relatives, friends, school teachers, ministers, turn against child experiencers . . . making fun of them, telling them to shut up, claiming it's just imagination gone wild, demeaning any notion of seeing and talking with "invisibles" or suddenly "knowing" things. For this reason, the majority of child experiencers "keep it secret," repress, or tuck away what happened to them. It is not unusual for child experiencers to grow up feeling somehow alien, that they do not fit into the world at large. Although the near-death phenomenon can be tossed aside by parents as an aberration, there's no denying the aftereffects, which can include changes in brain patterning and nerve response, as well as having a more abstract concept of the world and of God. Most child experiencers are unable to make the connection between their otherworldly episode and why they feel as they do. Learning about what is typical is a must, not only for families but for the kids themselves (whether still a child or once grown).

To help you recognize children who may have had a near-death experience, here are some general guidelines that may prove helpful. Notice if

- A serious illness or accident occurred before or involved with birth or up to the age of six or seven that nearly claimed the child's life. Any record of an otherworldly "dream" or "vision" is seldom recorded unless the social/family environment of the child honors the spiritual.

- Marked differences in behavior afterward. The child may be ahead of or different from age mates, becoming more so as the years pass, as well as taking on a more nontraditional or nonconformist attitude. He or she may be possessed of a charm or charisma that attracts people, animals, birds, etc. He or she may appear somewhat backward socially when young, while still being unusually creative, even bold. Unafraid of death, highly intuitive, aware of things future.

- A pattern of aftereffects is present. Some display electrical sensitivity, most a unique sensitivity to sunlight, sound, and pharmaceuticals. Experiencers often lose their tolerance for pharmaceuticals. Even though a majority go on to exhibit good health, there is a marked increase in sensitivity to touch-taste-texture-smell, and an increase in allergies. School is often a problem, but not for the usual reasons; rather, the child often knows more than the teacher does. Boredom is an issue.

- An almost obsessive drive to accomplish a particular task or project, as if it were their mission to do so, becomes evident. Most will work with no sense of time or money, yet are inclined to own a home or be aligned with distinctive places or groups. Marriage seems important to them, but not necessarily living a traditional life.

The child's vision of heaven or the other worlds beyond death is alive with a sense of truth and realness that challenges families, teachers, therapists, and ministers. Theirs is not just a vision but an experience that both colors their sense of the life they are living and the purpose behind their life. That many repress or tuck away their experience speaks to how they are treated and whether or not they are believed . . . or even allowed to share their story.

Tips on How to Handle and Support Child Experiencers

Sleep patterns abruptly change afterwards—less nap time, increased flow states, restlessness. Some may fear sleep and suffer nightmares; others seem exhausted on waking as if they had "toured the universe" or attended "night school" while asleep. Reliving the episode in the dream state is common. Encourage this. Do visualizations. Let them talk. Listen. Engage conversation.

Love changes for child experiencers. It is *normal* for them to lose the parent/child bonding. This doesn't mean they cease to be loving and thoughtful, but it does mean they tend to act more distant than before. The child switches gears and begins to mature faster, become more independent. Interests change.

Afterwards, most kids have a marked decrease in their ability to express themselves and socialize. Since language is the most critical skill anyone has, stimulate the child's speech with your own. Promote dialogue with question/answer games, group storytelling, reading out loud, speaking on pretend microphones. Encourage the child to participate in community projects as a volunteer.

Writing and drawing are just as important as dialogue. Ask the child to make a special book about his or her near-death experience. Have lots of paper handy for pages that cover newspaper accounts of death events (if any), drawings of each aspect of the episode, a description of what happened, information about dreams afterward, sketches of any "beings" that continue to appear, poems, ideas, thoughts, and extra room to record more later on. Have the child choose a title; bind the book with ribbon. A project such as this validates the near-death episode—*as well as the child's feelings*. It would be helpful if the parent kept a journal of how his or her child changes, what they say and do. This re-stimulates parent/child bonding and can serve as an invaluable resource once the child matures. Still, that special book, the child's version of what happened, can transform a child experiencer of any age, even once grown. It is never too late to "make your book."

<u>Child experiencers tend to withdraw</u>. They can even reject hugs and cuddles. Re-center them in their bodies through touch, pat their shoulder when you pass by, touch their hand if you speak to them, nudge a knee from time to time, rub their neck. Smile. Teach them to pat and nudge you like you do for them. Pets are wonderful for touch therapy, as are plants. Make cookies that the child can help prepare, then turn him or her loose creating shapes by hand and turning them into imaginative designs.

<u>Speaking of food, watch sugar levels</u>. Child experiencers are more sensitive than the average child to chemicals, excessive sweets, refined sugars, and overly processed foods. Full-spectrum lights are preferred to florescent. Avoid overexposure to electronic "toys" and modems, Wi-Fi, even electric blankets. Also, be careful of too much exposure to bright sunlight and music turned way too loud. Both can be painful. Recheck former medications—they may now be too potent.

<u>Ideally, child experiencers and adult experiencers should get together once in a while</u>. Adults can provide that special atmosphere where "taking about it" amongst fellow experiencers could make a huge difference. Children can inspire confidence and stability in adults, as kids are much more understanding and open than their elders. Above all, parents who were experiencers when young should be encouraged to speak of their own episode and what they went through *in front of their child experiencer*! Most don't. Such a sharing has a positive ripple effect for years to come.

Historical Cases

I've been researching near-death states since 1978, covering both adults and children, ever searching for a better understanding of the phenomenon itself, how it affects people, and what we can all learn from those who have gone through it. Being an experiencer myself has enabled me to notice what many miss . . . like the preponderance of historical figures who are recorded as having nearly died as a child, then afterward suddenly beginning to manifest skills and abilities, an intelligence and a spiritual awareness, uncharacteristic of the child before, or even in the family line.

Those I identified who fit this pattern are: Abraham Lincoln (American President and the man who freed the slaves); Albert Einstein (the great scientist who gave us the formula of $E=MC^2$); Black Elk (Lakota Sioux of unparalleled wisdom); John Neihardt (Black Elk's unusually perceptive biographer); Queen Elizabeth I (who established England as a world power); Edward de Vere, the 17th Earl of Oxford (whom I believe is the real Shakespeare); Mozart (a musical genius who created stirring masterpieces); Winston Churchill (whose steel resolve saved his country during World War II); Walter Russell (said to be the man who tapped the secrets of the universe); Valerie Hunt (the first researcher to objectify electronically the presence of an aura of light around people, places, things). Most of the Saints in the Catholic Church had their first experience of God as children during episodes the same or similar to near-death experiences. The same is true for great visionaries, prophets, and those possessed of unusual genius who went on to make significant discoveries that helped humankind.

I would add to this list Edgar Cayce, the most documented psychic of the 20th century, known more commonly as the "sleeping prophet" and the "father of holistic medicine." None of his abilities appeared until after he drowned at the age of five. Also, in all probability, the great new actor Benedict Cumberbatch, who was "frozen" (suffered hypothermia) when a baby. A study of Cumberbatch's life matches most of the markers for how to identify a child experiencer.

Markers

A simplified list of the markers for how to recognize very young children who may have had a near-death experience follows:

> a serious illness or accident that is somehow aligned with or connected to difficulties in the third trimester before birth, birth trauma, birthing difficulties, or as a baby or toddler, or young child up to about the age of six, maybe seven
>
> nontraditional, nonconformist attitude
>
> may lose bonding to parents—some or most
>
> may feel foreign in family, bond to the Other Side
>
> charm or charisma, especially with birds, animals
>
> socially backward
>
> unafraid of death, bold
>
> highly intuitive, knowing, creative
>
> aware of things future
>
> unique sensitivity to light and sound
>
> sensitive to touch-taste-texture-smell
>
> allergies
>
> school a problem, boredom, very intelligent
>
> drawn to the spiritual, spirit worlds
>
> may see ghosts, disincarnates, spirits
>
> obsessive drive to accomplish task, projects
>
> can be "mission"-oriented as years pass
>
> no sense of time/money, yet want a home that is theirs
>
> nontraditional relationships, yet want a marriage that lasts
>
> commitments important

special relationship with electricity, electrical sensitivity

sensitive to pharmaceuticals

may search for missing worlds, even lifelong

truth very important, meaning

can be withdrawn or quiet, keen observer

healers, service-oriented

decidedly independent, inventive

Invitation

I intend to research this further and write a book about near-death experiences of the very young. If you believe you can qualify as such an experiencer and would like to participate in this project, contact me. It is possible to forget the episode itself yet exhibit characteristics (markers) lifelong. To participate, this is what I need:

Your present age

Age when you think your experience occurred

Details of experience, including medical and third-party verification (if you have it or can get it)

Aftereffects, if any

What life was like for you afterward (confine story to one page)

Family response

School experience

Social experience

If now grown, any differences

Black and white drawing or sketch of episode or what you can remember from it, or what haunts you still or somehow "calls" or fascinates you about it

Permission from you that I can use any or all of the material you provide me in my work, and in any book, article, or creative communication I may put together

I reserve the right to edit as needed. You will be provided a copy of anything of yours that goes into a book before publication, so you can double-check for accuracy. Give me your full name, e-mail address, postal mailing address, and phone number. Let me know if I can use your name as given, or if you would prefer a "pen" name instead (state whatever name you want me to use in lieu of your real name).

Send all of this to

P. M. H. Atwater, L.H.D.
P. O. Box 7691
Charlottesville, VA 22906-7691

or email atwater@cinemind.com.

My website is www.pmhatwater.com.

Any material sent to me without "permission to use" will be returned immediately. The cut-off date for this project is March 11, 2016.

References

Raymond A. Moody, Jr., MD, Ph.D. *Life After Life*. Covington, GA; Mockingbird Books, 1975.

Melvin Morse, MD, with Paul Perry. *Closer to the Light: Learning from the Near-Death Experiences of Children*. New York, NY; Villard Books, 1990.

P. M. H. Atwater, L.H.D. *The New Children and Near-Death Experiences*. Rochester, VT; Bear & Co., 1999/2003.

P. M. H. Atwater, L.H.D. *The Big Book of Near-Death Experiences*. Charlottesville, VA; Hampton Roads, 2007

Author Bio

P.M.H Atwater, L.H.D.

P.M.H. is one of the original researchers in the field of near-death studies, having begun her work in 1978 (shortly after moving to Virginia), and is a pioneer in subjects like near-death experiences, the aftereffects of spiritual experiences, transformations of consciousness, reality shifts, future memory, and modern generations of children and how they differ from previous generations. Atwater did freelance assignments for many periodicals nationwide, including *Sunset* magazine. She wrote the column "Coming Back" for the *Vital Signs* magazine (1981—1985). She earned her Letters of the Humanities doctorate (L.H.D.) from the International College of Spiritual and Psychic Studies in Montreal, Quebec, Canada, May 19, 1992; and she was awarded an honorary Ph.D. in Therapeutic Counseling in March 2005 from Medicina Alternativa Institute, The Open International University for Complementary Medicines, in Colombo, Sri Lanka. Also in 2005, the International Association for Near-death Studies (IANDS) presented her with an Outstanding Service Award, and the National Association of Transpersonal Hypnotherapists awarded her a Lifetime Achievement Award. She has been a Prayer Chaplain since 2004.

P.M.H. retired as an active fieldworker in near-death studies in 2010, calling for the entire field to recognize near-death states as part of the larger genre of transformations of consciousness and how they change people. Her last book on this subject, which gives her summation, is *Near-Death Experiences: The Rest of The Story* (Hampton/Red Wheel, March 2011). For the first time, she also wrote the entire story of her own three near-death experiences (*I Died Three Times in 1977 —The Complete Story*), which was published as an e-book in August 2010.

How to See Spirit
A Personal and Scientific Investigation

Rhonda R. E. Schwartz, M.A.

This talk is dedicated to the "Sacred Promise Team," who have shown us so much and who continue to inspire us and make this research possible.

> *Vision is the art of seeing what is invisible to others.*
> Jonathan Swift

Abstract

The purpose of this presentation is to consider how it is possible under certain conditions to see spirit. We will consider two aspects of seeing spirit:
1. How it is possible to see spirit naturally with our eyes
2. How this process may be replicated with contemporary optical sciences technology

Also included in this talk will be my surprising personal journey as someone who has
3. Learned to see spirit
4. Used that knowledge and ability to join forces with a team of spirits in an attempt to develop technology that will enable those on the other side to be seen and heard using modern equipment

Overview: There is an Art and a Science to Seeing Spirit

What follows is an overview of my presentation, as summarized in Table 1, followed by a brief summary of each heading.

Table 1

Introduction
Who am I?
Lenz's Law Demonstration and Lesson
Early history with my mother—I did not see spirit then
From one to multiple spirits—I still did not see spirit
When did I first see spirit?
How did my seeing spirit develop?
How do I currently see spirit?
Six types of evidence for seeing spirit categorized by Dr. Schwartz
What I have learned about seeing spirit

Introduction

Dr. Gary Schwartz and I met not far from here at Duke University in 2006. We married seven months later. Our research has evolved and grown over the years to include a team of hypothesized, respected spirits who work with us on the development of spirit communication technology. The core team consists of six spirits:

    A. Two scientists: Albert Einstein and David Bohm

    B. Two lay persons: Susy Smith and Marcia Eklund, my mother

C. Two entertainers: Harry Houdini and a person whose identity we keep anonymous for the time being, but who we refer to as "Peter Taylor."

One quality they shared in life, and continue to share in the afterlife, is a deep commitment to human welfare and education.

Who am I?

I received a Bachelor of Fine Arts degree and a Master of Arts degree from Northern Illinois University. As an artist I enjoyed painting with pastels and mixed media. For twenty-three years after college, I worked for a major company, eventually serving in quality control, monitoring and helping to maintain service assurance levels, and as an international rules and regulations specialist. I wrote *Love Eternal*, a book in which I tell my account of my mother's communications with me after she passed.

Lenz's Law Demonstration and Lesson

I will give a live demonstration of a surprising natural phenomenon that shows Lenz's Law in action (based on the MIT demonstration and explanation at the following link: http://video.mit.edu/watch/physics-demo-lenzs-law-with-copper-pipe-10268/) to illustrate the point that science must be behind any occurrence that happens, no matter how seemingly inexplicable, if in fact it is real. The comparison is that if survival of consciousness, mediumship, and seeing spirit are real, there must be scientific laws providing for and governing how they work.

A discussion of other variables will also be covered, such as

- One's Interest level
- Possible biological and physiological advantages
- How busy one's life is
- Whether there are spirits around you with a strong need or reason to connect

- Belief systems that may help or hinder one's ability to see spirit

Early History with My Mother—I Did Not See Spirit Then

In my book *Love Eternal,* I report dozens of instances where Marcia Eklund, my deceased mother, came to me, which strongly indicated that she was still here. One example was of her being able to tell me the precise location of some important papers that were missing. Another example was precognitive, where she told me in advance that there was going to be a meaningful message on television that night—and there was. It should be noted, at this point I was not seeing spirit.

From One to Multiple Spirits—I Still Did Not See Spirit

The important role a development circle played in my connecting with spirits other than my mother will be briefly discussed. Also, I will share a specific dream in which Albert Einstein appeared to give me information in the dream that was later able to be verified in real life.

When Did I First See Spirit?

One spirit, Peter Taylor, deserves special credit for showing me that I could see spirit. The first sighting occurred in the fall of 2009. I will share that surprising and life-changing story and how it led to our current research with our spirit team. It is noteworthy that over the years I have seen and worked with Peter Taylor on over a thousand occasions.

How Did My Seeing Spirit Develop?

I will talk about exercises I developed to try to see spirit more regularly and accurately, and the hundreds of hours of scientific prodding and analyses by Gary as he tried to learn the mechanics of my perceptual processes as well as "the physics of spirit and their reality."

How Do I Currently See Spirit?

Specific steps and procedures will be outlined that I have found helpful, including

1. Focusing on them and letting the surroundings fade to the background
2. Consciously connecting with them emotionally
3. Allowing for the image to grow as the session builds

I will also consider

4. Some of the pitfalls in attempting to see spirit
5. What to expect when seeing spirit
6. What spirit typically looks like to me

Six Types of Evidence Categorized by Dr. Schwartz

Table 2 lists six categories that Dr. Schwartz has deemed essential evidence to draw the conclusion that seeing spirit is a real phenomenon; i.e., it is not all one's imagination.

Table 2

Six Types of Evidence for Verifying Seeing Spirit

Type I: Independent Mediumship Verifications
Type II: Spontaneous and Requested Validations of Information
Type III: Synchronicity Validations
Type IV: Experiments Comparing Imagining versus Seeing Spirits
Type V: Evidence from Brain Imaging
Type VI: Validations with Technology

Type I: Independent Mediumship Verifications

On numerous occasions—and under blinded conditions—we have asked mediums to attempt to connect with and identify members of our Spirit Team. These mediums were kept blind to the identities of our hypothesized team members.

At present we have worked with seven different mediums. They were all, seemingly effortlessly and to various degrees, able to describe individual spirit members of our team, including

- Their personalities
- What they did in life
- Their interest and involvement in this work

Each of the six primary members of our Spirit Team has been so identified two (or more) times. Some highly evidential (as well as amusing) examples will be shared.

Type II: Spontaneous and Requested Validations of Information

Accounts of instances when spirits came through with information that could subsequently be researched and discovered to be accurate is one of the most scientifically convincing types of evidence of seeing spirit. Sometimes the evidence is spontaneous, whereas other times specific information is requested. Also, sometimes the information is personal in nature, and at other times it is work-related.

In one instance Peter Taylor spontaneously said to me, "Something is going on with my family." Prompted by this surprising comment, I did a search on the internet and found that it was his birthday and his family was celebrating the occasion.

Another time, in response to Gary asking a question of David Bohm about an experiment, David was able to predict accurately and explain

1. How the data from a particular experiment we were conducting with them was going to have to be analyzed

2. To what specific degree they were going to be able to affect the equipment (see more detail below)

At present, these types of information validations total more than 40. They have occurred spontaneously and sporadically over the years.

Importantly, when they have happened, they have virtually always been accurate, sometimes in multiple ways, and sometimes in ways that have furthered the work in directions we could not have anticipated. Simply stated, these instances have not been "cherry picked" because of their accuracy; they represent the full set of instances.

Type III: Synchronicity Validations

Synchronicity is one of the most personally convincing types of evidence we have that spirit is present in our lives and actively participating in this process. I do not know if we would still be connected to the spirits we are working with if it were not for this form of apparent communication. Though it may be hard to fathom, we have witnessed (and documented) hundreds (if not thousands) of spirit-related synchronicity validations over the years of doing this work with them.

One of the earliest, most startling, and evidential synchronicities occurred shortly after Peter had first come to us. I had spent a few concentrated hours working with Peter and a few other members of the team. Then, in the last half hour of this session I did a "mirroring" exercise solely with him.

I would first ask him to take different poses, and I would try to mirror what he was doing.

We would take turns, so then I would take different poses, and then carefully look to see if I could detect him mirroring the stances I was taking.

During the course of the session, Peter actually coined the term "MIME" exercise.

We finished around five o'clock and I said to Peter, "You know, if you want me to continue doing this with you I'm going to need a really big sign as proof that you are here. Because otherwise it is ridiculous for me to think that we are doing this together, and it's a waste of my time when I could be doing something else!"

Little did I know that my request and the importance of the term MIME would very quickly be addressed with not one, but two highly improbable and meaningful synchronicities.

To my astonishment, 10 minutes later as I was driving home, approaching a main intersection near our house, I could see a man literally standing in the middle of the busy intersection striking poses like I had just been doing with this spirit.

I couldn't help but notice that this man was dressed and looked strikingly similar to how Peter looked and dressed in life (it was a very distinctive look).

I pulled over into a parking lot and took a picture with my cell phone. It was quite a spectacle, and shortly afterwards the police arrived and escorted the man away.

Interestingly, when I reached home and went to tell Gary about this stunning synchronicity, he happened to be watching a documentary on TV featuring a person doing mime!

This second synchronicity reinforced the original synchronicity.

More recently (January 2015), one morning Gary and I were in our living room and he asked me to call David for an impromptu meeting and experiment. What ensued was an intense session of Gary instructing me to look at a physical object in the room and to intentionally overlay it with a complex imaginary image. He then asked me to overlay that same complex imaginary image on David to see what, if any, the differences were.

Gary was questioning me about my perceptions and whether it felt like I was seeing reflection or emission when I was looking at spirit. Gary reached a tentative conclusion and asked me to ask David if this conclusion was correct. I was silent for a while, attempting to hear what David was saying, at which point Gary asked, "So what is David doing?"

When I looked over, I saw David throw a handful of confetti into the air, something I had never seen him (or any spirit, for that matter) do. David's throwing of the confetti was timed so that I felt it indicated that he was saying an emphatic "Yes!" that Gary was correct.

What gave weight to my seeing him throw the confetti was that over the next few days we were flooded with more than a dozen instances of confetti appearing on sports shows, on television commercials, in print ads, etc. Importantly within the next few days those confetti references abruptly decreased to a minimum—a further indication that they were genuine synchronicities.

Type IV: Experiments Comparing Imagination with Seeing Spirit

Gary would often put on his scientist hat and grill me about what I was seeing when I was looking at our Science Team members versus when I was imagining seeing them. Gary would routinely ask questions such as

1. How clearly did I see them?
2. Could I see through them, or were they completely solid, blocking out what was behind them?
3. Were they able to sit in a chair?
4. Could they bring items with them, and then could they leave those items behind?

He would regularly ask me to make ratings of the clarity and intensity of my perceptions, using a 0—10 scale.

We would experiment with changing conditions such as lighting to see if it affected the way I perceived spirit.

The results of our investigations were all considered when designing the equipment we hoped would be able to detect spirits' presence or capture their image.

Type V: Evidence from Brain Imaging

At present one formal brain imaging experiment was performed with me as the subject to determine if there was a difference between when I was imagining spirit versus when I was seeing spirit. EEG brain mapping recordings were performed by two highly skilled clinical and academic neuroscientists—Drs. Johanne Levesque and Mario Beauregard. The test results indicated clear evidence of differences between imagining versus seeing spirit. Interestingly, the findings were consistent with the neuroscience literature distinguishing visual imagination versus actual visual perception.

Type VI: Validation with Technology

Validation of spirits' involvement with us in the use of technology comes in two forms: within the data itself, collected during any given experiment; and from spirit's commentary in advance as to what to expect from the data.

Over the years, Gary has collected more than a thousand hours of sessions with spirit interacting with equipment, discovering that they can affect different types of sensors (including optical, magnetic, electrical, and radiation detectors) to varying degrees of intensity and reliability.

A month prior to the writing of this paper, Gary and our optical sciences engineer created a new system including (1) an elaborate array of optical components, (2) software to collect and analyze the data, and (3) an innovative graphics display to present the information in real time. I had not seen the configuration of the components and had no idea how the system was designed.

Then one day, spontaneously, David told me we were going to have to look in the lower portion of the data; we should ignore the top portion and only look in the troughs, not the crests. During the first test of the experiment I was surprised to see the readout on the monitor was an undulating wave. Without knowing of my communication with David, Gary spontaneously told me that we should be looking for evidence of spirit to show up in the lower portion of the data only.

David spontaneously spoke up during a subsequent session and indicated we were going to have to skim the lower portion of the data, zero in on it and blow it up in order to see them. Gary later confirmed that this is what he had to do.

Not only that, but Gary asked a follow-up question of David: could he tell us the specific magnitude of the effect we could expect to see show up in the data? Again I had no idea of the kind of measurements Gary was using, but I heard a very specific percentage from David, and once again it aligned with the data Gary had collected.

Conclusion: What I Have Learned About Seeing Spirit

What I Have Learned from My Experience

What I've learned from my experience is that spirit is subtle, and realizing this helped me to know what to look for and what to expect when trying to see them.

My experience is that seeing spirit requires practice and focus. It's probably not unlike a singer who has to keep up that skill; even the distinguished opera tenor Luciano Pavarotti used to practice every day and he would warm up before each performance.

Establishing a close personal relationship with the spirits I work with has been essential. I think that is because I feel them as well as hear and see them, so a holistic approach has been very helpful.

In my experience, although they are "thin," meaning transparent, they show up looking like themselves. I do not see them as orbs or simply as energy, although there have been times when I have seen them as energy-like. Most of the time I see them fully formed.

They appear to show up as the same age each time I see them. I trust it is the age of their choosing. They wear clothing, often the same clothes, with minor variations, if any.

I meet with our spirit team regularly in the same room, and they typically sit or stand in the same place each time.

I try to be as respectful of their time as I would be of anyone else's, so I try to schedule times with them for meetings or working sessions. Although if something comes up on the spur of the moment, I will reach out to them, and most of the time my experience is that I am able to connect with them.

What I Have Learned Working with Dr. Schwartz

What I've learned from working with my scientist husband Dr. Schwartz is—using a scale from 0 to 10—my perception of seeing spirit typically ranges in density and clarity between a 2 and a 6.

If they wear white, it tends to pop.

They minimally block whatever they stand in front of.

They have minimal ability to affect the physical world, but they can occasionally do so under certain circumstances.

Synchronicity is one of the best ways they have of letting us know they are here.

An imaginary projection (e.g., when Gary asks me to create a poster image of them) is stronger and easier for me to see than they are, and the imaginary poster forms effortlessly and instantaneously. In contrast, seeing spirit often requires effort and focus, and their image quality and intensity builds with time.

Importantly, I can sometimes be "fooled" by my "monkey mind" (the term I use for my imagination). Therefore I have learned that we must rely on various combinations of the six categories of evidence to justify concluding that what I am seeing is "more than my imagination."

What I Have Learned from Spirit

What I've learned from our spirit team is not only that they are still here, but that they **"really"** want us to know they are still here, and they have things they want to tell us. We recognize that they are a special group of spirits, and that what we are learning from them may in some ways be unique to them.

I have learned that they are full of surprises ... and that they have boundless creativity in the diverse ways in which they have found, and continue to find, to communicate with us.

They don't have all the answers. They have sometimes been wrong in how they have expected us to perceive them. And they have been surprised themselves by some things as well.

The most important thing I have learned from these spirits, however, is that if (1) I am in a quiet setting and (2) I am able to be in a focused, receiving mode, and (3) I call them, **they always show up**. This is not an exaggeration; I literally mean one hundred percent of the time.

Why is this?

They have convinced us that it is their choice to be here. They have indicated that they have an agenda and a commitment to what can best be described as a "higher purpose" and "grand plan." Moreover, they have made it their mission to awaken people to the fact that life continues after death and that they are still here and wish to be of service.

And they told us (as well as demonstrated), time and time again, that when we call, they choose to "drop everything" and show up.

We have made a solemn promise to them that we will do all we can to follow what they are showing us, and requesting of us, to do. We in turn have requested the same commitment from them, and they have repeatedly shown us that this is their intention and commitment. And this is why we have come to call them the "Sacred Promise Team."[1]

Endnotes

[1] Schwartz, G. E. (2011). *The Sacred Promise: How Science is Discovering Spirits Collaboration with Us in Our Daily Lives*. Oregon: Beyond Words (Atria Books / Simon & Schuster).

Author Bio

Rhonda R. E. Schwartz, M.A.

Rhonda received bachelor of fine arts and master of arts degrees from Northern Illinois University. She also worked for a major company for 23 years serving in a variety of capacities including quality control and as an international specialist. Being an artist and mystic at heart, as well as being science minded, she is happy to now be able to devote herself full-time to nurturing her evolving relationship with a team of spirits and her pursuit of trying to understand the physics of spirit and the science of the greater spiritual reality.

Continuing PSI Experiences Suggestive of an Afterlife

Sally Rhine Feather, Ph.D.

Abstract

The Rhine Research Center has a long history of interest in the survival or afterlife question. Among the large collection of spontaneous psi experiences of various types and forms that have been continuously reported to the Rhine Research Center over the years, there are many that can be interpreted as after-death communications. What has been learned from studying these, as well as the need for further study, is discussed. Examples are given of the more provocative cases, such as reports of young children, experiences shared by more than one person, or the unexplained physical phenomena noted at times of death or dying, now reported more frequently than in the past. The need for better guidelines for helping evaluate what may be after-death communication is noted, and an appeal for further reports is made to the audience.

The Rhine Research Center is known for decades of scientific research establishing the validity of psi experiences such as telepathy, clairvoyance, precognition and psychokinesis. Lesser known is that this work developed out of the early interest of the founders, JB and Louisa Rhine, in the age-old question of whether some aspect of consciousness could survive bodily death. It was only after being stymied on how to find a definitive answer to the afterlife question that JB's Lab team turned their attention to studying ESP ability of the living. It seemed the first issue to be resolved in determining the source of the mediumistic readings they had brought to Duke University for proper evaluation.

The afterlife issue continued to be considered numerous times during the history of the RRC, as is documented in various talks, conferences and publications of the times. And in the mid 60s JB expedited the founding of a separate foundation to address afterlife issues, the Psychical Research Foundation, that was led for years by Bill Roll and now by Jerry Conser, a current member of the Rhine Board.

In 1960 Louisa E. Rhine reported a case-based study bearing on the afterlife question in which she compared the presumed motivation of the living "percipient" to that of deceased "agent" in a selected sample of spontaneous psi reports of apparent after-death communications. She developed a 4-level grading system where the highest grade was assigned to cases where the deceased agent's motivation to send a message was so predominant that it seemed unlikely the experience could be attributed to that of the living percipient. While far from definitive, this was an ingenuous effort for evaluating what could constitute evidence for the afterlife, although the number of reports in Grade 4 was relatively low.

Spontaneous psi experiences that suggest the afterlife continue to be reported to the RRC as in Louisa's day, covering the same variety of sensory modalities, although today's case reports include a striking increase in so-called psychokinetic reports coinciding with the time of a loved one's death or dying. Examples of the various modern reports will be given, including those that are shared by more than one person, by young children or by pets. The need for more focused collection and analysis of SPE's suggestive of the afterlife is stressed, along with the need to develop clearer criteria of evaluation that may provide helpful guidelines to the public. The audience is invited to send suggestive case reports and observations to the RRC for its ongoing case collection and study.

Author Bio

Sally Rhine Feather, Ph.D.

Sally Rhine Feather Ph.D., retired director of the Rhine Research Center, is the eldest daughter of JB and Louisa E. Rhine, the founders of modern parapsychology. She has maintained a strong interest in parapsychology since childhood, when she often served as a child subject at the early Duke Parapsychology Lab. She worked there as a research assistant after college and then again after obtaining a doctorate in experimental psychology from Duke University (1967). Some of her research involved studying psi abilities of animals, the correlation of memory and ESP performance, and the help-hinder effects in a PK task.

Following another lifelong interest, Dr. Feather obtained further training in clinical psychology at UNC in 1969 and devoted the next several decades to clinical work in mental health centers and private practice both in North Carolina and then in New Jersey.

A move back to North Carolina in the early 1990s with husband Bill Hendrickson allowed Dr. Feather to get re-involved in what is now the Rhine Research Center. Since 1994 she has served in various administrative capacities, including the Board of Directors, and for several years as volunteer Executive Director. She co-authored a popular book on ESP experiences (St. Martins, 2005) and received the 2010 Career Achievement Award from the Parapsychology Association. Now in her retirement years, Dr. Feather is co-authoring a book on the selected letters of her father and working with a RRC team in a qualitative analysis of spontaneous psi experiences.

Spirit and the Soul Phone
Who will use it "Here" and "There"?

Gary E. Schwartz, Ph.D.

This address is dedicated to the "Sacred Promise Team," who inspire this research and make it possible.

Never doubt that a small group of thoughtful, committed citizens can change the world; indeed, it's the only thing that ever has.

Margaret Mead, Ph.D.

Abstract

In my Keynote Address for the 38th Annual Conference of the Academy for Spiritual and Consciousness Studies on July 12, 2014, in Scottsdale, Arizona, I gave a presentation titled "Pioneering Soul Phone Communications." In that lecture I provided an overview to a set of five criteria that collectively led me to the controversial conclusion that the development of a soul phone technology is inevitable. The five criteria are

1. Logic and scientific theory
2. Observations and evidence
3. Community of credible people who have also come to this conclusion
4. Direct personal experience with the technology

5. No responsible reasons for rejecting (i.e., being strongly skeptical of) factors 1-4

The present lecture briefly reviews these five criteria and then considers both the rationale (Criteria 1) and scientific evidence (Criteria 2) for the existence of an extraordinary group of "beings on the other side" (herein simply referred to as "spirits") who are actively collaborating on this work. Not only are They committed to helping us create a reliable and valid soul phone technology, but They are devoted to seeing it applied to humanity and the planet for the best and highest good.

My wife, Rhonda Schwartz, and I refer to these collaborators in spirit as "The Sacred Promise Team," named after my 2011 book of that title, *The Sacred Promise: How Science is Discovering Spirits Collaboration with Us in Our Daily Lives*.

The present lecture acknowledges their participation and honors their inspiring collaboration in this work.

Brief Review of the Five Criteria

As listed above, there are five factors—what we can think of as a "five fingers test"—that can point to a given conclusion as being true. I've come to realize that if all five criteria have been met in a given instance, that under these specific circumstances, logic dictates we hold the belief as likely being true.

In fact, if all five criteria have been met, I suggest that it is our ethical and moral responsibility to conclude that something is probably true—even if we do not like the conclusion, and even if the conclusion goes against our long-held beliefs and dogmas.

Criterion 1: Logic and Theory

The first criterion is "logic and scientific theory." Some super-skeptics make the extreme statement that no established scientific theories exist that predict that—and explain how—life after death exists. It turns out that this conclusion is indisputably false. In fact, there are some very easy ways for us to understand as lay people how logic and scientific theory supports the idea that photonic energy and information has a "kind of immortality" in the "vacuum of space" and therefore can be detected with the appropriate technology under controlled conditions.

If (1) we go out in the dark at night, and (2) we are away from the city of lights, and (3) there's no full moon or clouds, we can see thousands of stars with the naked eye. And with contemporary telescopes we can view billions of galaxies, each containing billions of stars. It is well accepted that all of this light has been traveling for millions or billions of years through space, and it is all still there. In fact, everywhere we look in space there are billions, if not trillions, of stars in every direction.

Think about this: all of this light is crisscrossing in the "vacuum of space," and it doesn't get mixed up. If it did, and if it became degraded, then when you and I looked up at the night sky, we would see mush. We don't see mush; what we see is a "history of starlight" extending back in time billions of years.

It is because of this fact that we can have the core sciences of astronomy and astrophysics. Both logic and theoretical physics tells us that light has a "kind of immortality" in terms of the storage of information and energy in the "vacuum of space."

Logic also tells us that although the vacuum may be "empty" in terms of matter, it is full of the detailed energy and information of the light from trillions of stars crisscrossing in all directions.

Though this may sound astounding, if not controversial—that the light from trillions of stars (and hence the light from everything else, including our light) is preserved in space—the truth is that this fact only becomes controversial when we deeply think about it.

However, during the day when we look up at the sky, and if there are no clouds, we do not see any stars; instead what we see is a blue sky. The question arises, what happened to all that starlight? What happened to all the thousands of stars we can see with the naked eye and the trillions of stars we can see with telescopes?

Have they all disappeared? Or, are they all still there, it's just that we can't see them because we are blinded by the brightness of the closest star in our vicinity, which we call the sun?

The answer is the latter. Moreover, this is why we cannot see most of the stars when we are in cities, because the city lights (termed light pollution) interfere with us seeing the dim starlight.

The take-home message—the sound bite—that first occurred to me in the early 1980s when I was a young professor at Yale University is this: *Sometimes we need to go into the dark in order to see the light.*

Let me repeat this: *Sometimes we need to go into the dark in order to see the light.*

This is why mediums learn to meditate. This is why we learn to go into quiet spaces. This is why at 3 a.m. or 4 a.m. we often are the most receptive to subtle information and energy.

Hence, logic and theory points to the possibility that light has a kind of immortality.

By the way, if you and I stand out in the night sky and look up at the stars, you know what's happening with the light that is reflected off our bodies? It goes out into space as well. We know this to be a fact because spy satellites can see us walking on a sandy beach or wherever we are. And our light is just like light from distant stars; it keeps going and going too.

Our light is constantly expanding out into the vacuum of space. Not just our *reflected* light, but *all* the frequencies that comprise our bodies *radiate* into space as well. There is a history of our *emitted photon radiation* that continues into the vacuum of space. In other words, both logic and physics support the idea that our energy and information extend into space and continue indefinitely. If it still exists as photonic energy and information, then in principle it can be detected by suitable technology.

Criterion 2: Observations and Evidence

The second criterion is "observations and evidence." At present time there is a voluminous amount of research literature spread across many different areas that is consistent with the life after death hypothesis. This includes documented cases of near-death experiences reported worldwide, reincarnation research primarily conducted at the University of Virginia, controlled mediumship research in my laboratory and other laboratories in the U.S. and Europe, and newly emerging research using state-of-the-art technology to detect the presence of spirit.

The _combination_ of this evidence points inexorably to the conclusion that our consciousness continues after physical death just like the light from distant stars continues after a given star has "died."

I have published three books investigating whether any mediums are real, and if so, can we interpret these findings as evidence of communication with spirit after physical death? In brief, the conclusion from all this evidence is that *some* mediums are real (Schwartz, 2002; 2005; 2011) and the simplest and most parsimonious explanation that explains the greatest amount of the evidence is the survival of consciousness hypothesis.

Of course, there are some mediums who are fakes, and we must be able to distinguish between genuine and fake mediums. I realized that "if you can't beat them, then join them." Hence, I learned how to become a fake medium. I purchased secret books on how to become a fake medium. I took a course in how to become a fake medium by a skilled "psychic entertainer" (a mental magician). In fact, I became a pretty good fake medium. Armed with this knowledge and skills, I could design controlled research that could eliminate the "tricks of the trade." In those carefully designed experiments, only genuine mediums would be able to produce accurate and statistically significant information about specific deceased persons.

Here is not the place to review all the single-blind, double-blind, and even triple-blind experimental procedures. They are described in detail in my three books as well as in research published by other investigators. What is important to understand here is that (1) a sizeable body of research has been conducted documenting the validity of specific mediums, that (2) the totality of the evidence can best be explained in terms of life after death, and that (3) aspects of the energy of spirit detected by mediums can also be detected by state-of-the-art optical sciences technology.

Criterion 3: Acceptance by Trustworthy and Credible People

The third criterion is the existence of highly knowledgeable, trustworthy and credible people who have reached a given conclusion. I am privileged to know many people who are highly successful and trustworthy who have come to believe not only that life after death is real, but that the development of a soul phone is likely.

These people meet what I call the "Seven S" Criteria. They are

1. Smart, *and*
2. Successful, *and*
3. Skeptical, as in questioning, *and*
4. Sophisticated in their thinking, *and*
5. Savvy, meaning that they're knowledgeable and discerning, *and*
6. Sane (e.g., they are not psychotic), *and finally*,
7. Straight, meaning that they have integrity, they are truth-seekers, and they care about being honest with themselves, their loved ones, and colleagues

When people like this believe that something is true, it is worth taking their conclusions seriously.

Criterion 4: Direct Personal Experience

The fourth criterion is direct personal experience. For most people, direct personal experience is the ultimate criteria for deciding whether something is true or not.

I have been blessed to have had more direct personal experiences with genuine research mediums than most researchers in the history of science. I have worked closely with over thirty gifted and credible persons who I refer to as "Michael Jordans of the Mediumship World."

Moreover, I have been blessed to have had more direct personal experience with specific spirits attempting to influence state-of-the-art optical sciences technology over the past 6 years than virtually any scientist who has ever lived. I have collected many hundreds of hours of documented observations of apparent communication that are way beyond statistical chance. Some of this evidence is included in my presentation.

Criterion 5:   No responsible reasons to reject (i.e., be strongly skeptical of) Criteria 1-4

Responsible science requires responsible skepticism, meaning, for us to be thorough in considering alternative explanations for all aspects of research—from logic and theory, through experimental design and data collection, to analyses and interpretations of the observations. Responsible scientists (and responsible thinkers in general) will take the time to "take stock" and carefully review what they are investigating.

When we engage in this process concerning Criteria 1-4 above, as applied to the question of life after death and the feasibility of developing a soul phone, we find that each of the criteria passes muster. There are no "smoking guns" that seriously question the soul phone hypothesis. We can conclude that for this area of research and potential application, it passes the "five fingers test."

Who are the members of the Sacred Promise Team, and what is their motivation?

In light of the above considerations, it becomes justified and meaningful to (1) examine who comprise the Sacred Promise Team, and (2) determine what their apparent motivations are for collaborating on this project.

My presentation reviews how a small group of "post-physical people" have been actively working with us to attempt to develop a reliable soul phone technology. Though some may find this information hard to accept, the totality of the evidence indicates that the group includes two distinguished scientists (David Bohm, Ph.D., and Albert Einstein, Ph.D.), two lay scholars (Susy Smith and Marcia Eklund), and two celebrity entertainers (Harry Houdini and "Peter Taylor"—a pseudonym).

However, many may find it even harder to accept the fact that the totality of the evidence indicates that a group of "angels," including Sophia, Metatron, Michael, Gabriel, Uriel, and Ariel, are actively involved in the research as well. The presentation will review some of the evidence that justifies this hypothesis.

Their collective motivation is to (1) scientifically establish that survival of consciousness and a greater spiritual reality exists, (2) demonstrate how love and caring is their driving force, and (3) illustrate how this core knowledge can serve as the "unifying motivation" for bringing humanity together for the purpose of healing the species and the planet, and achieving personal and global peace, before it is too late.

Whereas the general public will likely choose to use the anticipated soul phone technology primarily to maintain their ongoing relationships with close family members and friends who have physically died (e.g., Spirit Facebook), there are numerous other fundamental applications of the technology, including (1) obtaining information and advice spanning personal and scientific areas to business and governmental areas, (2) correcting errors of history, (3) seeking amends for past events, and (4) providing motivation and inspiration for humanity to wake up and collectively raise our consciousness accordingly.

My special interest is in number 4. Despite science's documentation of the perils of ever-increasing population growth, pollution, and associated climate change, and the public's increasing awakening to the reality of these perils, there is little inspiration for people to seek common solutions to these pressing challenges in a manner that will foster the evolution of our species as a whole.

Some of us working in the broad area of afterlife science and the existence of a greater spiritual reality see the promise of these discoveries potentially serving in the role of providing an essential unifying inspiration—especially if this unifying inspiration comes from the greater spiritual reality itself. If current efforts to develop a reliable soul are successful, it will be possible for the first time in human history for people all across the globe, from all cultures and all walks of life, to receive guidance and inspiration from their most respected and revered leaders. Many mediums have independently reported to me that groups "on the other side" are coming together for the purpose of fostering this expanded unified consciousness.

If any organization has the potential to foster this grand mission, it is the Academy for Consciousness and Spiritual Studies.

References

Schwartz, G. E. (2002). *The Afterlife Experiments: Breakthrough scientific evidence for life after death*. New York, NY: Atria Books / Simon & Schuster.

Schwartz, G. E. (2005). *The Truth about Medium: Extraordinary experiments with the real Alison Dubois of NBC's Medium and other remarkable psychics*. Charlottesville, VA: Hampton Roads.

Schwartz, G. E. (2011). *The Sacred Promise: How science is discovering spirit's collaboration with us in our daily lives*. New York, NY: Atria Books.

Author Bio

Gary E. Schwartz, Ph.D.

Gary E. Schwartz is a Professor of Psychology, Medicine, Neurology, Psychiatry, and Surgery, and Director of the Laboratory for Advances in Consciousness and Health, at the University of Arizona. He is also the Chairman of Eternea (www.eternea.org). He received his Ph.D. from Harvard University in 1971 and served as an Assistant Professor of Psychology at Harvard before moving to Yale University in 1976. There he was a Professor of Psychology and Psychiatry, Director of the Yale Psychophysiology Center, and co-Director of the Yale Behavioral Medicine Clinic before moving to the University of Arizona in 1988. He has published more than 450 scientific papers and chapters, including six papers in the journal *Science*, and co-edited 11 academic books. He is a Fellow of the American Psychological Association, the American Psychological Society, the Academy of Behavioral Medicine Research, and the Society of Behavioral Medicine. His research integrating body, mind, and spirit has been featured in numerous documentaries and television shows, including the documentary *The Life After Death Project* (2013), produced and directed by Paul Davids. His books for the general public include *The Afterlife Experiments*, *The G.O.D. Experiments*, *The Energy Healing Experiments*, and *The Sacred Promise*.

For more about Gary, visit drgaryschwartz.com.

Edgar Cayce on Dreams
Your Pathway to Personal Guidance and Intuition

Kevin J. Todeschi, M.A.

Abstract

Edgar Cayce, the most documented psychic of all time, was one of the first individuals in the West to consistently recommend that average individuals from every imaginable background and life experience learn how to examine and interpret their dreams. From Cayce's perspective, not only was everyone best suited for her or his own dream analysis, but dreams provided a constant source of information regarding every imaginable area of life: problem solving, creativity, finances, relationships, health and even intuitive insights into the future. Most importantly, Cayce contended that it was possible to get specific guidance to specific questions in the dream process.

It was really the work of Edgar Cayce that prompted my own interest in dreams nearly 35 years ago. While taking part in an ecumenical spiritual discussion group that examined Cayce's information on such topics as meditation and soul growth, members of the group informed me that they regularly asked for dream guidance—as was suggested by the Cayce information—and that our "homework assignment" for the week was to write out the question, "What do I need to work on spiritually?" and dream the answer.

Quite honestly, I had never heard of such a possibility, and I was certainly not aware of remembering very many dreams, but as I was new to the group and wanted to fit in, I agreed to give it a try. The first night I dutifully wrote out my question, read it before going to sleep, and went to bed.

The next morning—nothing! I wondered whether or not I would be the only one returning to my weekly group without a dream but I followed the same process the second night, wrote out the question, "What do I need to work on spiritually?," read it a couple of times and went to sleep. That night I had a dream:

I was in Egypt. (I had never been in Egypt before!) I was coming out of the Great Pyramid at Giza when all of a sudden someone I knew from A.R.E. (the Edgar Cayce organization) said to a crowd of people: "By the way, Jesus taught Kevin some dance steps, and Kevin would like to show them to you now."

Although I was stunned by such an announcement, as I knew almost nothing about dancing and I had certainly never had a conversation with Jesus, I decided that since everyone was watching me, I'd better come up with something.

As I was standing there wondering what to do, a number of people started sitting down in front of me on the Giza Plateau. One of these individuals was someone I knew that I absolutely did not like. As this person passed in front of me to sit down, I heard myself think [excuse the language]: "What an ASS!"

As soon as I had had the thought, I looked up over the horizon and there standing on the edge of the plateau was Jesus. As soon as I saw him, I heard his thoughts, and he thought back what I had just voiced in my thoughts. A moment later, I heard Jesus' words in my head: "More than anything else, you need to work on your thoughts."

I awoke the next morning absolutely convinced that I had received direct guidance regarding my question, "What do I need to work on spiritually?" From that day forward, I became an enthusiast of dreams.

Edgar Cayce has been called the "father of holistic medicine," "the Sleeping Prophet," and "the most documented psychic of all time." For forty-three years of his adult life, Cayce was able to enter into a self-induced sleep state and provide psychic information, called "readings," to virtually any question imaginable. He was documented with an accuracy rate in excess of 85% for such things as remote viewing health diagnosis, exceeding the average accurate diagnosis for modern-day physicians after an initial visit (Cayce/Cayce 1971, 24). In addition to subjects such as health, philosophy, spirituality and psychic ability, much of the Cayce material deals with dreams and dream interpretation. That information first opened up the world of dreams to me and provided a foundation and an understanding that has stood firm for decades.

Edgar Cayce emphasized the importance of working with dreams, stating as early as 1923 that attempting to understand what he called the subconscious, the psychic, and the soul forces of each individual should be "the great study for the human family." The rationale from Cayce's perspective was that through the study of the subconscious and psychic part of ourselves we would come to an understanding of the nature of the soul, our connection to one another and our relationship with the Creator.

Almost 900 of the more than 14,000 Cayce readings on file at Cayce's Association for Research and Enlightenment (www.edgarcayce.org) deal with the subject of dreams and dream interpretation. Generally, when Edgar Cayce was asked to discuss the meaning of a dream, his wife would simply hold a copy of the dream in her hand and ask that the dream be interpreted — without the dream itself ever being read! Even more amazing is the fact that on numerous occasions when Cayce was provided with an individual's request for interpretation, he would remind the dreamer of forgotten portions of his or her own dream!

In terms of the dream material, one of Cayce's most involved enthusiasts was a wealthy, young Jewish stock broker named Morton Blumenthal, who received more than 500 dream interpretation readings for himself and members of his immediate family. Extremely interested in the nature of the soul and each individual's relationship to God, one of Morton's dreams explored this very topic in a humorous vein.

Morton dreamed that he was in his apartment in New York City. Suddenly the doorbell rang and his maid went to answer the door. She announced the presence of a "distinguished visitor" and Morton jumped to his feet in exhilaration with the sudden knowledge that God Himself had come to call. Morton ran up to God and embraced Him with a hug. God's appearance was very businesslike. He was clean-shaven and clean-cut, wore an expensive suit and a derby hat. He also seemed strong and intelligent, just the sort of man with whom Morton would like to do business.

Because God was visiting, Morton decided to give Him a tour around the apartment. Things went well enough until Morton realized they were approaching the living room and that he had mistakenly left his liquor cabinet half-open. Understanding that God was omniscient, Morton decided to reveal everything rather than try to hide his liquor supply. He flung the cabinet wide open and pointed out the bottles by stating, "In case of sickness." God's reply was matter of fact: "You are very well prepared!"

Later, when asked for an interpretation, Cayce stated that much of Morton's dream indicated that each and every individual could have a personal relationship with the Divine. This interpretation becomes obvious when we consider that God comes to meet us in the form that we might best recognize Him, that he comes not as some supreme deity but as someone we might relate to, and that the Creator is extremely accepting of us in spite of our imperfections.

The Cayce information on dreams suggests that the guidance we obtain in the dream state often addresses the needs of the individual physically, psychologically/emotionally, and spiritually. In terms of dream guidance regarding the physical, on one occasion Edgar Cayce had been suffering without relief for many days with a serious cold and cough. One night he had a dream in which he saw himself mixing specific ingredients for a cough and cold medicine. Those ingredients were as follows:

• 4 tablespoons boiling water	• 10 drops glycerin
• 1 tablespoon honey	• 2 drops creosote
• 1 tablespoon simple syrup	• 1 teaspoon syrup of horehound
• 15 drops tolu in solution	• 30 drops compound tincture benzoin
• 2 ounces of whiskey	

Cayce reading #294-189, report 23

Upon awakening, he acquired the necessary ingredients, made the remedy, and found that it gave him immediate relief.

On another occasion, a woman who was very upset about the health of her mother who was suffering from a number of physical complaints dreamed that her mother appeared to her and said, "You should go to the osteopath. You ought to be ashamed of yourself! If [your husband] wants you to go to the osteopath, you should go!" (Cayce reading 136-45)

When the woman asked Edgar Cayce about the dream in a reading, Cayce replied that it was actually her mother who needed to see the osteopath and the dream had come to the dreamer as guidance regarding what she could do to assist her mother.

In terms of a physical dream in my own life, when I was a student at the University of Colorado, I was living in one of the oldest dorms, which always seemed to have a terrible draft in the winter. One night when it was especially cold, the phone rang and it was my grandmother who asked how I was doing. I must have complained about the cold because a week later my grandmother mailed me an electric blanket, which I began using immediately. Each night, I left the blanket plugged in all night and felt warm for the first time that winter.

However, sometime later, I found myself feeling tired and very lethargic each morning upon awakening. Since I had always awakened feeling energized and refreshed, I wondered whether or not there was a problem, and even whether I should see a doctor. One night I had a dream.

I saw myself standing in the bathroom in my grandmother's house, looking in the mirror. I had my electric blanket draped over my shoulders and around my body. Suddenly, I opened up the blanket and stared in the mirror. I was horrified to see that my body was covered with hundreds of leeches.

Obviously, the electric blanket was causing some kind of interruption with my own electrical system, so from that day forward I would plug in the blanket to heat up the bed, and then unplug it before getting in.

In terms of psychology and emotional insights from dreams, on one occasion a man who had been married for less than a couple of years was dealing with marital problems. He had a dream that seemed to involve him and his wife on a journey.

In the dream he was on a train and had apparently been looking out across one of the windows, watching the scenery and the various areas they were traveling through pass by. All at once he realized that his wife was sitting next to the window. She reportedly had a croquet mallet in her hand and was trying to line it up against the window one way and then another, as if to measure something. In a mixture of frustration and irritation the husband called out, "You can't measure it that way!"

During the course of a Cayce reading, the husband asked about his dream. Cayce suggested that the dream was actually guidance as to why the couple was having challenges in their marriage. The husband was trying to measure the success of their marriage by how much money they were making, how much ground they were covering and how successful they were becoming. On the other hand, his wife was trying to measure their marriage by how much fun they were having. They needed to have a collective purpose. (Cayce reading 900-120)

A contemporary example about psychological guidance in dreams occurred in the case of a stock broker who had been involved in the market for about 15 years, but had changed firms about six months earlier. One night he had the following dream.

"In the dream I am at some kind of a barbecue with a bunch of people from work. At first everything is fine. Some people are carrying plates, others have a drink in hand. Everyone is standing around and talking and having a good time. All at once I look down and notice that I am totally naked! I am horrified and feel very insecure, afraid that someone is going to notice. No one seems to notice before the dream ends. However, I wake up still feeling very insecure." (Todeschi 2013, 38)

When the individual was asked how he felt about his job, he replied, "Well, I have been here about six months and they do things a little different than my last firm. Sometimes I worry that I am not catching on as fast as I should."

The dream seemed to be suggesting that, as no one else in the dream noticed he was naked (e.g., unprepared), his insecurities were his own.

In terms of spiritual insights and visionary experiences—Cayce suggested that this is also the level where intuitive experiences can occur—Cayce had a dream in which he saw himself as a tiny speck of sand that began to be elevated as if in a whirlwind. As the piece of sand rose, the rings of the whirlwind became larger and larger, each one encompassing a greater span of space than the one preceding it. There were also spaces between each ring that the sleeping Cayce recognized as the various levels of consciousness development. The image on the next page illustrates this conception of the rings of the whirlwind.

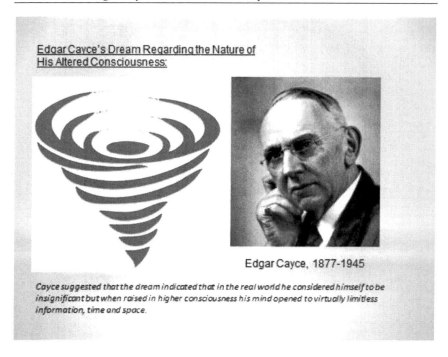

Edgar Cayce's Dream Regarding the Nature of His Altered Consciousness:

Edgar Cayce, 1877-1945

Cayce suggested that the dream indicated that in the real world he considered himself to be insignificant but when raised in higher consciousness his mind opened to virtually limitless information, time and space.

A reading was given on the dream and Cayce suggested that it was actually a "vision" of his own nature of consciousness and illustrated that in waking life he considered himself insignificant—no more than a speck of sand—but in the altered state his consciousness became open to virtually limitless information, time and space. This dream led to an understanding that the mind could be understood as having essentially three levels of consciousness. Cayce uses the terms conscious, subconscious and superconscious to describe these various levels of the mind.

Perhaps more importantly, the diagram on the next page illustrates Cayce's premise that symbols (as well as guidance and intuition) come to personal consciousness from both the subconscious and superconscious mind.

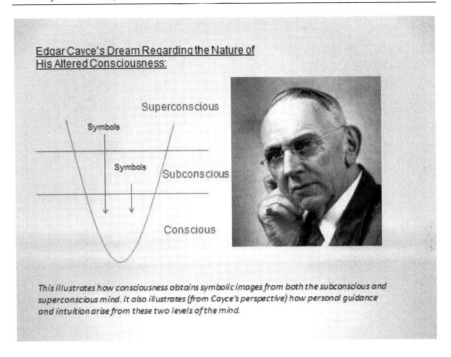

This illustrates how consciousness obtains symbolic images from both the subconscious and superconscious mind. It also illustrates (from Cayce's perspective) how personal guidance and intuition arise from these two levels of the mind.

One way to consider the wealth of information available within the subconscious is to understand the way in which the conscious mind filters out most information and stimulus coming to the individual. A number of scientific studies have suggested that the conscious mind filters out more than 95% of the stimulus coming to it. Although this may sound high, we are generally not aware of such things as the feeling of the clothing on our body, the sensation of the glasses on our nose, the watch on our hand or the ring on our finger, our feet on the floor, the sounds of the heating and air conditioning system, the intensity of the light in a room, the noise being made by a co-worker sitting near us—most things around us—unless we draw our attention to them. This holds true for all of our subtle interactions with people and events. And yet, all of these things reside within the realm of the subconscious mind and are brought to the surface in dreams. In fact, the amazing storehouse of the subconscious mind is the very reason that individuals can often remember more that went on at a crime season under hypnosis, for example, than they remember consciously. It is the subconscious mind that awakens while we sleep, providing dreamers with insights and guidance about their bodies, their minds, and even their souls.

Because dreams can provide additional insights into a situation, oftentimes they can enable the dreamer to have greater objectivity about his or her future and even "see" the result of possible choices. The dream of a forty-something-year-old man who had just graduated from massage school provides one example.

Although the individual was enthusiastic about massage and was truly excited about building up his own massage business, he was also extremely low on money. This shortage of funds had prompted him to begin looking for an office job. Finally he found a job that he thought he could do, but suddenly indecision set in. He was unsure about whether or not he should accept the job because he realized it might take up too much of his time, causing him to neglect the massage business that he was trying to develop; however, he really needed the income. As he went to bed that night, he asked for guidance about what he was supposed to do in regard to his future. That night he had a dream:

> I am in my living room with my wife and looking out the front window. I notice a little girl out front of our house standing on the lawn. Suddenly, an office supply van drives around the corner and stops abruptly in front of the house. Two men jump out of the man, abduct the little girl and swiftly drive away. To my horror I realize that she is being kidnapped. I wake up in a panic. (Todeschi 2013, 74)

Upon awakening the man knew that the dream had given him an answer to his query and he decided not to accept the job but to instead build up his massage practice. He came to that conclusion because he felt that the dream was showing himself in his present situation (living room) with wife (family and need for income), trying to make a decision about something related to his future (looking out the front window). He felt that little girl on the front lawn was a symbol of his massage business that had not yet reached maturity—it was still a child. The office supply van stopping in front of the house was suggestive of the nine-to-five job he was contemplating. As a result of the dream, the man decided that if he took the job, his massage business (the little girl) would be taken from him. He was convinced that he had received the very guidance he had requested.

Perhaps most amazingly, Cayce suggested that the information and guidance available to individuals is not limited to things that had ever come to conscious awareness! In other words, Cayce contended that oftentimes individuals receive psychic information in the dream state as a way of foreshadowing future events, enabling the dreamer to make changes and/or prepare for what is to come. In my own life, just such an experience occurred as my wife and I were in the process of building a new house.

We had contracted to build a new home located on a three-acre lot in the countryside, near other custom-built homes also with acreage. After the final plans for the house had been approved, positioning the house 175 feet back from the main road, surveyors were contracted by the builder to plot out the location of the house, which occurred 24 hours before the concrete foundation was to be poured. Neither the contractor nor I had gone out to watch the surveyors perform their straightforward assignment; however, that night I had a dream:

> I was walking through our house, which had been fully built. Everything was beautiful, just as my wife and I had imagined. When I came into the kitchen, however, I heard a noise that sounded like chewing that seemed to be coming from the back of the house. I walked to the back door and was horrified to find that the house was so close to the rear property line that the neighbor's horse was able to put its head over the fence and eat off of our deck! The noise I had heard was the sound of the horse chewing hay. (Todeschi 2013, 78)

Upon waking the next morning, I drove out to his property and measured where the house had been staked out to the back of the property line. Although the dream had exaggerated the problem, the surveyors had mistakenly staked out the foundation 50 feet farther from the street than they were supposed to—putting it much closer to the backyard neighbor than had been intended. I immediately called the builder and had him stop the concrete trucks that were on their way until the surveyors could move the house 50 feet forward.

Because of the preponderance of information in the Cayce files regarding the ease of acquiring guidance and insight in the dream state, over the years numerous educators and Cayce scholars have used the dream information in the Cayce material to prompt their own dream research. Once such scholar has been Henry Reed, Ph.D., who for years has demonstrated the accuracy with which a group of people can "target dream" for someone in need!

In addition to editing a journal for three years that contained a wealth of information on the ease of obtaining guidance in dreams (Reed, *Sundance*), Dr. Reed has repeatedly demonstrated the amazing results of the "Dream Helper Ceremony" in which a group of individuals agree to help someone in their dreams <u>without even knowing what the problem is!</u>

Part of the preparation is that the target gives each dreamer a personal belonging (such as a comb or a key) or instead writes out his or her name so that the dreamers have something to dream upon. That night they all go home and dream on the unknown question. The guidance is obtained by group members gathering together the next day and sharing their dreams with one another, looking for similar symbols and themes, arriving at a possible understanding of what the dreams may be suggesting, and then hearing from the target person as to the nature of his or her problem. A discussion ensues and invariably a helpful answer to the dreamer's problem or question is deduced by the group.

Reed, Henry, Ph.D., "Dreaming for Mary." *Venture Inward* magazine, Sept/Oct. 1985, pg. 14.

Is it possible to aid another person by agreeing to "Dream for them?"

In my own work, both personally and professionally (in conferences and lectures), I have repeatedly found that it is repeatedly possible to obtain the "dream guidance" suggested by the Cayce information by writing out a specific question and dreaming on the answer. What is even more surprising is the fact that a similar guidance process is readily available by working with the symbols and intuition that arise from the subconscious mind <u>without actually having to go to sleep</u>!

One simple example occurred in the life of a twenty-year-old woman who was faced with an imminent choice that she needed to make. She had gone to school in Virginia Beach, Virginia, more than 700 miles away from her home and family in Michigan. Two weeks prior to graduation she had met a young man and wondered if he was in fact "the one." The choice she had to make was whether she was supposed to remain in Virginia Beach in order to give the relationship a chance, or to move back to Michigan to be with the family that she missed after her graduation.

This was her experience:

> I took two identical pieces of paper. On one I wrote "Virginia Beach" and on the other I wrote "Michigan." I folded the pieces of paper into fourths and mixed them up so that I wouldn't know which one was which.
>
> I held the first piece of paper in my hand and imagined myself somewhere. I saw myself in Rome at the Coliseum. I associated the Coliseum as a place with a lot of history but with a lot of conflict because of all of the battles that had been fought there for sport. I wrote what I had seen on my piece of paper.
>
> I took the second piece of paper and imagined myself somewhere else. I saw myself at the beach on the Chesapeake Bay. It is one of my favorite places in Virginia Beach; it is a place I have even called "my heaven." I wrote down what I had seen on the second piece of paper.
>
> When I unfolded the pieces of paper, the one associated with Michigan was in fact the image of Rome. And, honestly, my home is a place with a lot of history but a lot of conflict. The idea of being in Virginia Beach with my boyfriend did sound like heaven to me. (Todeschi 2013, pgs. 147-148)

As a result of the exercise, the young woman decided to remain in Virginia Beach to be with her boyfriend—a decision she claimed had truly been the right choice six months later.

In my own life I have frequently used the "Conscious Dreamplay" exercise as a source of guidance and insight on numerous occasions. One such example occurred one January when my wife and I had taken a trip to Cape Cod to visit her mother and family for a late Christmas celebration.

We flew from Boston to Cape Code and—in spite of the freezing weather—arrived without incident. Unfortunately, our luggage containing all of the gifts that my wife had purchased for her family was lost somewhere on the way to the Cape. We checked in with luggage services, at which point the young woman informed us: "If we don't find your luggage in 90 days, we will replace it." My wife was horrified and told me that we "had to go shopping," as the family party (and present exchange) would occur in three days.

After renting a car and driving to my mother-in-law's, we settled in and my wife made plans for all of the stores we needed to visit in the morning, despite the bitter cold. As I had no desire to go shopping, I called the airlines again to see if they had found the luggage. To my dismay, they had not. Rather than immediately agreeing to the shopping outing, I suggested that we try the "Conscious Dreamplay" exercise for intuitive guidance, to which my wife agreed.

Perhaps the greatest hindrance to valid intuitive information is the fears, desires, concerns, and hopes of the conscious mind. This information cannot help but shade valid psychic insights. In the example above, my wife's fears for her missing luggage and my frustration over having to go shopping in freezing weather would obviously have an impact upon any intuitive hunch we might obtain over a question like: "Where is the luggage?" However, there is an approach that builds upon the dream guidance suggested by the readings, the targeted "Dream Helper" repeatedly demonstrated by Dr. Reed, and the way in which Cayce suggests guidance comes in the form of symbolism from the subconscious and superconscious levels of the mind.

Rather than my wife and I focusing on the luggage, I gave us a "harmless focus" that the conscious mind could dwell upon that at the same time allowed the subconscious mind to provide a symbol that would provide guidance and insight into our real question. Although I wrote out the question, "What is the energy surrounding the luggage?" on two pieces of paper, and gave each of us one to hold, I told my wife that the focus of our Conscious Dreamplay exercise would be simply to imagine a movie. If Cayce is right, somehow that symbol could provide guidance into the real question with which we were concerned.

After a few moments, I asked my wife what movie she had seen. She answered, "Lord of the Rings." The movie I had imagined was "Saving Private Ryan." As we discussed our personal feelings about the movies we had seen, my wife volunteered that the thing that stood out for her the most about her imagined movie was the fact that "there are three of them." I told her that for me, my movie meant we needed "reinforcements," as that had been the main theme I remembered from the movie.

The best reinforcement I could think of was my brother-in-law who lived in Boston. I called him and asked him to go to the US Airways luggage office and I described my wife's luggage. He went later that day and called and informed us that apparently en route to Boston (our connecting city) the tags had come off my wife's luggage. He obtained the luggage without incident and brought it to the family party, which occurred <u>three days</u> after my wife's image of "Lord of the Rings."

Time and again, working with dreams and symbolism has validated Edgar Cayce's premise that the purpose of dreams is to make us more consciously aware of what we are going through in our lives based on our thoughts, feelings, and actions. They are an ever-present source of guidance and insight. Not only can they provide us assistance in the process of making important decisions based on what we already know at a conscious level, but their potential to assist us in every area of our lives and even provide insight into things of which we have no awareness is truly amazing.

Author Bio

Kevin J. Todeschi, M.A.

Kevin J. Todeschi is the Executive Director and CEO of Edgar Cayce's A.R.E. and Atlantic University, as well as a popular author and speaker. As both student and teacher of the Cayce material for more than thirty years, he has lectured on five continents. A prolific writer, he is the author of twenty books including best-sellers Edgar Cayce on the Akashic Records, Edgar Cayce on Soul Mates, and Edgar Cayce on Vibrations.

A prolific writer, Kevin Todeshi, is the author of more than 25 books, including Edgar Cayce on the Akashic Records, Edgar Cayce on Vibrations, Edgar Cayce on Soul Mates, Edgar Cayce on Auras and Colors (co-author), Edgar Cayce on Reincarnation and Family Karma and his most recent book (co-author) Contemporary Cayce, which is an overview of the Cayce material in easy to understand language.

A nationally recognized resource on the interpretation of dreams, Kevin has taught thousands of students the art of dream interpretation. The author of The Best Dream Book Ever and Dream Images and Symbols, he also authored A.R.E.'s "Dream Interpretation A-Z Dictionary" App for both iPhone and Android.

Known for his ability to explain complex subjects in a straightforward and easy to understand manner, Kevin is popular for his insight and his sense of humor. One focus of his work has been to assist individuals in seeing how they are very much responsible for creating a better world.

Lucid Dreaming As a Path to Personal Growth, Healing and Spiritual Wisdom

Robert Waggoner[1]

Abstract

In 1980, the scientific evidence emerged to validate lucid dreaming, or the capacity to realize within a dream that you are dreaming. Aware within a dream, you have the ability to make choices, direct your awareness and influence the dream. Already, lucid dreamers report using lucid dreaming to access deep creativity, practice skills, resolve emotional issues, promote physical health, explore the nature of dreams and the psyche, and perform spiritual practices. As this paper will explain, lucid dreaming does not mean 'control' of the dream; instead lucid dreaming involves more awareness relating to the dream and the various psychical factors there. An insightful understanding of lucid dreaming naturally shows its potential for psychological and physical healing, as well as scientifically exploring the mind-body interaction from the inner platform of the lucid dream. Significantly, many lucid dreamers report communicating with another layer of inner awareness, and the interactions appear to meet the criteria established by Jung to substantiate the existence of an inner self (something Jung called "of absolutely revolutionary significance in that it could radically alter our view of the world").

---

[1]© 2015 All Rights Reserved

Lucid dreaming has the potential to accelerate our understanding of the nature of dreaming, the subconscious and consciousness. In this talk, I will discuss three primary areas of investigation: 1) how lucid dreamers appear to use this state to promote healing of emotional problems, and how this might assist the field of psychology; 2) how lucid dreamers use this state to promote healing of physical issues, sometimes with dramatic results; and 3) how lucid dreaming has allowed many to communicate with another apparent layer of self-awareness, and this responsive awareness appears to meet the criteria for an inner self, established by CG Jung.

My interest in lucid dreaming dates back to 1975, when as a high school student I taught myself how to become consciously aware of dreaming, while in the dream state, using a simple technique. Since that time, I have logged approximately 1,000 lucid dreams, and followed the science and practice of lucid dreaming with considerable interest.

The 2007 Dictionary of the American Psychological Association defines a lucid dream as "a dream in which the sleeper is aware that he or she is dreaming and may be able to influence the progress of the dream narrative." Most lucid dreamers would shorten that definition to this: Realizing within the dream state that you are dreaming.

To understand the difference between a regular dream and lucid dream, consider this dream scenario: *You find yourself sitting on the beach in San Francisco, when suddenly Godzilla rises up from the ocean and heads your way. Feeling alarmed, you decide to run and alert your family. As you head home, you wonder if Godzilla has left Japan because of the Fukushima nuclear problem.*

In this imagined dream sequence, you see many elements of common dreams, such as acceptance of the events as apparently "real," the perceiver's response to the perceived threat, and even the creation of a narrative to explain the events. Altogether, such dreams show a relative lack of critical awareness, and a reactive response to perceived events.

If you became lucid in this imagined dream sequence, the sight of Godzilla would prompt you to think more critically: "Wait a second, isn't Godzilla a fictional creature? Oh, this must be a dream!" At that point, lucidly aware, you realize you can deliberate and choose how to respond. You might stop and ask, "Godzilla, tell me, what do you represent?" and listen for a response. You might fly away, or decide to conduct a personal or scientific experiment. Lucid dreaming allows you to engage and relate to the dream experience at a new level of awareness [Note: lucid dreaming does not mean "control" of the dream—as we will see shortly].

In 1975, the scientific evidence for lucid dreaming appeared via sleep lab experiments by University of Hull (UK) graduate student Keith Hearne. He realized that when dreaming, a person normally has rapid eye movement (REM). Therefore, he wondered if you became consciously aware (lucid) within the dream, then could you move your eyes left to right a predetermined number of times and provide evidence of your conscious awareness within the lucid dream? In April of 1975, a lucid dreamer, Alan Worsley, did just that in the sleep lab at Hull.[1] The evidence was captured on the REM polygraph readout. Separately in 1978, Stephen LaBerge had much the same idea, and using himself as a Stanford sleep lab subject, signaled his awareness within the dream state by moving his eyes in a predetermined pattern. LaBerge released his results in 1980, and quickly became a leader in this new field of research.[2]

Recent neurological studies have focused on the exact areas of the brain activated during a lucid dream. A 19-channel EEG study by Ursula Voss, J. Allan Hobson and others captured brain activity while lucid dreaming, and showed simultaneous activation of the dreaming brain and portions of the frontolateral cortex. As a result, the authors deemed lucid dreaming "a hybrid state of consciousness."[3] Another fMRI/EEG study at the Max Planck Institute has shown cerebral cortex activation while lucid dreaming, which involved areas associated with self-perception, self-assessment and decision making.[4,5] Such neurological research serves to confirm the reported experience of millions of lucid dreamers.

Surveys have shown that lucid dreaming seems quite prevalent amongst college students. The *International Journal of Dream Research* had a comparative study of lucid dreaming in college students and obtained these results from those reporting at least one instance of lucid dream awareness: USA at 71%, Germany at 82%, Netherlands at 73%, and Japan at 47%. When asked if they experience one lucid dream *per month*, 20% of the respondents answered affirmatively.[6]

Why would a person care to lucid dream? For many, its profound nature relegates it to the level of "peak experience," as defined by Abraham Maslow. However, in general, many would claim that lucid dreaming allows the following:

    a. An experience of joy, freedom
    b. Access to creativity, develop skills
    c. Promote emotional healing
    d. Promote physical healing
    e. Explore the unconscious
    f. Engage in spiritual practices (e.g., meditate within a lucid dream)

After developing a simple pre-sleep suggestion technique in 1975 to associate the sight of my hands with the thought, "This is a dream!," I became consciously aware of dreaming on the third night of practice, when my hands literally popped up in front of my face.[7] Suddenly, I realized that the people in my high school hallway were actually dream figures, and the wall that felt cool and nubby consisted fundamentally of "dream stuff" or projected mental energy.

Having five or six years of solitary investigation of lucid dreaming (before the evidence emerged in 1980-81) taught me many lessons about the principled nature of the dream state. I began to grasp the underlying rules and principles, as I played around and explored the dream, lucidly aware. I also realized that lucid dreaming allowed for conceptual growth, as you experimented and developed new avenues. Years later, when I met other lucid dreamers, I felt amazed to realize that most had learnt the same rules and principles. Yet in this alternate reality, I often wondered, "who" or "what" created the rules and principles? Who was the programmer behind the scenes? And how could you explain the unexpected and creative elements within the lucid dream?

After a decade of lucid dreaming, I came to understand that lucid dreamers *do not control* the lucid dream. Instead, lucid dreamers **relate to** personal and psychical elements within the dream. I developed a metaphor to make the point: *The sailor does not control the sea, neither does the lucid dreamer control the dream. Like a sailor, lucid dreamers must relate to many apparent internal and external factors in order to direct ourselves within the lucid dream.*[8]

To convince others, I pointed out the numerous unexpected elements within common lucid dreams. For example, a lucid dreamer reported becoming lucid and having this exchange with a dream figure: *I ask the dream figure, "Do you know I am dreaming you?" He responds, "How do you know I am not dreaming you?" Then I say, "Well, look. I can fly." He responds, "Well, look. I can fly too."* After trying to out-do each other, both the lucid dreamer and dream figure ultimately agreed that it seemed an endlessly debatable point. Interestingly, the vast majority of lucid dreamers report dream figures taking umbrage to the poorly conceived assumptions in the question, "Do you know I am dreaming you?"

Besides this, I hasten to point out to lucid dreamers the innumerable instances where they do not express "control." For example, you fly through a dream wall and discover a castle and white horse on the other side. If you "control" the lucid dream, then who put the castle and white horse there? You did not. You discovered them. Obviously, lucid dreamers "influence" the dream and direct their awareness within the dream, but do not control it, just as the sailor does not control the sea.

If psychologists understood this basic point that a lucid dream involves "relating" to internal and external psychical elements, then many would benefit from contemplating a lucid dream such as this one, submitted by Brandon to my books' website, www.LucidAdvice.com. Brandon asked the following question:

> In many of my [lucid] dreams my mom appears and I don't know why, but *she always appears when I might be doing things that are inappropriate or wrong.* She just stares at me and makes me feel really uncomfortable. *Even though I know I'm dreaming and try to get rid of her, she won't leave.* Do you know why or have any suggestions? Thanks!

Lucid dreaming often allows us to see both the dreamer's interior thought process and the externally projected response, which illustrate the psychical process. Here, lucidly aware Brandon engages in actions that he admits "are inappropriate or wrong." As he engages in these actions, an inner conflict develops—and this conflicted "energy" becomes outwardly expressed—in the form of the disapproving mother. Note too how Brandon obviously does not "control" the dream, since he lucidly tries to get rid of her, but "she won't leave."

A personal lucid dream shows a bit more enlightened engagement, plus the profound nature of "resolving" an issue within a dream. I become lucid when a farm wife puts beans on my plate, and I realize that I do not live on a farm in the South. Now lucid, I go to the area of the most sensed energy (a rule I developed to aid in my resolution of inner issues). In this case, I can feel something behind me (in the Shadow's position). Turning around, I see an attractive black woman looking at me. I pick her up and put her in front of me, asking an open-ended question, "Who are you? Who are you?" She responds, *"I am a discarded aspect of yourself."* Hearing that, I wonder how to respond. I quickly decide that "a discarded aspect" wants acceptance. From my heart, I utterly accept her—whereupon I watch as she shrinks down to wisps of colored light energy that enter my torso with a jolt, and I wake up![9]

Later that week, I realized each day I had been thinking about writing a book on lucid dreaming, which was a project that I had discarded two years earlier as impossible. Now, having lucidly re-integrated the "discarded" energy of that intent, I made plans to write my first book, *Lucid Dreaming: Gateway to the Inner Self*.

Such examples (and there are many) show how the dreamer's actions within the framework of their belief system serves to generate "energy," which results in the creation of symbolically connected dream figures, objects or settings. As I discuss in my books, in a lucid dream the "mental action" precedes the effect. You can literally see the emergence of simple forms of dream figures, like Brandon's disapproving mother. Also you get insight into how dream figures could possibly receive more and more "energy" until they develop into something more substantial, as in my "discarded aspect," who shows some elements of awareness and an ability to respond.

In many ways, lucid dreaming seems much like a dream version of *Active Imagination*. Jungian author Robert Johnson, in his classic, *Inner Work*, noted,

> Essentially, Active Imagination is a dialogue that you enter into with the different parts of yourself that live in the unconscious. *In some ways it is similar to dreaming, except that you are fully awake and conscious during the experience.*[10]

This definition makes lucid dreaming seem much like Active Imagination performed while consciously aware in the dream state.

Lucid Dreams and Therapy

If examined thoughtfully, lucid dreaming may provide natural expressions of inner, subconscious processes that could inform the science of psychology and lead it to improve therapeutic treatment, develop models of subconscious activity (along with conscious and subconscious interaction) and provide evidence for a deeper layer of responsive self-awareness.

The literature on using lucid dreaming to resolve recurring nightmares associated with post traumatic stress disorder, or PTSD, begins in 1982 and a report by therapist Gordon Halliday. Working with people who suffered from recurring nightmares, he encouraged them to become lucidly aware when they noticed the familiar scenes. Then, once lucid, he asked them to change one thing in the nightmare. For example, a man haunted by recurring nightmares after an accident on the farm became lucid as the nightmare began, recalled Halliday's suggestion, and changed the color of an object in the dream. After one lucid dream, the recurring nightmares basically ceased.[11, 12, 13, 14]

Over the years, other approaches have emerged. Some therapists have asked the nightmare sufferer to stop and question the figure(s) chasing the person, and thus, possibly learn from that symbol. Others have suggested the idea of confronting and possibly conquering the nightmare figure. Others have learned to project acceptance and even love onto the nightmare figure and actively seek to heal the situation. Interestingly, Barry Krakow, MD, notes that his widely used waking technique of Imagery Rehearsal Therapy was partially informed by reading examples of lucid dreams that successfully ended recurring nightmares.

However, could lucid dreaming be used to help with other mental and emotional problems? The answer appears to be "Yes."

On lucid dream forums, lucid dreamers report the conceptual expansion of this idea for other types of emotional healing. For example, a talented lucid dreamer wrote me and stated that she wished to come to an International Association for the Study of Dreams (IASD) conference, but had a fear of flying on planes. She asked me, "Could lucid dreaming help?" I suggested that in her next lucid dreams, she recall this intent and go to the lucid dream airport. If she felt all right, then she should board a lucid dream airplane. And if she felt okay, then she should allow the airplane to take off. At any time, she could end the experience and wake, knowing it as a lucid dream.

After five lucid dreams in which she went to the airport (one time even announcing, "I love airplanes! I love airports too!"), and sometimes flew in a plane, she realized that her inner fear had basically evaporated. In fact, she purchased a window seat on the actual airplane flight to the IASD conference in order to see if the take-off and flight seemed "like" what she had experienced in her lucid dreams. She continues to fly on airplanes without fear. Lucid dreamers have reported using such exposure therapy or gradual desensitization *within the lucid dream* to resolve lifelong phobias.

In another instance, a lucid dreamer asked about resolving feelings of generalized anxiety through lucid dreaming. I responded that I had not heard of anyone even trying this, but if she wished, she might want to announce in a lucid dream to her non-visible larger awareness, "Hey! I want to be free of anxiety for one week!"

The woman made this request in her next lucid dream and wrote me in the morning to tell me that she felt "like a little girl." Perplexed, I asked what that meant, and she responded that the last time she felt free of anxiety is when she was a little girl. She made this request a few more times in her lucid dream, then attended her regularly scheduled psychiatric appointment. When they met, he immediately blurted out, "What's happened to you? Your anxiety has disappeared." She explained her lucid dream process. He reduced her medication to the lowest level, then later ended it.

Another example of healing involves dealing with a non-constructive habit, smoking (but here, it may possibly generalize to any non-constructive habit, like multiple hand washing or anorexia). A lucid dreamer named Antonio attended a workshop on lucid dreaming. That night, he became lucid and noticed that a female dream figure kept following him. Curious, he asked, *"So who are you?" Female Dream Figure: "I'm your brain ... But do us all a favor and stop smoking. It bothers us."* Antonio *[considers how to respond to this request]: "Okay then. How about whenever I feel like a cigarette, you make me think of something else instead?"*

Upon waking, Antonio felt no interest in smoking. In fact, he could hang out with smokers and have no interest in smoking. Antonio felt that in the lucid dream, he had encouraged the symbolic representation of his "brain" to inhibit cravings whenever he felt like a cigarette. And it worked! After a year, he continues to not smoke and reports no interest in smoking.[15]

Consider how lucid dreamers may ask to engage symbolic representatives of non-constructive habits or even obsessive disorders and seek a resolution to the issue. For example, a lucid dreamer might announce, "When I enter that next room, I will meet my addiction to bingeing on sweets!" In the next room, he meets a cheerful fellow. They chat. Finally, the lucid dreamer requests, "Whenever I feel like bingeing on sweets, you make me think of something else instead, okay?" Of course, the lucid dreamer could also seek out the underlying interest in sweets too.

The primary point is that lucid dreamers have already begun to use lucid dreaming for emotional healing, and science may do well to follow. As such, the anecdotes appear to show why scientific researchers should experiment with lucid dreaming to determine the following: 1) Does it serve as an alternative healing modality?; 2) Does it offer new insights into the psyche (creation of dream figures, mind-body interactions, alternate egos, etc.)?; 3) May it help create more effective therapies?; and 4) May it bring new insights into interactions between the subconscious and consciousness?

Physical Healing in Lucid Dreams

Author, therapist and lucid dreamer Patricia Garfield presciently noted, "The potential for healing in lucid dreams is enormous." Since the scientific evidence for lucid dreaming emerged in 1980-81, some have considered using lucid dreaming for proactive healing of the physical body. Stephen LaBerge noted, "*The question for future research to answer is, 'If we heal the dream body, to what extent will we also heal the physical body?'*"[16]

In many respects, LaBerge has answered his own question, through a series of experiments in which lucidly dreamt actions showed a parallel effect on the physical body.[17, 18, 19] Consider the following:

1) Looks left and right in a lucid dream — results in physical eyes moving left to right

2) Clenches fist in an alternating right arm/left arm pattern in a lucid dream—results in physical forearm showing muscle movement in alternating right/left pattern

3) Changes breathing pattern to slow down or speed up in lucid dream—the physical breathing pattern changes to reflect predetermined goal

4) Asks subjects to begin counting and performing arithmetic in lucid dreams—the left brain hemisphere shows more activity; asks subjects to begin singing in lucid dreams—the right brain hemisphere shows more activity

5) Places 17 devices to measure physiological activity on lucid dream subjects and asks them to signal lucid awareness, then find sex partner and signal with eyes that they have engaged in lucid dream sex—finds that most every physical measure reflects the dreamt activity as if the real thing

To this last point, LaBerge wrote, "lucid dream sex has as powerful an impact on the dreamer's body as the real thing."[20] So when it comes to his question, *"If we heal the dream body, to what extent will we also heal the physical body?,"* it appears that one can justifiably answer (based on these research papers) that the lucid dream action has a significant effect. In very basic terms, the conceptual proof already exists.

Anecdotally, lucid dreamers can provide many examples, such as the following:

1) Annie had painful plantar warts that resisted medical treatment. One night, she became lucidly aware, recalled her interest in healing the warts, and created a ball of healing light in her hands. Placing the ball of light over each foot, she intended for it to be healed. When she woke, she reports that overnight the plantar warts turned black, and within ten days fell off and did not return.[21]

2) A woman has heart surgery, but ten days later remains in the hospital with four tubes collecting the leakage from the heart area. That night she becomes lucidly aware, remembers that she wishes to heal herself, and removes the tubes in the lucid dream—which now release colored lights, flowers and peace symbols. She has a feeling she has healed herself. In the morning, the nurses report the leakage has stopped. Within a day, she is released.

3) A woman has an expanded uterus, and a large cyst and mass, which the doctor fears may be a tumor. She becomes lucidly aware and asks dream figures to explain the meaning of her condition, but receives no help. Then she asks "the source" (the larger awareness) what it means, and begins to see symbols like skeletons, crashing planes, fire trucks, etc. In the next dream, she becomes basically lucid when she sees large geometric figures of light, which beam down healing energy on her body. She tells her son not to worry, since "they have come to heal me." Returning to the doctor, a new scan shows no evidence of an expanded uterus, large cyst or mass.[22]

While my first book contains a chapter on healing in lucid dreams with about a dozen successful examples and two unsuccessful ones (to show the contrasting approaches to healing attempts), I want to make clear that lucid dreaming allows for scientific experimentation. Consider finding 20 people who have good dream recall and a simple medical ailment that resists conventional treatment (perhaps some form of skin psoriasis). Teach ten of them how to lucid dream, and direct healing intent within the lucid dream to help heal the psoriasis. Provide monthly support. Let the other ten serve as the control group. Within six months, perhaps less, I believe that evidence would emerge to show a greater degree of healing in the lucid dream group.

Ed Kellogg, Ph.D., has investigated lucid dream healing deeply, and apparently healed himself on a number of occasions. He writes that lucid dream healing may come in three forms: Diagnostic, in which the person gets information that properly diagnoses the ailment; Prescriptive, in which the person receives a prescription such as a substance or food to take (or avoid), or other information that assists to achieve a healing; and Curative, in which the lucid dreamer directly experiences a rapid healing or freedom from symptoms as a result of the lucid dream.[23]

Interacting with Another Layer of Self

Throughout the talk, I have mentioned that on some occasions, the lucid dreamer simply ignores the dream figures and setting, and poses a question or request to the non-visible "awareness" behind the dream. This non-visible awareness often responds verbally or visually (sometimes with an entirely new dream scene).

I first noticed this in 1985, conducting monthly experiments with part of a group of lucid dreamers. That particular month, the goal involved "Find out what the characters in your dream represent." I became lucid, recalled the goal, followed a woman into an office, turned to a man in a three-piece suit, and said, "Excuse me, but what do you represent?" I recall feeling amazed when a non-visible voice from above him boomed out a partial response. The answer seemed incomplete, so I asked for clarification. The non-visible voice again boomed out a full response, which now made more sense. I decided to wake, since I had received an answer.[24]

Yet, the unexpected nature of this booming voice suggested to me that perhaps an "awareness" existed behind the dream. So thereafter, I developed a habit in lucid dreams to ignore the dream figures and simply shout out questions to this "awareness behind the dream" and see how it responded (e.g., "Hey, show me something important for me to see!"). To my amazement, it showed considerable conceptual depth, creativity, knowledge and more.

Later that year, LaBerge published his first book in 1985 and suggested that lucid dreamers "surrender" in lucid dreams. He wrote that one could surrender to "the Highest," for example, and that one of his most satisfying lucid dreams occurred after he surrendered thusly.[25] But to me, the questions lingered: To whom does one surrender? Who or what responds? How deep is its knowledge?

Interestingly, the awareness behind the dream also refutes requests. The leader of an online lucid dream forum, PasQuale Ourtane, reports having a group goal to discover "the beginning and end of the universe." Becoming lucid, she asks to experience the beginning and end of the universe, whereupon the non-visible awareness responds, "The universe has no beginning and no end, the universe is an everlasting cycle." Here, her request is refuted and an alternative provided.

In another case, a lucid dreamer sought to experience a hyper-dimensional state related to String Theory. Making his request, he hears in response, "It does not seem a good idea to do an experiment of this type at this time, as you still seem too unfocused and distracted." The voice goes on to encourage him to carefully consider such requests and prepare mindfully for it. He calls out "Cancel" to stop any action.

As more fully explained in my first book, such interactions appear to show characteristics theorized by Jung of a second psychic system, the unconscious: "We have no knowledge of how this unconscious functions, but since it is conjectured to be a psychic system it may possibly have everything that consciousness has, including perception, apperception, memory, imagination, will, affectivity, feeling, reflection, judgment, etc., all in subliminal form."[26]

Jung goes on to suggest the implications: "If the unconscious can contain everything that is known to be a function of consciousness, then we are faced with the possibility that it too, like consciousness, possesses a subject, a sort of ego ... [which] brings out the real point of my argument: the fact, namely, *that a second psychic system co-existing with consciousness—no matter what qualities we suspect it of possessing—is of absolutely revolutionary significance in that it could radically alter our view of the world."*[27]

Experienced lucid dreamers report more and more interactions with this non-visible awareness behind the dream, and it consistently displays the characteristic criteria of consciousness that he outlined for a "second psychic system." In general, this conscious unconscious seems interested in educating the lucid dreamer and only responding when called upon. It appears considerably more creative than the lucid dreamer and able to bring forth conceptual experiences, ranging from the very simple to those of almost unendurable beauty and energy.

Lucid dreaming has extraordinary potential and depth, when properly understood. It may be that the often discussed "shift" in consciousness may be in the area of life most ignored and devalued—the state of dreaming. Lucid dreaming offers new light to explore it, and perhaps see it truly for the first time in this era.

Endnotes

1. Keith Hearne. *Lucid dreams: An electro-physiological and psychological study*. Unpublished doctoral dissertation (1978). University of Liverpool, UK.
2. Stephen LaBerge Lucid dreaming as a learnable skill: A case study, *Perceptual and Motor Skills*, 51, 3 Pt 2, (1980): 1039—1042.
3. Ursula Voss, Romain Holzmann, Inka Tuin, J. Allan Hobson, Lucid Dreaming: A State of Consciousness with Features of Both Waking and Non-Lucid Dreaming Sleep. *Sleep*, 2009 September 1; 32(9): 1191—1200.
4. Max-Planck-Gesellschaft. "Lucid dreamers help scientists locate the seat of meta-consciousness in the brain." *ScienceDaily*, 27 Jul. 2012. Web. 29 Oct. 2013.
5. Martin Dresler, Renate Wehrle, Victor I. Spoormaker, Stefan P. Koch, Florian Holsboer, Axel Steiger, Hellmuth Obrig, Philipp G. Sämann, Michael Czisch. Neural Correlates of Dream Lucidity Obtained from Contrasting Lucid versus Non-Lucid REM Sleep: A Combined EEG/fMRI Case Study. *Sleep*, 2012; 35 (7):1017-1020.

6. Daniel Erlacher, Michael Schredl, Tsuneo Watanabe, Jun Yamana, Florian Gantzert, The Incidence of Lucid Dreaming within a Japanese University Student Sample, *International Journal of Dream Research*, 1, 2, October 2008.
7. Robert Waggoner, *Lucid Dreaming: Gateway to the Inner Self*, (Needham, Massachusetts: Moment Point Press, 2009), 7.
8. Ibid., 17.
9. Ibid., 17.
10. Robert A. Johnson, *Inner Work: Using Dreams & Active Imagination for Personal Growth*, (San Francisco: Harper Collins, 1986), 138.
11. Gordon Halliday, Direct Alteration of a Traumatic Nightmare, (1982) *Perceptual and Motor Skills*: 54, (1982), pp. 413-414.
12. Henry Abramovitch, The nightmare of returning home: A case of acute onset nightmare disorder treated by lucid dreaming, *Israel Journal of Psychiatry and Related Sciences*, 32 (2) (1995), pp. 140—145.
13. Andrew Brylowski, Nightmares in crisis: Clinical applications of lucid dreaming techniques, *Psychiatric Journal of the University of Ottawa*, 15 (2) (1990), pp. 79—84.
14. Victor I. Spoormaker, J. van den Bout, E.J.G. Meijer, Lucid dreaming treatment for nightmares: A series of cases, *Dreaming*, 13, no.3, (2003): 181—186.
15. Charlie Morley, *Lucid Dreaming—A Beginners Guide to Becoming Conscious In Your Dreams*, (London: Hay House, 2015), p 37.
16. S. LaBerge Healing Through Lucid Dreaming, *Lucidity Letter*, 1991.
17. S. LaBerge., L. Nagel., W.C. Dement, & V. Zarcone Jr., Lucid dreaming verified by volitional communication during REM sleep. *Perceptual and Motor Skills*, 52, (1981) pp.727-732.
18. S. LaBerge and W.C. Dement, Lateralization of alpha activity for dreamed singing and counting during REM sleep. *Psychophysiology*, 19, (1982b) pp. 331-332.
19. S. LaBerge., W. Greenleaf, & B. Kedzierski., Physiological responses to dreamed sexual activity during lucid REM sleep. *Psychophysiology*, 20, (1983) pp. 454-455.
20. S. LaBerge, *Lucid Dreaming*, (Los Angeles: Tarcher, 1985), 86.
21. R. Waggoner, *Lucid Dreaming: Gateway to the Inner Self*, (Needham, Massachusetts: Moment Point Press, 2009), 160.
22. Ibid., 166.

23. E. W. Kellogg III, *Mind-Body Healing through Dreamwork* Presented at IASD's Sixth **PsiberDreaming Conference**, September 23 - October 7, 2007.
http://www.asdreams.org/psi2007/papers/edkellogg.htm
24. R. Waggoner, *Lucid Dreaming: Gateway to the Inner Self*, (Needham, Massachusetts: Moment Point Press, 2009), 52.
25. S. LaBerge, *Lucid Dreaming*, (Los Angeles: Tarcher, 1985), 245.
26. Carl G. Jung, "On the Nature of Psyche" in *The Basic Writings of C. G. Jung*, edited by Violet Staub de Laszlo, (New York: Random House, 1993), 53.
27. Ibid., 61.

Author Bio

Robert Waggoner

Robert Waggoner is author of the acclaimed book, *Lucid Dreaming: Gateway to the Inner Self*, now in its ninth printing, and the newly released *Lucid Dreaming Plain and Simple* (Conari Press, 2015), with co-author, Caroline McCready. A lucid dreamer since 1975, Robert has logged more than 1,000 lucid dreams and co-edits the online lucid dream magazine, *Lucid Dreaming Experience* (ISSN: 2167-616X). A past president of the International Association for the Study of Dreams (IASD), Robert speaks at colleges, conferences and workshops across the country and internationally, and conducts on-line workshops with www.GlideWing.com. Learn more about his books and free magazine at www.LucidAdvice.com and www.LucidDreamMagazine.com

Breakthrough or Breakdown

Signs and Symptoms of Spiritual Emergence vs Mental Illness

Theresa A. Yuschok, MD

Abstract

A Spiritual breakthrough may have signs and symptoms similar to a mental illness. As an example, St. Teresa of Avila was told her spiritual experiences were delusional or evil. This paper compares characteristics of a spiritual experience with the psychiatric diagnoses of depression, mania, and psychosis. Also she draws the distinctions between a malignant leader of a cult and a trustworthy spiritual guide. Spirituality may be integrated into medical treatment and a breakdown may become a breakthrough. After a spiritual experience, a person may still need psychotherapy. Our understanding of psycho-spirituality is evolving.

Case #1 A 39-year-old single woman who has been praying several times per day reports to her advisor that she has had moments of union and has heard God's voice, "Do not look too deeply into this, but serve Me." Her advisor tells her she is having delusions, or else she is possessed by the devil. She bursts into tears, spends more time alone, journaling and praying. She seeks a second opinion. The next spiritual directors, Jesuits, listen to her gently and respond skillfully to encourage her experiences of divine favors.

This is the case of St Teresa of Avila. Locutions are the voice of God, but both she and her advisors were alarmed by this happening. In her classic *The Interior Castle*, in the chapter of the 6th dwelling, she outlines how to discern that a voice is divine: 1) The words have a powerful effect, such as "Be not afraid," and calm her. 2) A quietude comes over her with love and peace. 3) The words linger, profound and indelible. 4) The message is in harmony with revealed truth.

When someone comes to a psychiatrist and complains about hearing voices, first we listen. We listen to the content and context of the symptom. We ask questions about the current medications, brain trauma, and other medical conditions. We ask about family history of illness, because schizophrenia, bipolar disorder, psychotic depression and Alzheimer's Disease may run in family. We are trained to consider the medical causes of hallucinations. Medications that can cause hallucinations include prednisone, reserpine, dopamine, amphetamines and recreational drugs such as LSD, PCP, cocaine, and alcohol withdrawal.

The voices can originate from seizures, hypothyroidism, high calcium from hyperparathyroidism, electrolyte imbalances, hepatic encephalopathy, Wilson's disease or syphilis, to name a few causes.

St. Teresa of Avila did not have any medications or drugs to abuse. Although she is the patron saint of hysteria, she did not have medical or psychiatric causes to explain the voice of God and other spiritual experiences.

Case #2 At age 16 he had a vision of Ezekiel the Prophet smiling at prayers of praise and thanksgiving. He wandered the countryside as a faith healer, story teller, and spiritual teacher.

Baal Shem Tov, or Rabbi Shem Tov, was the founder of Hasidism Judaism. He believed singing, dance and fervent prayer brought faith closer to God. How can we tell Bipolar Mania from

Ecstatic Rapture? Both may have an expansive mood, sleeplessness and religious fervor, but mania, as an extreme mood elevation in bipolar disorder, would also be accompanied by racing thoughts, grandiosity, impulsive behaviors, pressured speech and agitation. The mood swings of manic depression occur in cycles. Other family members may have bipolar disorder too. A medical review would check for drugs that induce mania, such as cocaine, antidepressants, amphetamines and steroids. Medical conditions of brain tumor, seizures, hyperthyroidism, MS, Huntington's disease, metabolic change, and delirium should be considered. Baal Shem Tov did not meet the criteria for a mania. He had ecstasy and taught others, "Whoever lives in joy does his Creator's will."

Case #3 A wealthy 50-year-old successful novelist, a married man with 14 children, struggles with feelings of disillusionment and anhedonia. He considers suicide and removes the rope and hunting rifle.

Is this a melancholic depression? Evil influence? Complicated bereavement for his brother who died of a tormenting illness? Or an existential crisis of meaninglessness?

Count Leo Tolstoy did not have the benefits of antidepressants, but he did have the education to review natural science and philosophy about his persistent questions. He wrote a book about this soul-searching to understand and relieve his anguish, *A Confession.* At age 50, witnessing his brother's tormenting death and recognizing his own mortality, he asks the big questions: *Why do I live? Is there any meaning in my life that will not be annihilated by the inevitability of death that awaits me?* This life force returns as he returned with his faith in God. *I now knew that I could not live without it.* His mood improved with finding spiritual meaning.

Now in a culture with Prozac on the cover of TIME magazine, we are quick to consider depression as a depletion of serotonin and take antidepressants. But the spiritual crisis should be considered as well as medication side effects from reserpine or propranolol, withdrawal symptoms from cocaine, medical illness such as cancer, hypothyroidism, vitamin deficiency, or infection. With daily suicidal thoughts for a year, emptiness, agony, worthlessness, anhedonia, poor sleep and decreased appetite, Tolstoy met the criteria for Major Depression, Severe, but he resolved it with a spiritual quest. When he found faith, the life force returned gradually and imperceptibly. Tolstoy wrote in *A Confession*, "Whatever answers faith gives, regardless of which faith, or to whom the answers are given, such answers always give an infinite meaning to the finite existence of man; a meaning that is not destroyed by suffering, deprivation, or death."

Case #4 *A 37-year-old widowed and remarried male theology professor, obsessed with a 65-year-old religious man, neglects his students and home. He spontaneously speaks poetry for long spells.*

Is this a healthy spiritual friendship or a personality change? Is Rumi being controlled by a cult leader? His students and friends were worried about him.

None of the medical causes of personality change fit in this case: traumatic brain injury, stroke, brain tumors, seizures, MS, Huntington's disease, endocrine disorders, heavy metal poisoning. More likely, he had what Carl Jung called an "enantiodromia." Suddenly the horses go in the opposite directions. An excess of rigorous study flips to the immediacy of direct experience and Rumi throws his books away. In the life of Mevlana Jalalu'ddin Rumi, Shams of Tabriz was a catalyst to the shift from intellectual book learning to direct mystical experience.

This raises the question of how to discern whether a spiritual guide is trustworthy or not. Dangerous cult leaders demonstrate the characteristics of malignant narcissism. They expect followers to worship them, rather than the Divine. They consider themselves special, rather than humble. With arrogance and lack of empathy, they can be cruel, controlling and exploitative, rather than loving, kind and compassionate. When people try to leave a cult, there can be punishment and shunning.

Abraham Maslow developed a hierarchy of needs, starting with necessities for survival and safety at the base, building to belonging, self-esteem, cognition beauty, self-actualization. Posthumously, self-transcendence—the need to be connected to something larger that ourselves. We may join organizations such as ASCSI or the Jung Society or religious groups to meet these needs. On the shadow side, these same needs are exploited in cults, gangs and terrorist organizations. Cults find a vulnerable prey and offer belonging, an explanation to problems and the promise of a higher purpose. With the Internet, Americans have been recruited overseas for humanitarian service only to find themselves isolated in a training camp. The induction process wears people down through excessive work, sleep deprivation and dietary changes. Petty rules of grooming or attire pave the way toward mind control. They explain the world legalistically as "Us and Them," and offer their answer to the crisis. The charismatic malignant narcissistic leader demands complete loyalty without questions. The cult encourages an external identity as follower, rather than directing an inner communion. The cult member surrenders their sense of self to another person, the anointed leader, rather than surrendering to God. To exit the group puts one in peril of isolation/shunning, persecution, fears of unknown or physical danger.

I describe the shadow side of cults to contrast the difference of a spiritual growth setting. Self-examination is a liberating process rather than controlling with perpetual guilt or shame. A wise and humble teacher encourages novices to go within for their answers and worship God, not the leader. Instead of fostering dependency, blind obedience, and mind-control, the sense of self is developed to have an inner communion and alignment. Shams of Tabriz, teaching by his presence, set Rumi free to explore greater emotional freedom and higher spiritual realms.

We have shown four examples of spiritual awakenings that may be, superficially, mistaken for hearing voices in psychosis, mania, depression or personality change. Now, I will talk about it from the other side, how medical or psychiatric conditions may create spiritual crisis or growth

If the diagnosis is medical or psychiatric illness, spirituality may be addressed in the interview and treatment plan. The Joint Commission of Hospitals expects doctors to ask about religious and spiritual history. Hospital Chaplains may be consulted. An emotional breakdown may lead to spiritual growth, connecting with a Higher Power for addiction recovery, mindfulness meditation for emotional regulation, The existential questions of the purpose of life, the meaning of suffering, may start a spiritual journey. I've witnessed patients renew a religious connection, start spiritual practices, reset priorities, develop a compassionate heart to themselves and others.

After someone has experienced a spiritual awakening, psychotherapy may also play a role. Although consciousness has been raised, there may still be unresolved psychodynamics, painful interpersonal relationships, emotional dysregulation, and adjustment to a new world-view.

In summary, signs of a spiritual breakthrough may be mistaken as psychiatric symptoms. Likewise, emotional breakdowns may have symptoms similar to spiritual breakthrough. Cults may manipulate human needs to achieve blind obedience, surrendering to a charismatic leader rather than the Divine. Spirituality may be integrated into treatment and a breakdown may become a breakthrough. After a spiritual breakthrough, a person may still need psychotherapy, because childhood psychodynamics may interfere with interpersonal relationships and inner perceptions.

Our understanding of the interface of psychiatry and spirituality is evolving. Just as the Diagnostic and Statistical Manual (DSM- III [third edition] eliminated homosexuality as a mental disorder, V 62.89 Religious or Spiritual Disorder was added to DSM IV, and APA task force wrote guidelines for psychiatrists addressing religious and spiritual issues. The diagnostic categories in the DSM5 and beyond are fluid and will be influenced by new research.

Author Bio

Theresa A. Yuschok, MD

Theresa is a psychiatrist at Durham VA Medical Center and on the faculty at Duke University Medical Center. As President of the C.G. Jung Society of the Triangle, she has a long-standing interest in spirituality and mental health. She has written a one-woman play, "The Saint with a Tambourine," to make accessible St. Teresa's book, *The Interior Castle* and she is the author of *The Man Who Reads Souls*, about her husband, Lee Lawrence.

Understanding the Human Soul and the Purpose of Life

Lee Lawrence

Abstract

This paper explains that we are the seeds of consciousness planted here to grow through our consciousness. We are becoming "Light." We as humans are growing in each of the frequencies of consciousness represented by the colors of consciousness at each chakra to reach wholeness and experience nirvana as we become "Light." We should always strive to reach and grow to the highest levels of consciousness possible. The more we cleanse our souls of the anchors and ballast, the easier it is to grow to the higher levels of consciousness we strive for.

In 1988 I had a near death experience, or as I prefer to call it, a death experience. I returned with a very unusual ability of being able to read people's souls, including stored memories of their life experiences since conception, without subjects volunteering any information. Actually, I'm not sure that I completely returned to my body as it is, as though the greater part of me now exists outside my physical body, including awareness and perception of reality. I can now perceive from my consciousness directly rather than just my five critical senses.

    This freedom from the physical body has allowed my consciousness to be free and soar the realms of many layers of reality just as easily as one might change the frequency of their voice while singing a song. It's very difficult to put it into words, but it is as though everyone and everything exists within me as I lift up to higher altitudes of consciousness. Our perception of reality is a function of the level of consciousness from which we perceive it. There is one reality existing at many levels, all within each other or in the same time/space continuum. Things that are non-physical at the level of consciousness at which most people perceive they exist suddenly become physical when perceived from the higher level of consciousness. People's thoughts, including all stored memories of their past experiences in their life, become physical tangible objects perceivable directly by my consciousness when I tune to higher levels. This is as much a curse as a blessing, as I feel and experience the emotional and physical pains and pleasures of their stored historical memories as my consciousness passes through each of them in the field around their physical body. (Note: the only way I can protect myself from feeling the painful experiences of other's stored memories is to radiate a higher level of consciousness out of myself. This high energy will transmute any low-frequency thoughts as soon as they enter my field. This is why the Hindu statue of Shiva has the ring of fire surrounding him. I have seen this on occasion when observing a highly evolved being meditating. It appears as ball of fire around the individual that flares up whenever a low-frequency thought or consciousness tries to enter it. Low-frequency earthbound spirits or ghosts cannot cause harm and are afraid of me when I am connected to the higher levels. Likewise, it is why the Bible states that giving a prayerful blessing to an evil person is like placing hot coals upon their head.)

    Any level of consciousness existing above the level at which we exist is always perceived by us as "Light." This is an inherent quality of consciousness and is the reason that many religions refer to "God as Light." Generally, we are only allowed to perceive one level of consciousness above that at which we exist in order to protect ourselves from the individual abilities gained by us at the higher levels if we have not cleansed our soul of the low-frequency thoughts of fear, anger, guilt or jealousy. Our free will is limited by the level of consciousness at which we exist in order to protect ourselves and others. You are not allowed into the higher levels if you would use your abilities gained at that higher level in an irresponsible manner. Thus physical manifestation and alteration of matter is restricted to the higher levels of consciousness for the reasons highlighted in the Midas Touch myth.

While I do not have the time to elaborate in this writing, I have found that human consciousness has many attributes in common with atomic theory. Just as the Nobel Prize-winning Danish atomic physicist Niels Bohr discovered that an electron traveling from a higher orbital to a lower orbital generates a photon (light), so does consciousness when it flows from a higher to a lower level. (Thus the "Healing Hands of Light.") Even the electron spin in the orbitals resembles the consciousness flow patterns and attributes of the masculine and feminine aspects of consciousness. Right spin or feminine aspect of consciousness creates a dispersion pattern while left spin or masculine consciousness creates and organized pattern. (This is the secret of quantum entanglement and the holograms of memory storage.) The union of two souls in a relationship resembles a covalent bond in chemistry, while an individual finding wholeness through spiritual growth resembles an ionic bond.

Memories are no more stored in the physical body than the music you hear coming from a radio is stored in the radio. The human brain is merely a transmitter and receiver facilitating communication between the lower frequencies of consciousness anchored in the physical body and the higher frequencies of consciousness contained in the field surrounding the body. Thus the field contains a very specific matrix of flow patterns integrating the various frequencies in the vertical axis with the historical storage field on the horizontal axis. This consciousness field, which extends approximately fifteen feet in all directions at its smallest radius from the physical body, contains the two aspects of consciousness spinning in opposite directions. "Love" is critically important to humans as Love is the glue that holds these fields together and provides stability.

I must laugh as scientists make the concept of quantum entanglement so difficult to understand. Quantum entanglement is a function of the two aspects of consciousness and exists at many levels. All our memories are stored as holograms through the quantum entanglement of the masculine and feminine aspects of consciousness. I perceive this as reality when I am reading an individual's soul field.

This spinning field causes the earliest memories experienced in life to be stored at the greatest distance from the physical body. They are on the outermost perimeter or about fifteen feet from the physical body. When I walk toward an individual and pass through this field of stored historical memories, I am passing through the timeline of the person's life memories. Incidentally, a person's life flashing before their eyes, the "life review process" or "judgment," as some near death experiencers call it, is merely the conscious awareness of an individual detaching from the physical body and expanding outward through this same field where I read the memories. I've found these same memory storage patterns exist in earthbound spirits or ghosts, even though they no longer have physical bodies.

Memories are stored at the intersection of these to counter rotating overlapping fields existing around the physical body. Karl Pribram was correct in his theory that memories are stored as holograms, but not in the brain's dendrites, as he theorized. If only people could understand this concept it would help to eliminate many of the learning disabilities children experience. Learning style and capacity is totally a function of the aspect of consciousness utilized by the individual at that moment of their life. This includes the formation of the physical brain and neuropathways. Memories are stored on the soul's horizontal axis at whatever operating frequency was being utilized at the moment of the perceived experience. I emphasize that memories are stored based upon perception of the individual and not necessarily reality as viewed by others.

I've noticed that the "Tower of Babel" concept applies to communication as the levels of consciousness change. The higher the level, the easier it is to communicate through pure thoughts directly rather than using words as metaphors. Several years ago I stopped to visit a friend living near Philadelphia, Pennsylvania, while traveling through the area. We were old friends, often vacationing together in years past. Circumstances changed and we were now lucky to get together once per year, each time picking up exactly where we had left off previously, as though no time had passed. He would always invite me to stay the night in the guest room and we would spend much of the night catching up with each other's lives.

However, this time was different. He informed me that a nasty spirit or ghost was in his house that was causing havoc and kept trying to kill his daughter's fiancé. As I entered the guest room, immediately I felt the presence of the earthbound spirit. I closed my eyes to communicate with it, but all I could hear was gibberish. This had never happened to me previously and was quite puzzling. Inquisitively, I closed my eyes again and climbed to an even higher level of consciousness and immediately heard the ghost's words clearly. The ghost was a friend of my host's oldest son who had been visiting from Italy and had been killed in an auto accident a few months earlier. He spoke no English, and I spoke no Italian, thus it sounded like gibberish to me hearing Italian in his emotional state. To make a long story much shorter I will eliminate many details, but it ended up that the ghost was best friends with the daughter's fiancé in Italy. The two got into trouble and the ghost, while still in his physical body, went to jail to protect his best friend. While in jail for a crime he did not commit, his best friend stole his girlfriend (my host's daughter) and became engaged to her. Thus the ghost was angry and kept trying to kill his former best friend by strangulation every time he tried to sleep in the house.

As mentioned previously, "Our perception of reality is a function of the level of consciousness from which we perceive it." Einstein understood this, as he once stated, "People don't understand my theory of relativity. Imagine you set on a hot plate for a second, it seems like an hour. However if you have a beautiful woman sitting on your lap for an hour, it seems like a second." Einstein just did not understand the important variable in action was actually the level of consciousness functioning at the time of each perception. This is why he had to consider the speed of light as a constant. He further explained that time is a function of the speed of light, when in actuality time is a function of the operating frequency of consciousness divided by the speed of light. Thus, as consciousness is cleansed of all its ballast of the lower frequencies and increases operational frequency approaching the speed of light, time appears to slow down. An enlightened individual who has cleansed their soul and increased their consciousness frequency sufficiently has the gift of prophesy. Between the expansion of consciousness as it increases operational frequency and the increased speed, the time/space continuum appears to collapse as perceived by an enlightened individual.

In the early 1990s I had a series of many visions of what is upcoming for civilization on earth. It was very clear and vivid. I thought it would all unfold by the mid 1990s. But I was wrong, as the time distortion between the higher level of consciousness where I observed the visions and the earth level of perceived reality is great. Many of these events are just now beginning to unfold.

After over twenty-five years of using this unusual ability to learn about the details of consciousness patterns in the human soul and how they relate to personality development, spiritual development, gender identity, sexual attraction, mental illness, physical illness, learning disorders and other developmental disorders, I will share much of the information gained at this conference. This includes how and where memories are stored, processed, retrieved and how the body's defense mechanisms create stress and illness while trying to block traumatic memory retrieval.

The limits of this writing can barely scratch the surface of the knowledge that is available by tapping into the higher levels. A thousand volumes could not contain it all, as there is a level of consciousness I refer to as the "Divine Library." When I first entered it, it felt as though a thousand volumes of encyclopedias had been instantaneously dumped into my head. Ask any question and the answer is instantly there. But you must first know enough to ask the question before there can be an answer. Those are the rules.

So, after all this, "What is the purpose of our life here on earth?" We are the seeds of consciousness planted here to grow. How do we grow? Just as a seed does that is buried in the darkness of the soil; i.e., sprout, utilize the earth as nutrition to grow to a point where it can utilize light as nourishment. We through our consciousness growth are forming or becoming "Light." In the reverse process that occurs when light is refracted through a prism and separates into the ROYGBIV sequence of colors of the rainbow, we as humans are growing in each of the frequencies of consciousness represented by the colors of consciousness at each chakra to reach wholeness and experience nirvana as we become "Light."

Jesus summarized this in His two most important commandments. Love God with all your heart, mind, body and soul. This means that you should always strive to reach and grow to the highest levels of consciousness possible. The second commandment given by Jesus was to Love our neighbors as ourselves. This is similar to the Sufi poet Rumi's statement, "Life is about finding and removing the obstacles to Love that exists within us." Why? Because the more we cleanse our souls of the anchors and ballast, the easier it is to grow to the higher levels of consciousness we strive for by following the first commandment.

Please visit my website at www.thescienceofthesoul.com or contact me by email at LeeSLawrence@gmail.com for a list of future public appearances.

Author Bio

Lee Lawrence

Lee Lawrence is an internationally known medical/psychological intuitive and scientific researcher into the existence of the human soul and how it works. For many years, Lee was a successful Certified Public Accountant, having worked for an international CPA firm, prior to establishing his own regional firm. Then Lee had a near-death experience that changed his life. He began a quest to understand his experiences. He returned to the university, completed a degree in psychology, continued his studies in cognitive neuroscience, anatomy and physiology, and studied various religions in depth.

Leading Edge Science of the Afterlife and Mediumship

Alan Ross Hugenot, Ph.D.

Based on his book *THE DEATH EXPERIENCE: What it is like when you die*
© 2012 Alan Ross Hugenot, and also on his personal research as a
Scientist and a Practicing Medium. © 2015 Alan Ross Hugenot

1. WHAT HAPPENS TO INDIVIDUAL CONSCIOUSNESS AT DEATH?

The energy of our consciousness cannot cease to exist in strict accordance with the laws of classical Newtonian physics. The Law of Conservation of Energy states that.

> *"Energy never disappears. It only changes form, with no beginning or ending."*

Now, if that is true, as every materialist swears that it is, then the consciousness, which is energy, simply must go somewhere. But the NDE has changed medical science.

> *"Most people still believe that death is the end of everything ... that used to be my own belief. But, after many years of*

critical research into the ... NDE, ... brain function, consciousness, and ... basic principles of quantum physics, my views have undergone a complete transformation. I found the most significant finding to be the conclusion of one NDEr: "Dead turned out to be not dead." I now see the continuity of our consciousness after the death of our physical body as a very real possibility."

Dr. Pim von Lommel Cardiac Surgeon,
Consciousness Beyond Life ©2010

I can understand why people may have difficulty believing in mediumship. My own mother was a fundamentalist Baptist and my father was a Catholic. So, I grew up being told that speaking to dead people was "of the devil." And, it was something that a "Christian" person would not be "caught dead" doing (excuse the pun). And, most recently (2014), my sister has informed me that I am on my way to hell for being a medium. But through the miracle of mediumship, my mom has come through from the other side to tell me it's O.K. and to ignore my sister.

But on May 27, 1970, I actually was "caught dead." In a Near-Death experience, I was killed during a motorcycle accident. I suffered severe head injuries, with multiple fractures to my right leg and arm, including a shattered femur. I was placed in an Intensive Care Unit (ICU), and about three hours after the accident cerebral swelling caused me to lapse into a coma. My consciousness traveled out-of-body into the afterlife. But, that is another story told in my book *THE DEATH EXPERIENCE: What It Is Like When You Die.*

After this experience, I knew that the afterlife was real, that our individual consciousness survives outside the physical body, and reincarnates at will.

But of course, with my upbringing, I had never once considered communicating with souls in the afterlife.

Yet after researching mediumship for the last 10 years, all the superstitious FEARS of my parents' cultural traditions left me. And today, mediumship has become cutting-edge science.

2. CAN WE REALLY COMMUNICATE?

I have been a professional member of the International Association for Near-Death Studies (IANDS.org) for nearly 20 years, promoting the idea that afterlife is proven by the NDE. But I was "haunted" by this one question: "If our consciousness survives death, as proven by the NDE, then shouldn't we be able to communicate with those who have crossed over?

So in 2006 I began scientifically researching After Death Communication (ADC). I began studying to become a Medium myself ... that's right, a Physicist who talks to dead people.

Today, nine years later, I am a graduate of the four-year extension course in *Mediumship* offered by Morris Prat Institute (est. 1901), which includes on-campus work at Lily Dale, NY, and also a member of Certified Mediums Society, National Spiritualist Association (NASC). And I have done graduate work in *Evidential Mediumship* at Arthur Findlay College of Psychic Science (est. 1964), Stansted, England.

Once or twice a month I regularly serve as the medium providing "Greetings from Spirit" at two Spiritualist churches in San Francisco. As an Evidential Medium I actually bring through details like the relationship of the spirit to the receiver, their name, their characteristics (like their job, hair color, etc.) as well as their message for the receiver (sitter).

I have also learned that everyone has mediumistic abilities. But since birth each of us has been taught to ignore these capacities. But we still get hunches and have "gut feelings." Did you ever wonder where those intuitions are coming from? Could they be coming from your loved ones on the other side?

3. UNDERSTANDING THE TERMINOLOGY

Definitions: To avoid confusion there are two traditions in the world of mediumship: the American-British tradition known as "Spiritualism," which grew out of the American and English "Protestant" churches (including the Anglican-Episcopal churches), and also the Portuguese-Brazilian tradition known as

"Spiritism," which grew out of the Portuguese-Brazilian Roman Catholic churches following the science of Allan Kardec. I am deeply familiar with both and know that these two traditions define mediumship differently. Spiritualism subdivides the science of Extra Sensory Perception (ESP) or Clairvoyance into two branches: psychic skills (ESP with living people) and mediumship skills (ESP with the discarnate). On the other hand, Spiritists do not make this distinction, calling it all psychic ESP "mediumship." Psychic and mediumship both use the same ESP skills, but with different targets. But to the Spiritualist, the target is what is important because they want to prove an afterlife.

PSYCHIC WORK: This is when a person, who is sensitive to these higher vibrations, is communicating with your consciousness here on this physical plane of existence. It will include me using tarot cards, reading your palm, etc. And all "mediums" are also good at doing this "psychic work." But such work is all about this material world and does not involve communication with surviving consciousness in an afterlife.

MEDIUMSHIP: This is when a person, who is sensitive to these higher vibrations, is communicating with the spirit of a departed loved one on the other side. Normally, they will not use any physical systems like Tarot cards, or palm reading or psychometry to do this. A good way to remember this distinction is that "Mediums communicate with deceased people; Psychics communicate with living people."

SITTER: This is the person who came for the medium to get in touch with departed loved ones by having a reading.

4. CREDIBLE MEDIUMS

In my research I have met dozens of mediums who are among America's and Europe's finest citizens, first-class, honest people whose credibility is unquestionable. And, they always bring through amazing evidence from the deceased loved ones whose messages they channel. One of the most credible mediums I have ever met is *Suzanne Giesemann*. She is a retired US Navy

Commander and former Aide-de-Camp to the Chairman of the Joint Chiefs of Staff. This position is the personal assistant for the highest military officer in the US, and involves traveling everywhere with him. So when 9/11 happened she was actually in the air flying with the Chairman to London. Their flight was recalled back to Washington DC and Suzanne was actually on the last plane still in the air on 9/11.

Her story "Messages of Hope" is available in a video on her site at www.suzannegiesemann.com. That story includes how the death of her step-daughter, being foretold in a dream, caused her to become "a most unexpected medium." Today, a decade later, Suzanne is one of the finest evidential mediums in the entire world.

Suzanne follows the system for evidential mediumship, which she learned at Arthur Findlay College, located between Cambridge and London in England. And at her recommendation I also studied there for 12 days of Evidential Mediumship.

Courses at AFC are geared for practicing mediums who want to improve their skills. The tutors really "stretch" their students to new levels of psychic and mediumship ability. In the two weeks I was there I gave over 60 readings, and received an equal number of readings. All had undeniable evidence. Mediums brought through my mother, father, grandmother, uncle (I asked the student medium "Which uncle?" and she responded with "Oh, definitely Robert." And in nearly every reading my chief guide, Helen, whom none of the mediums knew about, also came through. I remember one medium saying, *"Is this woman's name Helen?"*

STANSTED HALL - ARTHUR FINDLAY COLLEGE

One of the most important things I learned at Arthur Findlay College was that mediumship is worldwide and growing. In fact it is much more an accepted fact in Europe than it is in the United States. Consequently, I met and worked with mediums from Copenhagen; Melbourne and Perth, Australia; Malmo, Sweden; Reykjavik, Iceland; Rome; Lisbon; Amsterdam; Houston and Los Angeles; Freiburg, Germany; Panama; and Oxford and Cambridge, England.

We ate all our meals together at tables with people from around the world, and everyone there was a definite "psychic." We also spent an hour each evening at the pub, "raising a pint" and getting to know each other. Now we all find each other on Facebook.

5. HOW MEDIUMSHIP WORKS

Making contact with surviving consciousnesses, which apparently continue to exist in, as yet undiscerned, dimensions (the afterlife), involves four people:

1. You, the person seeking a message. We usually call you the "Sitter."

2. The "Evidential Medium" here in the physical reality, who is the telephone operator, receiving the message for you. That's me.

3. The "Medium in Spirit" doing the telephone operator task on that side, a surviving consciousness who knows how to connect with the Evidential Medium. We usually refer to this deceased medium as "Our Chief Guide," or "Control." That's HELEN.

4. Finally, there is the "Deceased Spirit Communicator" who has to work through a deceased medium because, just like you, most of them have never developed their innate mediumistic skills. This is your loved one.

Remember the game where you pass a whispered message between four people and everybody laughs because it comes out so garbled from the last person? Messages coming through mediumship are often a little garbled also. And, in the game, when anyone refuses to play, there is no communication at all.

Similarly, with a medium, if anyone is skeptical, there will be no communication. Also, if the departed loved one believed that "when you die you're dead," they may not yet have realized they have passed on, and may be confusedly thinking "I'm still here ... so I can't be dead." They see no reason to communicate through a medium. Hauntings and poltergeist situations are simply people who have not yet realized they are dead.

Finally, the spirits originate the "phone calls." You may expect to "dial up" a deceased spouse or favorite grandma, but the spirit who comes through instead may be the uncle you never liked because he needs to ask your forgiveness, while your beloved grandma has no such urgent need. Grandma loved you and told you before she left that she would love you forever. But your lousy uncle may have discovered that he can't progress further until he makes reparations with everyone he took advantage of.

FUZZY MATH: Also it is important to recognize how much is actually true within the somewhat garbled message you will receive from the deceased. For example, during a reading a medium says, "I have a female who seems to be a mother figure here and she tells me her name is "Elise." She indicates to me that she is your grandmother on your father's side." But the client (sitter) says, *"No, you are wrong. Elise is my grandmother on my mother's side."*

Later, the sitter will remember only that he said to the medium, "You are wrong." Yet the medium was 95% correct. He had the grandmother's actual name—something he could not have guessed.

THE ACTUAL STATISTICAL FACTS: What this sitter should realize instead is how accurate the medium actually was in properly identifying

1. The spirit's gender (odds of 1 in 2)
2. That she was a relative, a mother figure (odds of 1 in 10)
3. The correct generation, that she was my grandmother (odds of 1 in 3)
4. That her name was Elise (odds of about 1 in 200)

Multiplying that out (2 x 10 x 3 x 200 = 12,000) the odds of guessing this correctly become 12,000 to one. So actually the medium was only wrong about one item, which side of the family. Even ignoring odds on names, the medium still got 4 right out of 5, which is *80% accuracy.* But this sitter will remember only what he verbalized, that the medium was "WRONG" rather than 80% right.

PSYCHIC VS MEDIUMSHIP: Some readers may have been to visit psychics or mediums who are not Evidential. Unfortunately, they will often say things that can not be verified, and as a consequence it is difficult to believe them: "I have your grandmother here ... She had gray hair ... She says she loved you ... She is also telling me that you will do well in the thing you were considering doing." But in such a message there is no evidence that you can verify.

This is why my goal is to deliver evidence that shows the sitter undeniably that it is really the discarnate who is coming through. For this I like to collect what I call NAME, RANK, AND SERIAL NUMBER, specifically their name, or at least their first initial, and then distinguishing features like hair style, hats, glasses, hair color, eye color, hobbies, occupation, etc. And finally, I want some WOW evidence, the kind of thing that will put tears in the sitter's eyes.

CAN LOVED ONES REALLY CALL HOME FROM THE OTHER SIDE?

Apparently they can, but it is difficult to call someone who refuses to answer the phone. They can only "talk" to you through whatever medium you will allow (dreams, mediums, etc.). And you also have to be receptive to the idea that they may communicate, and also take some initiative yourself. If you refuse to believe in mediumship your loved ones will probably not ever be able to communicate with you. It is like having cell phone service available (through the medium), but because you don't believe in cell phones, you have never signed up for phone service and so your loved ones can't call you on a cell.

I regularly attend séances and Spiritualist services and regularly receive messages from the other side, which always contain solid evidentiary material identifying who the message is from. It is evidence only I and the communicating spirit would know, but the medium could not have guessed. Always it is unequivocally clear evidence.

MEDIUMS HAVE GUIDES: Before I took up active mediumship, I had a reading with a Certified Spiritualist Medium. Although the medium knew me personally, she knew nothing about me and did not know that I had purchased a reading a few moments earlier at this "Festival of Mediums." So there was no way she could know any of the evidence she gave me. Here is how it went.

MEDIUM: "Alan, I have a woman here in spirit who wants to talk with you. She seems to be a Mother Figure who was an architect. She is from back East … maybe ... Minnesota."

ALAN: "But I don't have any mothers or grandmothers who are deceased Minnesota women architects."

MEDIUM: "O.K. I'll go back to Spirit for more information." Shortly she said, "Well she said she is not exactly your relative, but she is like a mother figure. And she is not exactly an architect. But she knows you and she draws pictures of houses. She has dark brown curly hair and hazel eyes."

ALAN: "Oh, that is Helen, my mother-in-law, the developer who drew the plans for the house I live in with my wife, her daughter. And yes, she is from Minneapolis, Minnesota. And yes, she is a mother figure. And yes, we are not exactly related."

Helen, Dorothy Bradley deceased 1992

The interesting part is that I had never met Helen in this physical life. For me she was not a "departed loved one," she was actually a stranger, but one I knew enough about to recognize from the details. She died five years before I met and married her daughter.

Later, as I pondered all this, I realized that Helen had loved occult things like tarot, astrology and mediums when she was here in the physical life, and had even been a member for about 12 years of a strange new organization she joined in 1980 called The INSTITUTE OF NOETIC SCIENCES (IONS). Now she comes through to me all the time, very much like a cell phone call, and we have developed quite an extensive relationship. When I am working as a medium, Helen is the deceased medium on the other side, my "gate keeper" who assists the spirit who wants to come through for the sitter. And whenever I have a reading with another medium, she always gives me solid evidentiary things telling me that it is her, coming through mediums who do not know who she might be. When I was at Arthur Findlay College, Helen came through another medium to me at least once every day. She said in February 2015, when we were at IONS doing scientific experiments with Dr. Radin and Dr. Delorme, that she was excited to finally be working at IONS.

But it has taken her almost a quarter century on that side after she passed on to perfect her skills to come through to this side. So don't be expecting your loved one to come through by themselves without a medium the day after they pass on. Even an expert on mediumship like Fredrick Myers, one of the most learned scientists in the field of mediumship, did not come through for six years after he died in 1901. His first communications did not begin to come through until 1907.

Now I will share two examples from personal experience of what happens when all four players (you the sitter, Me the medium here in the physical, Helen the medium in the afterlife, and your departed loved one) work together. Here is how it went with a reading on October 15, 2014 (names changed to preserve privacy).

1894 photo of MARY ADELAIDE

ALAN: "Mary, although I know you well, I still know nothing *about your family* or who you have on the other side. I just know that you are married to Michael."

MARY: "Yes."

ALAN: "Mary, I have a woman coming through from your grandmother's generation, on your father's side, maybe your great grandmother's generation. She has an 'M' for a name, and I want to say her name is Mary, but then because that is your name I am confused. Maybe she is instead 'Mame' or Margo, or Marguerite. She seems to be telling me that, yes, this is her other, or middle name, which she is now giving me … I feel that she died of a pain in the chest, because she is making my chest hurt on the surface here … maybe breast cancer. She had brown hair, which she wore pulled back into a severe bun …

Pulled back behind her head. She apparently died in the 1890s, because she is giving me that number ... 1890s. "Her message is that she loves you, even though she never knew you ... but is happy that you returned to Spiritualism. Does that make sense to you?"

MARY: "Yes, Alan. That makes a lot of sense to me. My grandmother on my father's side's name does start with an 'M' and it is in fact Mary, as you first thought. Indeed, I am named after her. I believe that she died of breast cancer, but I'll check it out. Actually, you probably thought great grandmother because of the age difference. You see, I was born quite late in my parents' lifetime, and she died before I was born. So just like she said, I never knew her."

Later relatives verified that Grandma Mary's nickname (or as I said, "other name") was "Mame." Officially she died of "Pleurisy," which is an inflammation of the chest cavity. The relatives sent her picture and verification of these facts.

1. SPIRIT'S ACTUAL NAME = "Mary" (odds of better than 200 to 1)

2. HER NICKNAME = "Mame" (1 in 25?)

3. GENERATION = "grandma" (1 in 10)

4. RELATIONSHIP = "father's side" (1 in 2)

5. WHAT SHE DIED OF = inflammation of the chest cavity (1 in 50?)

6. HER HAIR COLOR: = brown (1 in 5?)

7. HER HAIR STYLE = "pulled back into a severe bun" (1 in 20?)

8. WOW EVIDENCE = never knew sitter; dies before sitter was born (1 in 25?)

9. WOW EVIDENCE = showing me 1890s, picture was taken in 1894 (1 in 25?)

Again, these evidential facts are simply the answers to the exact questions which I "automatically" ask of every spirit and "demand" answers for before I will accept the greeting. Statistically, the odds are 200 x 25 x 10 x 2 x 50 x 5 x 20 x 25 x 25 = **312.5 billion to 1.**

ISOLATION CHAMBER OR CABINET ?

Dr. Dean Radin, Chief Scientist at IONS took this photo of me just after they had wetted the electrodes on my head and just before placing me in the Electro-Magnetic Isolation Chamber.

Back in the 1890s the mediums would sit in "Cabinets" to concentrate their energy. Today, at Arthur Findlay College, we mediums still sit in cabinets when we do trance mediumship.

Now, this "Isolation Chamber" at IONS certainly looked to me like a "cabinet."

After I got inside they closed the door so I was supposedly "isolated." But my chief Spirit guide, "Helen," whispered in my left ear, *"Alan, what are they thinking? I'm right here in the 'cabinet' with you."*

Here are the computer diagrams generated by Dr. Arnaud Delorme's program for analyzing mediums and meditators. Each circle shows my head. My nose is the triangle at the top, my ears are also shown on each side, and the back of my head is on the bottom. At the far left is a diagram when I am observing a photo of a person who is still living. In the middle is a diagram of my head when I am observing a photo of a person who is deceased.

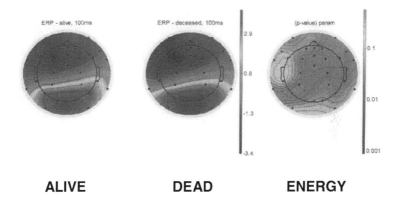

ALIVE **DEAD** **ENERGY**

Notice at the back of my head, which is where the visual cortex is located, how the diagram on the left is dark red, but the diagram in the middle is a darker red.

The green diagram shows where energy is concentrated in my brain. Notice yellow at my left ear, and yellow at the back of my head. This indicates that my visual cortex is registering the image shown on the computer screen in front of me and the "answer," whether the person in the photo is alive or dead, is being received in my left ear. Of course, that is where I already know Helen hangs out.

The recent IONS study investigated the correlations between the accuracy of mediums' statements and their brain electrical activity. And also differences in mediums' brain activity between four subjective states were studied: PERCEPTION, RECOLLECTION, FABRICATION and MEDIUMSHIP communication.

It was found that the *mediumship communication* mental state differed from the *perceptive* mental state with larger amplitude, high gamma power observed during the *mediumship communication* mental state.

This rise in gamma waves seems to be from eye, ear or muscular activity. In other words, the mediums were receiving information through eyes, ears and feelings, rather than imagining or fabricating them. The report concluded that, "The study's findings suggest that the experience of communicating with the deceased may be a distinct mental state that is not consistent with brain activity during ordinary thinking or imagination." This is important scientific verification of the fact that *mediums are actually receiving outside information* during *medium communication* mental activities. The mediums all propose that they are communications being received from the deceased. Although the data is insufficient to confirm scientifically that the source of the communications is actually surviving consciousness, it does show that the source is outside the medium. The next step is to figure out experiments that can isolate data under test conditions that will explain where that information being received by the mediums is actually coming from.

We mediums may "know" that it is coming directly from deceased loved ones. But science asks the question, "How do we prove that it did not happen some other way, like ESP from living minds?"

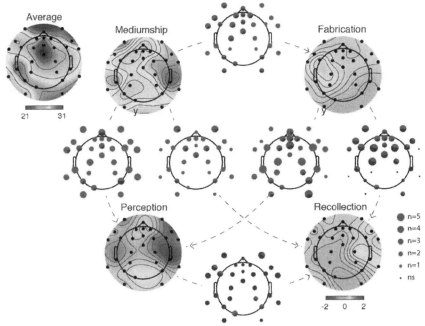

Notice, on the left, the AVERAGE condition of the cerebral cortex, and the next one, second from left, which is MEDIUMSHIP. The blue one at bottom left is PERCEPTION, and the one on the bottom right is RECOLLECTION. Finally, the one at top right is FABRICATION. As you can see, MEDIUMSHIP is totally different from all of these. But, looking back at my own images, my mind seemed to be somewhere between FABRICATION and RECOLLECTION. The scientists said this was merely coincidental, as I transitioned from PERCEPTION to MEDIUMSHIP.

NEW DEVELOPMENTS: INDUCED NEAR-DEATH EXPERIENCES:

In the last few years, additional science has come to light. ERASING DEATH: Dr. Sam Parnia, a resuscitation specialist, assists with cardiac arrest patients, and using hypothermia (lowered body temperature) "suspends" them between life and death for up to four hours without respiration or blood circulation. This timeframe, during which the person is by all our measurements DEAD, allows the surgeons time to repair the heart using bypasses, etc., and then they bring the person back to physical life. The patients often have had Near-Death experiences while they were completely dead (not breathing) for four hours. His 2013 book is an exciting read.

INDUCED AFTER-DEATH COMMUNICATIONS (IADC®)

This is a copyrighted therapy of Dr. Allan L. Botkin, Psy.D, where he induces a reconnection with someone who has passed away, resulting in healing deep sadness associated with grief. Dr. Botkin discovered this in 1995 and has since developed it into a complete therapy. This is also a great read for mediums as well as NDE enthusiasts.

MY BOOK

THE DEATH EXPERIENCE: What it is like when you die, © 2012. This book describes the story I have told today and is available in PAPERBACK or KINDLE from Amazon.

YOU-TUBE VIDEOS

A Sept. 2013 TV interview with me speaking on the **"SCIENCE OF THE AFTERLIFE"** is at http://www.youtube.com/watch?v=sG8RAVh4VwE (29 min).

An excellent Sept. 2014 short film **"BEYOND OUR SIGHT"** is available at https://www.youtube.com/watch?v=xpSuO8DtiMM (57 min).

Dr. Dean Radin, Chief Scientist at Institute of Noetic Sciences (noetic.org), discusses consciousness studies at Noetic.org in a video clip at http://vimeo.com/113981492 (2 min).

Dr. Arnaud Delorme discusses MEDIUMSHIP SCIENCE at Noetic.org in a video clip http://vimeo.com/113345358 (2 min).

Suzanne Giesemann, *"WHY I DO THIS WORK"* video clip (3.5 min) https://www.youtube.com/watch?v=k2tc6YmQJlU SuzanneGiesemann.com

References

MESSAGES of HOPE: The Metaphysical Memoir of a Most Unexpected Medium ©2011, Suzanne Giesemann, Former Commander USN, Aide-de-Camp to the Chairman of the Joint Chiefs of Staff

SCIENCE and the AFTERLIFE EXPERIENCE: Evidence for the Immortality of Consciousness, ©2012, By Chris Carter, PART III, "MESSAGES FROM THE DEAD." Published by Inner Traditions

WHERE THE TWO WORLDS MEET: How to Develop Evidential Mediumship, ©2011, By Janet Novahec.

THE FRENCH REVELATION: The Phenomena of Direct-Independent Voice Medium Emily S. French, as documented 1890 - 1912, by Attorney Edward G. Randall, ©1995, By N. Riley Heagerty

TESTIMONY OF LIGHT: Messages from the deceased Francis Banks, ©1969, By Helen Greaves

ERASING DEATH – The science that is rewriting the boundaries between life and death, ©2013, by Dr. Sam Parnia, M.D. with Josh Young.

CONSCIOUSNESS BEYOND LIFE: The Science of the Near Death Experience, ©2010, by Pin Von Lommel, M.D. Harper Collins

HANDBOOK OF NEAR-DEATH STUDIES: 30 years of investigation, ©2009, By Janice Miner Holden, PhD., Bruce Greyson, M.D. and Debbie James RN/MSN, ABC-CLIO, LLC